The Australian Garden

First published in Australia in 2002 by Bloomings Books, Melbourne, Australia

This edition published in UK in 2003 by Garden Art Press a division of the Antique Collectors' Club Ltd.

Designer: Danie Pout Design
Editors: Jane Holth and Julia Stokes
Botanical Editor: David Cameron
Indexer: Malory Weston
Principal Photographers: Simon Griffiths, Diana Snape
Publisher: Warwick Forge

ISBN 1 870673 46 8

British Library Cataloguing-in-Publication Data
A Catalogue record for this book is available from the British Library

Garden Art Press
Sandy Lane, Old Martlesham, Woodbridge, Suffolk, IP12 4SD
Tel: 01394 389950 Fax: 01394 389999
e-mail: sales@antique-acc.com website: www.antique-acc.com

PREVIOUS PAGE: A natural garden Vic. An ancient Snow Gum (*Eucalyptus pauciflora*). Many eucalypts have superb trunks but one as majestic as this would require at least a human lifespan to develop.
PHOTOGRAPH DIANA SNAPE

PHOTO RIGHT: Hanson garden Vic. Designed by Bev Hanson. An inviting path leads into the serenity of a cool, green garden. Beneath a sheltering canopy, among the ground flora, ferns, sedges and rushes thrive, suggesting the lure of a nearby pool.
PHOTOGRAPH SIMON GRIFFITHS

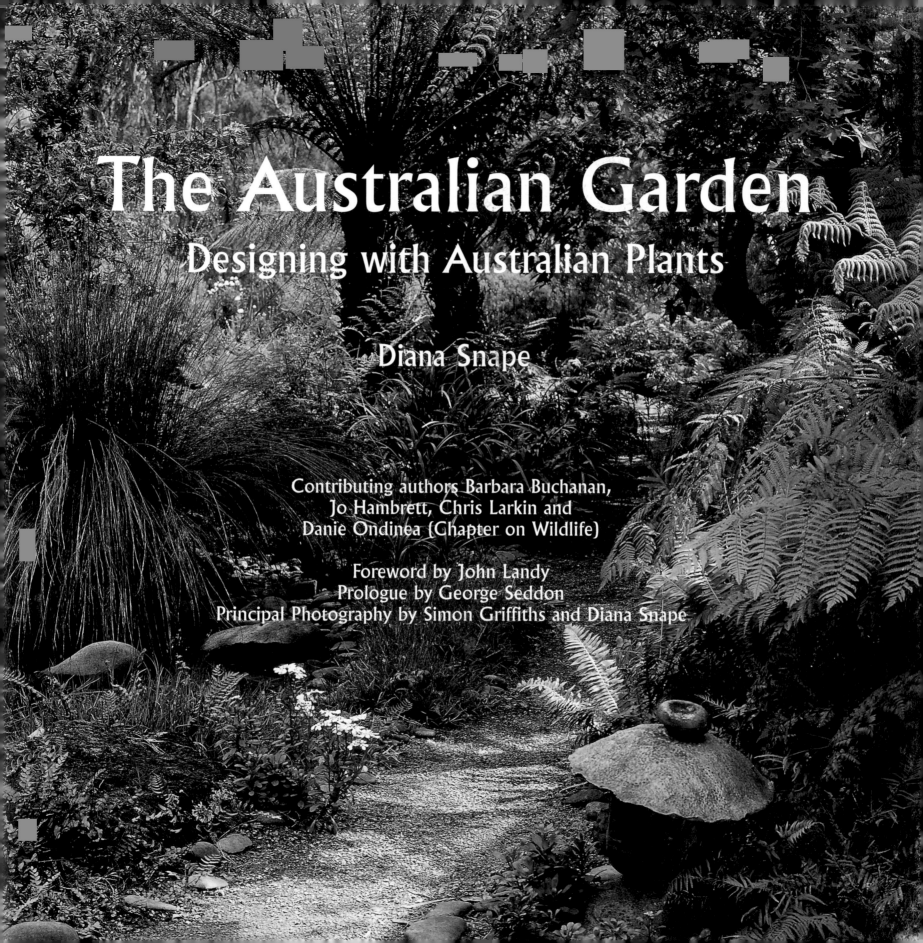

The Australian Garden
Designing with Australian Plants

Diana Snape

Contributing authors Barbara Buchanan,
Jo Hambrett, Chris Larkin and
Danie Ondinea (Chapter on Wildlife)

Foreword by John Landy
Prologue by George Seddon
Principal Photography by Simon Griffiths and Diana Snape

The publisher desires to gratefully acknowledge the assistance of the Garden Design Study Group of the Association of Societies for Growing Australian Plants (ASGAP) and the Australian Plants Society of Victoria.

PHOTO: Myall Park Qld. The exquisite *Eucalyptus crucis* (Silver Mallee).

PHOTOGRAPH BRIAN SNAPE

CONTENTS

ACKNOWLEDGMENTS

I wish to thank my wonderful colleagues and contributing authors, Barbara Buchanan, Jo Hambrett, Chris Larkin and Danie Ondinea. I have enjoyed our collaboration.

We all wish to thank John Landy AC, MBE, Governor of Victoria, for kindly writing the apposite Foreword, and Professor George Seddon AM for his Prologue – as thought-provoking as ever.

We are grateful to John Armstrong for drawing the plan for Chapter 5 and to all members of the Garden Design Study Group of the Association of Societies for Growing Australian Plants (ASGAP) who have contributed ideas and information over the years. Unfortunately we cannot acknowledge each of them individually but we wish to mention: Joan Barrett, Trevor and Beryl Blake, Lynne Boladeras, Jennifer Borrell, Jane Calder, Lindsay Campbell, Bev Courtney, Peter Cuneo, Glenda Datson, Kay Dempsey, Cherree Densley, Catherine Drew, Grahame Durbidge, Rodger and Gwen Elliot, Vanessa Elwell-Gavins, Shirley Fisher, Linda Floyd, Peter Garnham, Margaret Garrett, Marilyn Gray, Doris Gunn, Caroline Gunter, Jan Hall, Monika Herrmann, Jeff Howes, Colleen Keena, Paul and Barbara Kennedy, John Knight, Margaret Lee, Margarete Lee, Nicole Lenffer, Bryan Loft, Ann and Geoffrey Long, Neil Marriott, Doug and Margaret McIver, Ian Percy, Shirley Pipitone, Anne Pye, Tony and Joy Roberts, Nicky Rose, Gordon Rowland, Betty Rymer, Geoff Simmons, Roger Stone, Gloria Thomlinson, Paul Thompson, Pat and John Webb, Merele Webb, Aliki Zouliou.

Others from outside the Garden Design Study Group who have generously contributed helpful information, including Leaders of other ASGAP Study Groups (SG) are: Hazel Blackney (Hakea SG); Tony Cavanagh and Margaret Pieroni (Dryandra SG); Col Cornford (Melaleuca and Allied Genera SG); Maria Hitchcock (Correa SG); Colin Jennings (Eremophila SG); Esma Salkin (Australian Daisy SG); Judy Barker, Jane Burke, Ivan Holliday, Peg McAllister, Dean Nicolle (eucalypts); Jane Shepherd, Jan Simpson, Geoff Sitch; Yvonne and Don Wignall and Ian Anderson, John Delpratt, James Ross and Phil Watson (grasslands).

We also wish to thank those who have kindly helped prepare sample lists of indigenous plants for each of the capital cities: Lynette and Peter Reilly and Paul Donatiu (Brisbane); Kris Schaffer (Hobart); Bob Dixon and Nathan McQuoid (Perth).

I would also like to thank the many gardeners whose gardens I have visited, including all those who have kindly allowed photographs of their gardens to be reproduced in this book; Celia Rosser and Monash University for permission to reproduce Celia's wonderful painting; Mary White for her map of Gondwana, from *The Greening of Gondwana* (Kangaroo Press); May Gibbs Spastic Centre Trust; Simon Griffiths as the lead photographer and other contributing photographers, whose pictures reflect the enormous variety of Australian gardens around this continent; Peter Bailey for his willingness to initially check plant names for changes and errors. This difficult task was completed with great dedication and thoroughness by David Cameron as botanical editor.

I am also grateful to Jane Holth for her patience and expertise as editor; Julie Stokes for her additional expertise; Danie Pout who, as the designer, added her touch of magic; and Warwick Forge for his encouragement, commitment and guiding hand as publisher.

Finally, I want to thank our partners for their unfailing support. I especially wish to thank my husband, Brian, who proof-read the manuscript at many stages and accompanied me on numerous garden visits. I could not have completed the book without his help.

Diana Snape

FOREWORD

The publication of *The Australian Garden* is very timely. Water shortages are becoming critical throughout Australia, particularly in the cities of southern Australia. Native gardens had a period of considerable popularity during the 1960s and 1970s but interest waned at least partly because of a lack of understanding of management and design. But now enthusiasm for Australian plants, encouraged by the need to find plants that are more efficient users of water, that are adapted to thrive on soil of low fertility and require minimum maintenance, is again evident.

This book covers in a very comprehensive way Australian plants suitable for growing in gardens and describes how to establish specialised gardens such as grassland, heathland and coastal gardens.

Emphasis is placed on the use of local native species because they are easier to establish and more likely to persist and also because they provide a natural habitat for indigenous birds, mammals and insects. As a rule, in establishing an Australian garden, it is best to first seek local plants before searching further afield. Gardens with local plants can form linkages between remnant vegetation along creek and river frontages, bushland reserves and national parks.

Many people will not want to switch entirely to Australian plants, particularly if they have a well-established garden of exotic species, and emphasis is given in the book to 'blending' Australian plants with exotics. With the current interest in Mediterranean-type plants that are adapted to hot dry summers and cold winters, such as lavender, rosemary, sage and echiums, which have somewhat similar requirements to many Australian species, 'blending' will be relatively easy.

At a critical stage in the evolution of Australian gardens, Diana Snape provides an invaluable guide on how to utilise our own extraordinarily diverse and beautiful flora.

John Landy AC, MBE

ABOVE: Firewheel Tree (*Stenocarpus sinuatus*) is a handsome tree which blends well with exotics.
PHOTOGRAPH DIANA SNAPE

7

PROLOGUE

That 'Australians should be growing more plants from their own country in their gardens' is the theme of this book. But why should they? The case has been argued in the past from a mixture of good reasons and bad, and this has resulted in some good gardens and some very bad ones; lemon-scented gums pushing into the foundations of valuable nineteenth-century terraces in their minute front yards in the inner suburbs of Sydney and Melbourne, for example.

The bad arguments led twenty years ago to a belief that the 'bush garden' was self-maintaining: you bought the plants, put them in the ground, and your task was over. Neither gardening nor plants are like that, nor ever have been, but the failures may have set back by a decade or more the campaign to persuade Australians to grow more plants from their own country. So before we begin planting, let us first turn to a little weeding: some of the arguments we have heard are overstated, need qualification, are incomplete, or in conflict with other beliefs, and some of the terminology is imprecise or misleading. Then we can turn to the good arguments based on knowledge, experience and understanding, the substance of this book.

To write or speak of 'Australian plants' is to use a convenient fiction, sometimes useful, sometimes not, leading to serious confusions. The term has its uses, but its use always requires caution. The caution is needed because plants know nothing of nationality. Nations and nationality are the outcome of political history, of conquest, invasion, change, chance, all of which might, in our own case, have led to quite different boundaries. The French might well have claimed the western third of the continent, the Dutch Van Diemen's Land, the Germans and the Dutch or the Indonesians or the Japanese, the northern third of the continent. So the words 'Australia' and 'Australian plants' might have applied only to the land and flora of the south-eastern mainland.

The nation of Australia, however, now comprises a continent, the only nation state to do so. Thus the political boundary coincides with a natural boundary, with the exception of a few bits and pieces that we will come to presently. This colours our thinking in many odd ways, usually unconscious. North America has eight nation states plus Greenland (Danish) and another five Caribbean countries, just counting the larger ones, while all the other continents have many more. Yet our continental unity is also misleading; it encompasses many highly diverse environments and the plants from one often fail to survive in another, although there are also many interesting exceptions, discussed later.

Europe is called a continent, even THE Continent (although strictly a mere subcontinent of Asia, like India). Now that the political boundaries grow close to the natural ones by courtesy of the European Union, we could be tempted to speak of 'European plants' and urge that these should dominate European gardens. But of course we do not, for two very good reasons. One is environmental and one cultural. The cultural reason is that gardens are human constructs, and Europeans have ransacked the world for 'garden-worthy' plants, and then bred and refined them.

The second is ecological. *Quercus suber*, the cork oak, is indigenous in Portugal and southern Spain, but there would be little point in planting it in Finland, nor in planting birches in Portugal, although both are European plants and European countries. In Australia, by contrast, it is common enough in gardening literature to see statements like 'Australians should plant Australian plants in their gardens' with the implication that it is a patriotic duty. There is no moral

RIGHT: Should Australians be growing more plants from their own country in their gardens? Subtle colours of *Eucalyptus doratoxylon* (Spearwood Mallee) from WA.
PHOTOGRAPH BRIAN SNAPE

imperative. Nationalism of this kind belongs essentially to the nineteenth century.

Plant affinities often ignore national boundaries. They may also ignore natural boundaries. For our region, the most significant natural boundary is Wallace's Line, the dramatic gap in the Indonesian Archipelago between Lombok and Flores, dividing the biotic realm of South-East Asia and Australasia. It works well for the fauna (tigers and monkeys to the west of it, kangaroos and their kin to the east) but less well for the plants. The flora of Australia has many shared characteristics at the continental scale, but there are also many plant species and genera that 'look outwards' rather than inwards to the centre.

Popular speech reflects this sense of a continent and a people looking out from the coastal fringe rather than inwards. It makes sense to speak of the 'American heartland', a powerful political and cultural force, but here the heart is dead. We call non-coastal Australia 'the outback', and if it is well out, 'beyond the black stump'. What it is not is 'in'. We even define ourselves by the oceans we face. Sydney fronts the Pacific, Perth the Indian Ocean. America and Europe have transcontinental railroads. We have one too, but we call it 'The Indian Pacific', ocean to ocean.

Many plants look out across these seas. Kangaroo Grass (themeda), which we think of as quintessentially Australian, is common in southern Africa, as I once discovered to my surprise. The distinctive boabs (*Adansonia*) of the Kimberley have close relatives in Madagascar and southern Africa, but none in eastern Australia, while some of the evergreen figs of tropical and subtropical Australia have their nearest relatives in India. Tasmania has a suite of gymnosperms that

LEFT: A natural garden WA. The Australian Boab (*Adansonia gregorii*), from north-western Australia, is a highly distinctive deciduous tree with close relatives in Madagascar and southern Africa.
PHOTOGRAPH DIANA SNAPE

Dicroidium – Triassic

Triassic Reptiles

Triassic Amphibia

Glossopteris – Permian

Mesosaurus

Devonian Freshwater Fish

are unknown in south-western Australia, but with related species up the east coast, across the Tasman to New Zealand and even further to Chile. The greatest concentration is in New Caledonia. To give a few examples, we have one species of kauri (*Agathis robusta*) on the east coast of Queensland, and New Zealand has one (*A. australis*). We have three *Araucaria* (*A. heterophylla* from Norfolk Island, *A. bidwillii* and *A. cunninghamiana*) while New Caledonia has many species of these two genera, especially *Araucaria*. The western four-fifths of the continent has none. Tasmania has *Lagarostrobus franklinii*, formerly *Dacrydium franklinii* (the Huon Pine), *Phyllocladus aspleniifolius* (the Celery-top Pine) and *Microcachrys tetragona*, all members of the Podocarpaceae; most of the related species are in New Zealand.

All of this is the outcome of the geological past, Gondwanan links, including linkages through a more temperate Antarctica, chance seed dispersal by birds or waves, and so on. The point is that the current geographical location of plants in Australia may provide only limited significant information. To talk of 'Australian' plants is therefore accurate and tolerably precise only if it is intended to mean no more than those plants now growing naturally in Australia. Even then we have to exclude recent introductions that have naturalised. We also have to exclude from the concept of 'Australia', Christmas, Heard and Macquarie Islands, while including Norfolk Island, Tasmania, Rottnest, Kangaroo Island and so on, by criteria that are obviously quite arbitrary, since if we restricted ourselves to the Australian continent, they would all be out too. Beyond that imperfect geographical sense, the word 'Australian' applied to plants is a joker, sometimes rich in meaning, sometimes poor and misleading.

ABOVE: A map of Gondwana indicates how the geological past has strongly influenced geographical location of plants in Australia.

Courtesy of Mary White *The Greening of Gondwana*

The lecture

that Diana Snape uses with precision). Such plants are likely to need no or little supplementary watering, immensely important as water becomes an increasingly scarce resource. They are adapted to local soils and should rarely need the mineral fertilisers that lead to excess nutrient build-up in our waterways: (the nutrients lead to algal blooms, which deplete the water of oxygen, the fish die, and so on down).

Local plants are usually resistant to local pests and are therefore less demanding of toxic pesticides, although this, alas, is not always the case. There are few general statements in either horticulture or ecology that do not admit of exceptions. Where plant breeders are able to cross two related species the F1 hybrids often show hybrid vigour and are tougher than either parent. More often, however, the nurseries even of 'native' plants practise selective breeding within a given species, aiming for showy flowers or a longer flowering season. The resultant cultivars may need more care in the garden than in nature, more nutrients, more water – and of course they are not necessarily resistant to all the plant pathogens and predators we have introduced into the garden environment, especially in the towns and cities where most of us live.

A second and powerful reason for using the plants of your own locale is that they cannot become 'garden escapes', by definition. In one sense, that of the last paragraph, it is wise to use plants, whatever their source, adapted to your immediate environment (soil, rainfall, hours of sunshine, temperature range). Thus plants from comparable Mediterranean zones in the other continents are generally well suited to southern Australia, but these are also the plants most likely to become invasive (feral, if you like). Bulbs and corms from southern Africa are among the worst, but there is a long list, rapidly getting longer, of introduced plants that are

The danger of confusing political with natural boundaries can be illustrated with birds which, like the plants, know nothing of nationality. The kookaburra is an alien in Western Australia introduced from the eastern seaboard, and much hated by bird lovers. It is a rapacious predator, more disposed to eat the eggs and nestlings of the indigenous birds that have a different evolutionary past and are not adapted to its presence than it is to eat the lizards and snakes of popular illustration. Birds know nothing of the nationality of plants, either. My wife and I treasure the singing honeyeaters in our garden. Their preferred winter food is the abundant red pea flower of the big old coral tree, *Erythrina* cf. *indica*. That it is an exotic is of no concern to the honeyeaters.

There is, however, a strong case for using plants from your immediate locality (literally indigenous plants, a term

ABOVE: May Gibbs' endearing kookaburra from *Snugglepot and Cuddlepie*.

invading the bushland of south-western Australia, and many are now out of control. This problem can also occur with 'native' plants used in a new setting. One well-known case is *Pittosporum undulatum* from Gippsland, now regarded as a serious invasive weed in the Dandenongs, where it is not indigenous. But if you live on the coastal limestone in Fremantle, as my wife Marli and I do, our garden templetonia or spyridium might yield seeds that are spread by birds, but if they grow they will be indistinguishable from the survivors still to be found in adjoining pockets of bushland.

A third reason for experimenting with Australian plants in the garden is the 'love 'em or lose 'em' proposition, of which the Wollemi Pine is a spectacular example. It has been found in two small and almost inaccessible natural habitats in the Blue Mountains, but is now being busily propagated in a Queensland nursery, to be released shortly to the gardening public. This is an interesting case, in that the 'conserve biological diversity' argument runs head-on into the purist approach to environmental conservation. For instance the anti-pittosporum case in the Dandenongs is essentially an argument against the increasing homogenisation of the natural world and the blurring of the distinctive character of specific habitats. The outcome, however, is beyond doubt: the Wollemi Pine will sell like hot cakes, and will be tried all over the place (if I were younger I would be tempted to try one myself, since *Podocarpus elatus* does so well here in Fremantle, so far from 'home'!).

There are similar examples from the western side of the continent. Some of the Mountain Bells such as *Darwinia collina*, *D. leiostyla* and *D. macrostegia* occur only on one or two peaks in the Stirling Ranges. Another example of a valuable and beautiful plant with a very limited natural distribution is the Qualup Bell (*Pimelea physodes*). All of these are vulnerable. They are not yet common in cultivation, but *Corymbia ficifolia*, the Red-Flowering Gum, does so well in southern Victoria that it is sometimes called

ABOVE: Qualup Bell (*Pimelea physodes*) from WA has delicate, soft pastel tones. In the east, it can be grafted and grown in a pot for greater success.
PHOTOGRAPH BRIAN SNAPE

the Melbourne Gum. It is restricted naturally to a small area in the extreme south-west of Western Australia that gets some summer rain. Its distribution has been pushed steadily southwards as the climate has become drier over the last ten thousand years and it will be pushed right off the edge of the continent if this trend continues, as is generally predicted. The western half of the continent runs out of south too soon for further migration, whereas southern Victoria offers ideal habitat for this and other vulnerable species from the extreme south of Western Australia. If they had properly understood that they are 'Australian' species, they might have moved to Victoria of their own accord!

Many plants are increasingly vulnerable in the natural environment, for a whole raft of reasons, of which limited natural habitat is only the beginning. Increased fire frequency and intensity and clearing for agriculture have had a massive impact. In areas of pastoral leasehold, which take up a third of the continent, stretching from the Pilbara and the Kimberley across to north-west Queensland and western New South Wales, selective grazing and trampling by sheep, cattle, goats, donkeys and camels have eliminated or threaten many species. In southern Australia, garden escapes often out-compete the indigenous flora, and there are also introduced insect predators and pathogens, of which the worst is *Phytophthora cinnamomi*. Dieback has done immense damage in some of the floristic treasure houses of Western Australia such as the Stirling Ranges and the Fitzgerald River National Parks. The Proteaceae are especially at risk ('jarrah die-back' is a misnomer) so if you live on the Mornington Peninsula and can grow *Banksia coccinea* (not easy, but I have seen it growing there) you might be rendering a service to posterity. So the 'love 'em or lose 'em' argument can be compelling.

A fourth reason for growing 'Australian' plants is that it is fun. Gardening is rewarding when it is experimental: there is not much challenge in growing petunias, but there is in growing *Leschenaultia formosa*. I have seen some strikingly successful experiments in Diana and Brian Snape's own garden. For example they grow and flower several species of the prostrate banksias from the south coast of Western Australia. They are not ecologically appropriate so they have recreated a suitable environment by importing a mound of free-draining sand. This is exactly what traditional gardeners do – artificially recreate the conditions that are natural for the plant, be it a rhododendron or a cattleya orchid. Success has come through skilled gardening. So the lovely little banksia cones enrich their manufactured environment thousands of kilometres from their natural home, but nonetheless both a delight and a triumph.

Sometimes Australian plants are surprisingly versatile and can be grown in a wide range of environments, even though their natural habitat may be severely restricted. An extreme case is the Norfolk Island Pine (*Araucaria heterophylla*) which has been grown almost right around the coast of temperate Australia from Brisbane to Geraldton and beyond. The Silky Oak (*Grevillea robusta*) and the Geraldton Wax (*Chamelaucium uncinatum*) are other examples, and there are more. The Silky Oak comes from well-watered subtropical Queensland, but it can tolerate environments that have cold winters and hot, dry summers: it lines the main street of Heathcote in central Victoria, for example. Marli and I have in our garden three Plum Pines (*Podocarpus elatus*). This species also comes from a humid climate with summer rainfall in coastal Queensland, and it has no right to grow in Fremantle, with its searingly dry summers in 'soil' with a pH that approaches 11 – a thin layer of grey, water repellent sand that overlies dense limestone caprock. Yet they flourish, and show that they are quite 'at home' by reproducing prolifically, with unwanted seedlings requiring constant removal.

So there is great scope for experimenting with Australian plants from environments remote from our own, so long as we remember that this is not different in kind from trying to grow roses or Chilean bell-flowers. Strictly speaking, the podocarpus in our garden and the prostrate banksias in the Snape garden are exotics. In the main text, to follow, the author has an outstanding section on garden styles, in which she quite properly distinguishes between indigenous gardens, using local plants only, and 'blended gardens'. She adds that all gardens that include non-indigenous plants are blended gardens, even those that are restricted to Australian plants. Her garden is therefore a blended garden, as is ours. But we need to remember that such plant transfers from one part of Australia to another can themselves become 'garden escapes' like *Pittosporum undulatum* in the Dandenongs. The banksia and the podocarpus are unlikely candidates, since the banksia needs its sand pile for drainage, and the podocarpus some summer water.

Apart from the pleasure of successful experiment there are other reasons for wanting to grow podocarpus in Fremantle so far from its natural habitat. Were we to grow only the plants indigenous to the limestone hill on which we live, we would be restricted to heathland plants. We do have them, too, abundantly: Cockies Tongue (*Templetonia retusa*); *Melaleuca acerosa* with its generous yellow flower heads; and Native Dusty Miller (*Spyridium globulosum*), a plant that should be used much more widely, in my view, since it is both attractive and very undemanding; and so on. But for trees, only *Callitris preissii*, of which we have about twenty, and *Melaleuca lanceolata*, which prefers more shelter than we can provide. We needed more trees, some for shade and privacy and others chosen for design or functional considerations; some deciduous to allow winter sun and summer shade, like the old mulberry and several coral trees (*Erythrina* cf. *indica*) with its red pea-flowers

Banksia blechnifolia   F. Mueller

ABOVE
Celia Rosser
Banksia blechnifolia 1994
Vol.111, No. 1
Watercolour and pencil on paper
76.0 x 58.8 cm
Courtesy of Monash University Collection

15

bright against the winter-blue sky. (There are at least four species of Erythrina indigenous to Australia – including *E. vespertilio* and *E. phlebocarpa* – so perhaps this one from India can be allowed in under the 'family reunion' clause.)

In any case the mulberry and the coral trees were here when we bought the house and are part of its history. We have introduced other exotics ourselves, for example some evergreen oaks (*Quercus suber* from the Iberian Peninsula; *Q. ilex* from Italy, and *Q. agrifolia* from California). Why? In part for horticultural reasons and in part for design reasons. The practical problem is that very few Australian trees can tolerate the hyperalkalinity of our soil; Diana Snape notes later that although plants from alkaline soils can often adapt to soils that are neutral or weakly acid, the reverse does not hold. Most eucalypts, for example, like a neutral or slightly acid soil, whereas these oaks from Mediterranean climes are familiar with limestone. The design reasons are the usual ones; for contrast, form, colour. In our strong light, a green so dark as to be almost black helps to give solidity and substance to the design in summer, but there is also a wonderful flush of new foliage in spring, especially with the podocarpus, a burst of lime green against the sombre black-green of the mature foliage.

And that brings us to design, the exciting part, yet in many ways the most difficult to do well and the most difficult to talk about sensibly, given the scale and diversity of the continent and the range of social and cultural settings. Good design is good design. We do not need, it does not make sense to talk about, an Australian garden style. What we do need is better design, which, like all good design, is sensitive to local environmental and cultural settings. The author argues this case persuasively in the text to follow, but the broad proposition that 'good design is sensitive to local environmental and cultural settings' is subject to a range of interpretations. Some of these are in partial conflict with her

preference for what she identifies as 'the informal' as against 'the formal'.

Her usage is pretty much common practice in much current Australian garden writing, but these are nevertheless imprecise terms. If by 'formal' one means design that demands control and manipulation of both the natural environment and the introduced plant material, then all gardening is 'formal': that is the nature of gardening. Growing prostrate banksias from the coastal sand plains of the south coast of Western Australia in Melbourne is formal in this sense, a triumphant act of control and manipulation (with, of course, an attractive outcome). The difference lies, not primarily in the degree of control exercised, but in the extent to which it is visually displayed or artfully concealed, as in the latter case. The most obvious characteristic of consciously displayed manipulation is the use of a rectilinear layout, of plane surfaces (as in many hedges), and geometrically precise shapes such as balls and pillars, achieved by clipping. We have a helper in the garden for a couple of hours a week, and I have told him that when he is reducing the bulk of a plant that is getting too big for its boots, it should look when he is finished as if he had never touched it, which may actually be more time consuming than a simple clip-over. This reflects the Snape view, too; she shows a marked preference for what she calls 'informality'.

But she also argues, rightly, that a garden should be compatible with the house and sensitive to the local physical and social context. These two attitudes may conflict. The typical Australian house is rectilinear in plan, and it sits on a rectilinear block of land amongst other rectilinear houses on rectilinear blocks of land. This is the immediate context of most gardens in Australia. I do not automatically prefer to conceal this rectilinear format, and in at least some respects it should be embraced. Where, for example, a path has a clear destination and is much trafficked, as in front gate to front door, anything but a straight line is perverse. The same holds for the driveway unless you have a very large block.

The social context also includes the neighbourhood. If you live in one of the older suburbs, for example, there's likely to be an overall likeness between at least the front gardens, and perhaps good manners might suggest that you respect this. You can dare to be different, of course, and could find yourself a trendsetter, but at least you should give the overall context some thought. What is rare and valuable in Diana Snape's book, however, is that despite her strong preference for the 'informal' she nevertheless offers constructive detail about the Australian plants that will withstand regular clipping to make satisfactory geometrical shapes and plane surfaces. You don't have to use *Buxus sempervirens*: there are Australian alternatives.

Strong light intensities prevail in much of Australia, and especially in the southern sweep from south-western Australia across all of South Australia, through most of Victoria, and then north through New South Wales and southern Queensland west of the Divide. This, along with the need to conserve water, has led to adaptive consequences in the natural environment, and they are significant for design. Foliage is often fine, sometimes very fine, as in nearly all the plants of the heathlands (micromyrtus, for example).

The colour range is highly distinctive; grey, grey-green, blue-green, black-green, and then translucent copper reds in the new flush of growth (because in nutrient-poor soils, the production of anthocyanin outstrips that of the more

RIGHT: Glazebrook/Cox garden Qld. Colourful shrubs such as grevilleas and daisies have been introduced and blend beautifully with a background of local trees and Grass Trees. Grevilleas have abundant nectar for insects and birds, with a variety of other food sources present too so that birds in particular can get a 'balanced diet'.

PHOTOGRAPH FRAN BRIGHT

nutrient-demanding chlorophyll). Foliage is often pendent and tough (sclerophyllous) as a protection against insolation; prickly or harsh as a protection against grazing and browsing animals. Foliage is often resinous, too, a fresh fragrance to our Australian noses, but a deterrent to many insect predators. Flowers may be exquisite but small: even banksia cones are made up of a multitude of small individual flowers. Flowers are often rich in stamens, like tiny pincushions, but poor in petals. In less brilliantly lit climes, large petals guide the fertilising bees and moths to the functional core of the flower, stamens and stigma, but such crude traffic signals are rarely needed here. Our flowers are often rich in honey, too, easy to manufacture in a sun-rich world.

What we do not commonly find in this world of the sun are plants with large mid-green leaves, wilting as soon as their water-filled cells are thirsty; nor large flowers like those of, say, the rhododendrons, and prolific to the point of covering the bush or tree, going all out to get fertilised in their native murk. I have seen groves of rhododendrons growing under sheltering deciduous trees in Bodnant, one of the great gardens of the British Isles. The flowers glow like jewels in the low light. If you were able to grow them in Bendigo you would

need to keep them under a humidifying spray through the summer and they would look gross, lacking all decent restraint.

The point I am making is that such foliage, such flowers, look out of place in much of this country, not just horticulturally and ecologically, but visually. Of course there are exceptions like Mount Macedon and Mount Wilson – but they are indeed exceptions. By contrast, designing with a palette of indigenous plants can allow a subtle harmony of all the foliage colours listed above, and more; some are very pale grey, almost white, like *Leucophyta brownii* (which used to be *Calocephalus*) and some of the Emu Bushes (*Eremophila* spp.), which are good for accent or contrast, just as the black-greens are so good for giving solidity, anchoring a composition that might otherwise etherealise in the heat-haze and float away.

Gardens must serve all kinds of people, with differing needs in different places, so it is unwise to be prescriptive about design. A common design model in suburban

ABOVE: Standing garden NSW. On a relatively flat block, this beautiful garden is designed to link with and retain borrowed landscape. Plants respond well to the open but sheltered conditions and trees such as a young Native Tamarind (*Diploglottis cunninghamii*) are kept away from the house to reduce fire risk.
PHOTOGRAPH JIM STANDING

Australia is what I call the 'clearing in the forest', a lawn opening out from the rear of the house, backed by a half-circle or irregular u-shape of shrubs and trees. When much of Europe was densely forested, a clearing gave some security – approaching predators could be seen in advance. The study of human behaviour in such settings has led to the 'prospect and refuge' hypothesis (Appleton, 1975): that people going for a picnic in a park, for example, will generally choose to sit, neither in the middle of the open space, nor in the encircling trees, but at the edge, exhibiting a behaviour pattern that has a long ancestry. We have in-herited this design model, along with much else, from Britain, and it survives perhaps for primeval reasons (it offers a com-fort zone), but also for more practical ones: the surrounding trees give privacy, while the open space, usually under grass, is well suited to the needs of children, dogs, family life.

Natural clearings in the forests of western Europe were usually the outcome of lightning strikes and local fire, but such clearings are almost unknown in the Australian bush, where fire is rarely local. Away from the coast, moreover, forest soon gives way to grassy woodland, heath, grassland or shrub steppe. If you are intending a naturalistic use of indigenous plants, therefore, the 'clearing in the forest' is not an appropriate model (although that does not mean that you cannot follow that model and yet include indigenous plants). A naturalistic design will not be that of a static composition seen through a picture window. Such gardens are to be enjoyed from a preferred viewing point, with all those formal elements so deeply embedded in our culture: foreground, middle ground, back-ground, asymmetric framing elements on each side, a 'picture' more or less conforming to the golden mean of the Greeks – which is roughly the proportion of most paintings, most photo-graphs of landscapes, even of the view-finder of the camera.

Fred Williams, the landscape painter par excellence, broke with this painterly convention by painting strip pictures, his contention being that the Australian landscape is often a seamless continuity rather than a series of set views. Naturalistic gardens using Australian plant material also break with this convention, but in a different way; they will be intricate and dynamic, not static. Diana Snape writes of 'walkabout gardens', a good term. They can be quite small, like her own. You move around them, apparently at will, discovering hidden treasures, and the scale of attention is often minute. You are constantly tempted around the next corner, all apparently artlessly, although of course the artistry lies in concealing the art.

Even this is not new: Guilfoyle designed the Royal Botanic Gardens at South Yarra on just such principles, although on the grand scale, and not in the naturalistic mode. The English poet Robert Herrick once wrote of a young woman that 'there is a sweet disorder in her dress', and this might apply to such a garden, which can accept, be enhanced by, fallen twigs and leaves, although once again with hidden management in the background to ensure that treasured plants are not smothered. 'Leaf litter is not litter' might be a new slogan in such a context.

This book covers much ground, not all of it well trodden, so it is in part exploratory. There is room for debate over some of its assertions. The author is a campaigner for a cause in which she believes passionately. It is a cause with which I sympathise and believe to matter. It is a strength of this book that it challenges the reader to look again, to think again. We are all on a steep learning curve about a country of which we still know so little, and of which we have destroyed so much. So a book such as this is welcome.

Now let the trumpets sound, the curtain go up, the show begin. The Prologue is at an end.

George Seddon AM

Reference: Appleton, Jay 1975,
The Experience of Landscape, Wiley, New York

INTRODUCTION

My colleagues and I are passionate about our very different Australian gardens. Each is unique, a product of its site and sense of place interpreted through the owner's experience and creativity. Barbara Buchanan cares for an expansive area in the country, while Jo Hambrett in Sydney and Chris Larkin in Melbourne tend large gardens in the outer suburbs. Danie Ondinea's inner suburban garden in Sydney is just 170 square metres. Over one hundred other members of our Garden Design Study Group from all over Australia have contributed their knowledge and ideas to assist in the writing of this book. We all belong to the Australian Plants Society (APS) or the Society for Growing Australian Plants (SGAP).

My husband, Brian, and I began our Australian garden almost thirty years ago on our standard suburban allotment of 0.1 hectare, 9 kilometres from the centre of Melbourne. Its creation was a gradual process – no overnight transformation but an exploration over many years of the exciting possibilities of our site and the array of wonderful plants available. We have tried to reflect the pristine beauty of untouched natural areas, an elusive goal that still inspires us. We designed garden rooms – separate areas with different microclimates, characteristics and uses. For practical purposes, we have grouped plants in zones according to their water needs. After initial watering and fertilising, the plants require no further fertilising and almost no watering.

All plants in our garden (outside the vegetable garden) are Australian including a number that are indigenous to our area. The enormous variety of Australian plants – about 25000 species – and their versatility offer great scope for the design of gardens for every purpose and location. By contrast, in Britain fewer than 1800 native species remain. The Australian flora is unique – the drift of the continent from other land masses millions of years ago resulted in the evolution of many unusual and beautiful plant forms. Grass Trees, Bottle Trees and banksias have arresting sculptural forms to rival any. They belong only here, while many showy exotic plants and flowers are as widespread as Big Macs.

In our garden, the seasonal changes are more subtle than in gardens of the northern hemisphere. However, in their turn, buds, flowers, fruits and the magnificent new foliage of many species provide wonderful colour. When plants flower in sequence, an area can be bathed in the yellow of acacias, the white of tea-trees, or in pink and purple. Summer features grasses that play with light – silver, golden or tawny. Winter is never bare and bleak but green and often colourful with flowers, for example grevilleas, hakeas and banksias.

Australian plants are the basis of our natural ecosystem and a garden containing local plants helps keep the ecological landscape intact. Interrelationships between organisms and the environment they share are precariously balanced. Even a small Australian garden, with a safe birdbath, automatically supports a mini native ecosystem; birds are good indicators of the ecological health of an area. In a busy suburban area, our garden welcomes over sixty species of native birds, including colourful Eastern and Crimson Rosellas and clamorous lorikeets. We greatly enjoy seeing small birds such as Brown Thornbills, White-browed Scrubwrens and Eastern Spinebills, and have been thrilled by visits from a Pink Robin and a Regent Honeyeater.

These are some of our rewards for creating an Australian garden. There are also evocative sounds – a magpie's call, wind whispering in casuarinas; perfumes too – scent of eucalypt leaves,

OPPOSITE: Snape garden Vic. My husband Brian and I began our Australian garden almost thirty years ago, inspired by natural landscapes though not a 'bush garden'. Its peace and harmony depend in part on the woven blend of form and foliage. *Eucalyptus mannifera* ssp. *maculosa* (Red Spotted Gum) shades the house in summer and established melaleucas offer western shade. In the foreground, *Isopogon anemonifolius* (Broad-leaf Drumsticks) and a Guinea Flower (hibbertia) add colour.
PHOTOGRAPH SIMON GRIFFITHS

fragrance of a prostanthera; and textures – papery bark of melaleucas, furrows in ironbark trunks. Generally plants thrive here and the birds, insects and wildlife that respond to them are inherent components of it. We replaced all lawns with mulched areas, groundcover plants or hard landscape and this has saved much water and work. Our whole garden follows sound ecological principles and is easy to manage, with recycling of nutrients from prunings and leaf-drop.

Cooperation with nature is satisfying but the greatest reward is the deep, all-pervading sense of harmony in our garden. Its calmness and cohesion reflect the timeless (but now threatened) nature of our natural environment. The total ambience is absorbing and relaxing but beauty also lies in intricate details. An ornamental beetle sits on a leaf; a colourful dragonfly projects from the stem of a reed beside a small pool. These insects are descendants from dreamtime ancestors and this is their home. New foliage shyly reveals its colour, or a flower bud unfolds. Individual plants link us to memories of favourite places.

Despite its highly urban population, Australia is still defined by its landscape, 'the outback' and 'the bush'. Like thousands of Australians we enjoy travelling throughout our country and appreciate the beauty of its wilderness areas – our natural landscapes and their plant communities. We can all gain inspiration from the Australian landscape – its peace and harmony; the light and space; its infinite variety of colours, often subtle; the sculpturing of the land surface; the massing, forms and patterns of rocks; the fascinating liquid textures of water; and, of course, the plants – a weeping tree, a tufted grass.

Those of us who experience this beauty are privileged. We can design gardens that respond to such natural landscapes and their plant communities. We do not have to repeat the familiar, stereotyped images drawn from gardens of exotic origin. Most Australians enjoy gardening (70 per cent in a recent survey), one of the three top lifestyle choices. Yet few gardeners aim to capture or distil the essence of natural landscapes; most are still missing out on the peace and tranquillity that could be theirs.

Forty years ago, when we first grew Australian plants, gardeners had to be propagators and horticulturists. They collected cuttings or seeds and then experimented with horticulture. It is much easier now to use Australian plants successfully in garden design. Nurseries stock an increasing range of species, especially exciting small plants. Knowledge about cultivation is amassed in reference books such as the *Encyclopaedia of Australian Plants*. Horticultural invest-igation has expanded into the selection of special forms and cultivars and the recognition of provenance and ecological relationships. We now know that we can design an Australian garden with confidence and it can blend Australian and exotic plants. It can, for example, even be strikingly formal – it does not have to be a 'bush garden'.

In designing our garden we have incorporated elements derived from nature and from other gardens, then interwoven our own inspiration and ideas. Brian and I seek to work in partnership with nature, not in conflict. We benefit from recognising and accepting what the Australian environment has to offer, and working within its dynamic but delicate equil-ibrium. Our garden celebrates nature's charms and strengths. However, it is a garden – we enjoy the natural forms of plants but, where necessary, we shape them to grow as we wish, so that we find their blending attractive. No garden can be a slice of pristine wilderness because people are part of that garden.

In the stillness and serenity of the late afternoon, I think our Australian garden acknowledges and shows our appreciation of our place in this lucky country. I am deeply conscious of our good fortune.

Diana Snape

OPPOSITE: A cluster of individual flowers of *Pimelea* 'Pygmy White' shows a high degree of symmetry. It is a delightful small plant in the garden.
PHOTOGRAPH BRIAN SNAPE

Beginning with Design

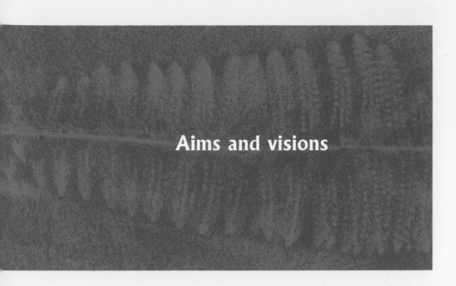

Aims and visions

The garden must be prepared in the soul first or else it will not flourish.

Old English proverb

A beautiful garden designed with appropriate Australian plants has many special and appealing qualities. It can be home for a variety of native birds, animals and insects. It can display an array of colours, stunning or subtle, and tantalise with a variety of scents. A garden of Australian plants has practical advantages with modest requirements of resources such as water. Significantly, it has a serenity often hard to find elsewhere.

Before you start planning, it helps to identify your aims and to find an overall vision for your garden that will continue to inspire you. Visiting other gardens, especially local ones, may prompt ideas. Remember your family's needs may change, just as your aspirations may also evolve as your garden develops. Australians relax, entertain, work and play in their gardens, so the design must suit your lifestyle. A garden can extend the boundaries of a home in a distinctive way, with no hard division between inside and out. Achieving harmony in the total home environment involves good design, centred in simplicity and tailored for you.

A special entrance garden, sunny mounds for flora from arid areas, or sheltered areas for ferns may be among your aims. In hot climates, you may long for the coolness of a shady summer garden with trees, dense planting, rainforest flora and water in a pond or pool. In colder climates, gardeners welcome maximum sunshine or a sunny winter courtyard. You may wish to maintain open sunny areas between swathes of trees and shrubs that, later on, could shelter an array of smaller plants from wind and frost.

What style of garden would you like to achieve? Do you want a hard or soft look, bold use of colour or prevailing shades of green? You may plan your garden for specific local conditions, such as coastal or arid. An informal garden landscape might be easy to maintain and compatible with a growing family, or you may prefer a neat and tidy formal garden. Repeating form and foliage from surrounding natural landscapes will ensure an integrated and harmonious result or you may decide to follow a theme such as foliage or flower colour or interesting textures.

Increasingly Australians look to their garden not just for its beauty but also as a haven, a source of comfort and reassurance. A beautiful garden may soothe a troubled mind or encourage a creative spirit. A living space that respects the environment and its natural cycles can make us feel better mentally and physically – just as we try to provide optimum conditions for the health of our plants, so we can for ourselves. Gardens managed in harmony with nature will be serene with a palpable 'sense of place'.

Establishing a garden with Australian plants enables a more efficient management of soil, water and energy. If this management is combined with design skills, we can anticipate the development of gardens that function well and enjoy a certain look or style, so that instinctively we say 'That's a great Australian garden!'

PREVIOUS PAGE: *Anigozanthos flavidus* hybrid (a Kangaroo Paw) PHOTOGRAPH BRIAN SNAPE

OPPOSITE: Adams garden Vic. Designed by Gordon Ford. This special, welcoming entrance area links garden to house and is beautiful to look out on from inside. A timber frame outlines the space where a lily pond provides coolness and humidity in hot weather. A waterfall has been created among skilfully placed rocks. PHOTOGRAPH TRISHA DIXON

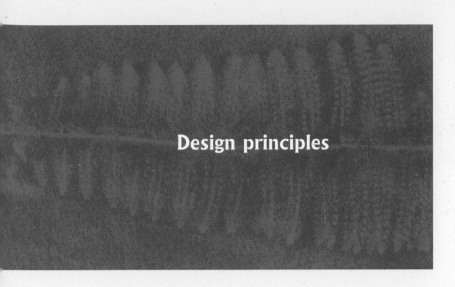

Design principles

Gardening calls for an artist's eye for colour and form coupled with a musician's sense of developing a theme over time – something the visual artist can't do.

Kevin Nicolay, quoted in *Horticulture*, January 1990

Garden design is as much an art form as painting or sculpture. Some gardeners claim it is the highest form of art because plants change with the seasons and the years, so the designer is working in four dimensions. Underlying all art forms are a few basic design principles. Successful garden design depends on the application of these principles, while fulfilling your aims, and responding to the demands of available material (including plants), the site, climate and budget.

There are two main phases in designing a garden. First is the development of your vision of the desired effect, the way you want to use the space. This is the broad design. It involves identifying the roles that plants will play and how they will be arranged to achieve your vision. The second phase involves choosing the actual plants. Then the real joy begins!

Scale and proportion

A garden of appropriate scale can enhance the buildings within it – it can emphasise the best features, and disguise or hide poor ones. The house and garden should work as one visually pleasing space. If the surrounding landscape or the building dominates, a garden on too small a scale will look limited and insignificant. Planting of extensive areas should be bold, for example with stands of tall trees and an array of middle- and lowerstorey plants. In contrast, a large shrub in a small cottage garden is likely to look incongruous and be too dominant.

The size of each component – paths, steps, rocks, pool and seats – should be appropriate for the dimensions of the garden and the house it surrounds. Wide front doors need wide approaches; tall trees look best in large gardens.

There are many ways to solve problems of scale. You can bring a large garden back to human scale by subdividing it into separate spaces, either outdoor 'rooms' or less regular areas, each serving a specific function or enjoying different characteristics. If you plan a cottage or wildflower garden as part of a much larger garden, you could contain it with a formal or informal hedge, or a pergola; then the whole becomes a unit within the overall design.

Proportions or ratios will help determine the 'feel' of a garden. One significant ratio is between open space at ground level, including paths, and the ground space occupied by garden beds or planted areas. Another is the comparison of space and vegetation at head height, which affects visibility through the garden. A third ratio is that of relative heights of plants – trees, shrubs, groundcovers and tufted plants. Harmonious ratios contribute to the serenity of a garden. For example, is this poa (Tussock Grass) the right size to place next to this rock? The answer will depend on ratios of sizes and your personal response to them – for example, a ratio of one-half or one-quarter

OPPOSITE: Hanson garden Vic. Designed by Bev Hanson. A Bower Vine (*Pandorea jasminoides*) arches over a pathway, framing the vista beyond. This climber is attractive with large, glossy leaves and pale pink trumpet flowers but requires pruning each year to keep it in shape.
PHOTOGRAPH SIMON GRIFFITHS

may be less pleasing to the eye than one-third (closer to the 'golden mean').

Symmetry, asymmetry and harmony

Harmony relies on proportion and symmetry. Formal gardens have symmetry about an axis. Informal or naturalistic gardens are asymmetrical. Both styles require elements to be in pleasing proportion but you can obtain balance about an axis by means other than symmetry. Balance depends on the arrangement of masses and voids, horizontals and verticals, forms protruding and receding. Where balance is aesthetically pleasing, the effect is harmonious. Formal gardens have strong appeal for their obvious balance and order; however, they may suffer from being too predictable. Symmetry often works best on a large scale where there are enough individual features to sustain interest.

An asymmetrical scene that achieves harmony generally intrigues the eye longer, especially in restricted areas. Asymmetry need not be a total absence of symmetry, which may appear as an unsettling and undesirable hotchpotch of plants, but a balance achieved by an equivalence of components. For example, the mass of a dense shrub on one side of a pathway may visually balance a group of more wispy shrubs on the other side; the vertical dimension of a tree on one side might be equivalent to the combined heights of a group of shrubs or a swathe of strap-leaved plants on the other; the 'negative' space of a reflective pool may be balanced by sky.

Of course in all gardens (even formal ones) everything grows, at varying rates, and the effect of time is likely to alter proportions and balance, so you need to manage growth to maintain harmony.

Line, shape and form

Line is a primary element in creating shapes and may be used in an infinite number of ways – straight and curved lines, complex patterns of lines. Converging lines may be used to focus inwards, diverging lines to open out. Parallel lines of plants can form a partial screen. Crossing lines can create shapes and patterns. Broad-scale horizontal lines of water, grass and distant low hills produce a tranquil effect. In a small garden, the flat surfaces – water, mulched open space, ground-hugging plants, a mown lawn – contrast with the vertical dimension of strap-leaved or tufted plants such as reeds, lilies, grasses and Kangaroo Paws. Their upright stance reinforces other vertical lines. The white trunks of eucalypts like Lemon-scented Gums (*Corymbia citriodora*) planted together in a lawn make the statement on a grander scale. Light produces silhouettes of trees and a tracery of shadows of branches as a secondary series of lines. Lines outline surfaces and, in three dimensions, describe regular or abstract shapes.

Shapes or forms come in a limitless variety, hard- or soft-edged, on their own or in combination with lines and circles. Picture a mountain, a bushy tree, a shrub – you are mostly aware of shape and solidity. The composition of shapes in a garden should sit comfortably within the surfaces and shapes of the surrounding landscape. Some plants are regular in shape – spheres, ellipsoids or cones – but more are irregular and few, other than pruned hedges, have the flat surfaces characteristic of hard landscape. Australian plants display an infinite variety of growth patterns – upright or weeping, rounded or spreading, single or multi-trunked, graceful or sturdy. An ability to relate shapes well will produce visual strength in garden design.

Form is often referred to as the 'bones' of a garden and good gardens invariably have 'good bones'. The form of an individual plant is just the starting point, as you can mass groups of plants to create simple or complex shapes. If the plan calls for a tall thin plant, only one may be needed but a

rounded mass could be filled by one large plant or a series of smaller ones. Several similar species may be introduced without disrupting the unity of the overall design. Plants with similar foliage blend into the larger plant mass, while shapes of plants defined by contrasting foliage – in colour, leaf shape or size – stand out from the overall form.

Another element could be dots or circles, as in traditional Aboriginal artwork or the landscape itself – all sizes of rounded pebbles or rocks, plants or groups of plants.

Masses and voids

The question of balance between material and space, or mass and void, must also be considered. What the eye sees as open space depends partly on the scale of the garden. In large gardens, you see space between groups of trees or shrubs; in a rainforest garden you see beneath the canopy and along paths; in intimate town gardens the space between individual plants is more significant. Whatever the size of the garden, space is the counterpart of the solid masses of vegetation. A pleasing balance between material and space and the shapes so created is essential to achieve harmony. A fence or wall gives space a straight edge, while the convex surface of a shrub gives space a concave side. Open space provides a natural setting – a stage – for a feature plant, garden furniture or sculpture.

Many conventional gardens, with their high proportion of open space and relatively narrow garden beds around the margins, do not inspire. At the other extreme, a garden with no open areas looks overcrowded and cluttered. Without open space there are no views, from within either the house or the garden. Gaps between foliage allow you to observe framed vistas, providing visual links between separate parts of the garden and giving a sense of space. The appropriate balance between material and space will be determined by the type of garden, sheltered and intimate or expansive and open, and the plants you choose. It is amazingly easy to over-plant and have open spaces shrink as plants grow, though this is part of the natural development of any garden. Pruning and replacement can maintain the desired balance.

ABOVE: Davidson garden Vic. In a coastal garden, rounded forms of correas such as White Correa (*C. alba*), grevilleas and taller banksias are massed to create a pleasing overall form in the landscape.
PHOTOGRAPH DIANA SNAPE

Unity and repetition

Your personal touch will help ensure unity in your garden, especially as you develop firm ideas about design and the confidence to follow them. The strong appeal of a formal garden lies in its unified order. In a naturalistic garden, repetition is just as important but the rhythms are more subtle.

While you may choose to treat various areas differently, links will assist in creating unity. A gardener can enhance harmony by repeating some elements from space to space, for example the form and texture of a particular indigenous eucalyptus or leptospermum (Tea-tree) species; of groundcover plants, rushes, sedges or grasses; or of the material used for hard surfaces. You might use border plants to link one site to the next. Too much repetition of elements can be monotonous but the complete lack of it creates disharmony, which might be exciting but is difficult to live with.

Focal points and framing

Focal points to draw the eye are valuable features to include in a garden. In a large landscape a focal point could be a sculpture or feature tree; in a small intimate garden a moss-covered rock or beautiful plant in a pot. Items appropriate for formal gardens will differ in style from those for naturalistic ones. In a formal setting, avenues, hedges or sculpture may lead the eye to a focal point; in a naturalistic one the gardener can use more subtle elements, perhaps silvery or other distinctive foliage. If you create one major focal point in each vista, there will be a series of highlights to enjoy as you move through the garden.

Every picture is enhanced by a frame that encourages the eye to focus on the composition. Frames are straightforward in formal gardens – an arch, a wall or a solid background of dark-green foliage. 'Doors' or 'windows' cut into a screen increase interest as you glimpse framed views of another part of the garden. Chinese and Japanese gardeners effectively use Moon Gates, circular openings onto a view beyond. In a naturalistic garden, focal points should be less dramatic as gardens are viewed from different angles. There is less scope for formal framing but a uniform green background will highlight any feature plant. Natural-looking frames can be created with skilful pruning. If you are lucky enough to have dramatic scenery, such as mountains, as a backdrop, you may enhance the view by carefully framing it with trunks or foliage.

Screening

If your garden is without mystery and all can be seen at first glance, it may soon lack interest. Consider subdividing a large garden into separate compartments, each with its own character. Partial screens can allow glimpses of what is beyond while obscuring the details, enticing you to explore further. Discovering the whole garden, section by section, is a gradual and exciting process. Screening can also work in small gardens so that we feel enfolded by nature. It can make small gardens feel larger and more remote from the noise of city life and nearby vehicles.

Choosing the essentials

Gardeners need to be discriminating, to choose the essentials and not try to pack everything in. This discrimination and the ruthlessness needed to exercise it develop with experience, so don't ever feel guilty about your mistakes, just learn from them.

As the renowned garden designer Gertrude Jekyll put it: 'The way to enjoy beautiful things is to see one picture at a time, not to confuse the mind with a jumble of too many interesting individuals'. Elsewhere she wrote: 'In all kinds of gardening … the very best effects are made by the simplest means'. Jekyll, writing in Victorian England, also believed strongly in the use of local (indigenous) plants and her message of simplicity is equally valid today.

ABOVE: Hanson garden Vic. Designed by Bev Hanson. On either side of a path, planting is asymmetrical but harmony is achieved by a satisfying balance. Tufted plants include a fine lepidosperma and groundcovers such as Creeping Myoporum (*M. parvifolium*) in the foreground, adding variety to taller shrubs behind. Rounded forms, colours and particular species are repeated and the planting near rocks is of appropriate scale. In bloom on the left are two grafted darwinias, *D. meeboldi* and, in front, *D. macrostegia* (Mondurup Bell) with spectacular red and white streaked flowers.

PHOTOGRAPH SIMON GRIFFITHS

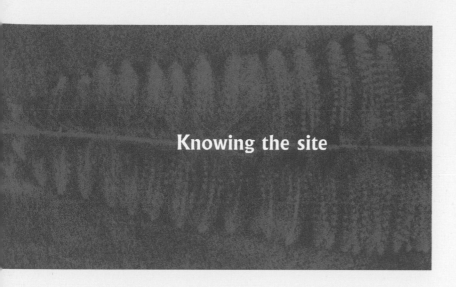

Knowing the site

Unlike the weather, soil can be improved.

Hugh Johnson, *Hugh Johnson's Gardening Companion*, 1966

Garden design must respect the existing site conditions.

Topography and soil

Is the land flat, sloping slightly or steeply, or irregular and interesting with higher and lower areas? Whatever the surface and its contours, they can be manipulated. The characteristics of surrounding landforms may also influence design.

Soil provides the foundation for the garden and much will depend on its nature – whether it is a product of alluvial deposition or the underlying geology and rock character. For a plant to reach its full potential the roots must be healthy, without disease or stress. Both sandy and clay soils have their advantages but a wide range of Australian plants prefer sandy loam because of its intermediate particle size. Although it may be tempting to bring in soil from elsewhere to 'improve' poor soil, this is generally not a good idea. It is preferable to improve existing soils by, for example, adding gypsum to heavy clay to improve the texture.

Some plants can grow in a range of areas and the occasional experiment can be worthwhile. Alkaline soils are more restrictive than acid, as generally plants from alkaline areas will grow in more acid conditions but the reverse does not apply. The situation in which a plant normally grows provides valuable guidelines – those found on ridge tops generally demand good drainage but also put down deep roots to endure drought. Plants from valley floors where water lies longer after rain are usually more shallow-rooted and susceptible to drought, while periodically tolerant of water around the roots. Ridge-top plants are also more likely to be frost-tender than their valley neighbours, because cold air drains downhill.

Water and climate

Water and climate will also restrict the choice of plants from other areas of Australia that will grow well for you. Rainwater is a precious resource that you should aim to retain in your garden wherever possible. Early in your observations you will quickly determine the directions and force of prevailing winds so that you can position important windbreaks to shelter the house and later plantings. A double row, not too dense, can be very effective. Consider wind deflection and local breezes. Plants may be sensitive to heat or frosts (especially when conditions are dry), so try to identify frost pockets. Observe the movement of the sun as it changes throughout the year. Consider the orientation of the garden and the resulting light patterns, as they will determine how growing trees and large shrubs change the distribution of shade.

'Borrowed' landscape

If you look out to wide open spaces or attractive suburban

OPPOSITE: John Hunt's garden NSW. A natural sandstone shelf and an old, gnarled *Banksia serrata* (Saw Banksia) have been retained on the site and contribute great character to the garden. Massed annual *Rhodanthe chlorocephala* ssp *rosea* (Pink Paper-daisy) add contrasting colour and delicacy against the background of solid rock.
PHOTOGRAPH DIANA SNAPE

gardens, you may want to enjoy your 'borrowed' landscape and restrict planting to low shrubs, tufted plants, or trees carefully spaced with an array of splendid trunks to frame the view. If the outlook is less appealing, a formal or informal hedge of shrubs can block the sight and create an enclosed area that is sheltered and cosy.

Starting with a block of land

Even a bare block of land has a history that may influence your options. It may have been used for grazing, an orchard or market garden, a sanitary land-fill, or a pine forest now burnt. Weeds, temporary or persistent, sometimes tell the story. They are best tackled early. A weed-infested area may eventually become the most prolific garden bed! Building a house, even with minimum disturbance, will also affect the distribution of soil and water on the block.

Starting with a house and an existing garden

Look at the house from many points in the garden. The style of house does not predetermine the style of garden, though the lines and mass of the building should certainly be taken into account. Check views from your windows too and identify those you want to retain, rescue or hide. The forms, textures and colours of plants and their combinations should create a picture in harmony with the building, or be designed to contrast.

Renovating an existing garden provides an excellent opportunity to remove unhealthy plants or those in the wrong position. (It's less painful when you haven't planted them yourself!) It's easier to design on a clear canvas but established plants, if suitable, will provide the 'backbone' for any new garden. Inheriting a well-established garden has its blessings. First, there is less urgency to get started. You have time to consider the strengths and weaknesses of the existing design and plantings, which may tell you a lot about the site

and its features. Secondly, you can create a new garden 'inside' one that is many years old. But an existing garden can often tempt the designer to compromise, as it can be difficult to see the garden with new eyes and not be strongly influenced by what is already there.

A 'bush' block

A block of natural vegetation may include trees, shrubs, groundcover plants, strap-leaved plants and grasses that could all contribute to a beautiful natural garden. The importance of such local indigenous plants is discussed later. The less land is cleared, the more unspoilt (and maintenance-free) the natural garden will be. If this area is large enough to be sustainable, eight hectares or so, in some states it can be protected forever by a covenant. Covenants originated in Victoria in 1972 with the Trust for Nature and more recently have become available in some other states.

The nature of the 'bush' will influence decisions. Grassland or heathland provides a wonderful open garden if disturbed as little as possible. Woodlands with large trees are shaded and enclosed, so you may have to remove some trees to obtain space and sunlight for the garden as well as buildings. Such clearing will affect local wildlife. The ecology of the site depends on the types and sizes of plants present and how they associate with each other. Look for evidence of animal life, remembering that it may be seasonal. Try to identify dominant plant and animal communities, their dependence on the existing conditions and their sensitivity to change.

A 'bush' block, or one next to a National or State Park or other conservation area, provides a ready-made, natural garden into which your garden can flow. Avoid using plants that can 'escape' and become weeds, either exotic plants or Australian plants from other areas. The attractive *Acacia baileyana* (Cootamundra Wattle), which occurs naturally in a very restricted area near Cootamundra, NSW, self-sows

abundantly and flourishes in many parts of Australia where it has been introduced. It is an example of an Australian plant now considered a pest. So check on potential nuisances before you plant and become attached to them.

Another responsibility for pet owners, particularly of cats, is not to allow them to wander at any time. Cats can be devastating killers of birds and other wildlife.

LEFT: Terrace garden Vic. Bought in the 1960s as *Eucalyptus nicholii* (Willow Peppermint) and supposed in those days to be a small tree, although beautiful in itself this tree now dwarfs the building and front garden.
PHOTOGRAPH DIANA SNAPE

RIGHT: Webb garden Qld. A steep site reveals an expansive borrowed landscape. A garden of Australian plants includes a young *Brachychiton acerifolius* (Illawarra Flame Tree), with grevilleas and Kangaroo Paws colouring the bed close to the house. A rainforest garden has been created higher on the site to avoid blocking the view.
PHOTOGRAPH DIANA SNAPE

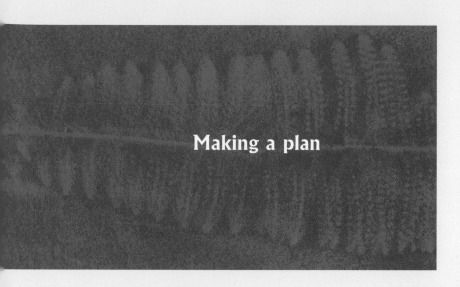

Making a plan

You have to have an idea. If you don't have a concept, you're just making goulash.

William Brincka, quoted in *Horticulture*, May 1990

Beginning a new garden or re-working an old one can seem a challenging task. The secret is to decide first on an overall broad-scale plan, without worrying about all the details. Set your priorities, then implement the plan in stages, taking one step at a time.

At an early stage, decide how much time you want to spend maintaining your garden. Both the style of garden and your standard of maintenance will affect this decision.

Determine whether you will need walls, fences, a driveway, access to the rear of the block, paths to doorways, steps or paving – all items of 'hard landscape'. These need to be completed early, so you are ready for the first rain and not surrounded by a sea of mud. Do you want areas for specific uses or activities (for example sitting, children's play, swimming pool, barbecue, clothes drying)? The initial layout of a garden should provide for such areas, connected by paths linked to the house.

The introduction of large rocks is also much easier prior to planting. If you need to use machines to create major changes in ground level, try to do so early in the process. Also at the planning stage it is worth deciding whether you can harvest water in low-lying areas or if you wish to create any features with water.

Planting trees is another priority as windbreaks and screens take several years to be effective and, until trees are above head height, a garden will appear young and unfinished.

Another consideration is the extent and shape of open areas and the surfacing or types of plants you'll choose for them. Mowing grass keeps an area tidy and useable while your ideas change and evolve – grass can be replaced without too much effort at a later stage.

Envisage a plan for the positions and shapes of garden beds and planted areas. Consider proportions and balance, vistas and screening. Design for an attractive arrangement of foreground, midground and background views. Then develop one area at a time, probably starting close to the house and relating each new section to the last. This will save time and energy. It is worthwhile measuring sizes and drawing a sketch plan of individual areas even if you can't manage this for the whole garden. If you plant all or most plants in one area at the same time, you will find that area easy to look after and the plants will have an equal share of rain and sun.

When you have finished planting one area, relax and enjoy what you have accomplished before starting the next.

OPPOSITE: Hall garden NSW. A treehouse in *Eucalyptus haemastoma* (Scribbly Gum) offers adventure for a growing family. The surrounding lawn provides space to play and, as needs change, the owner plans to extend the mulched garden to gradually reduce or eventually replace the lawn.
PHOTOGRAPH DIANA SNAPE

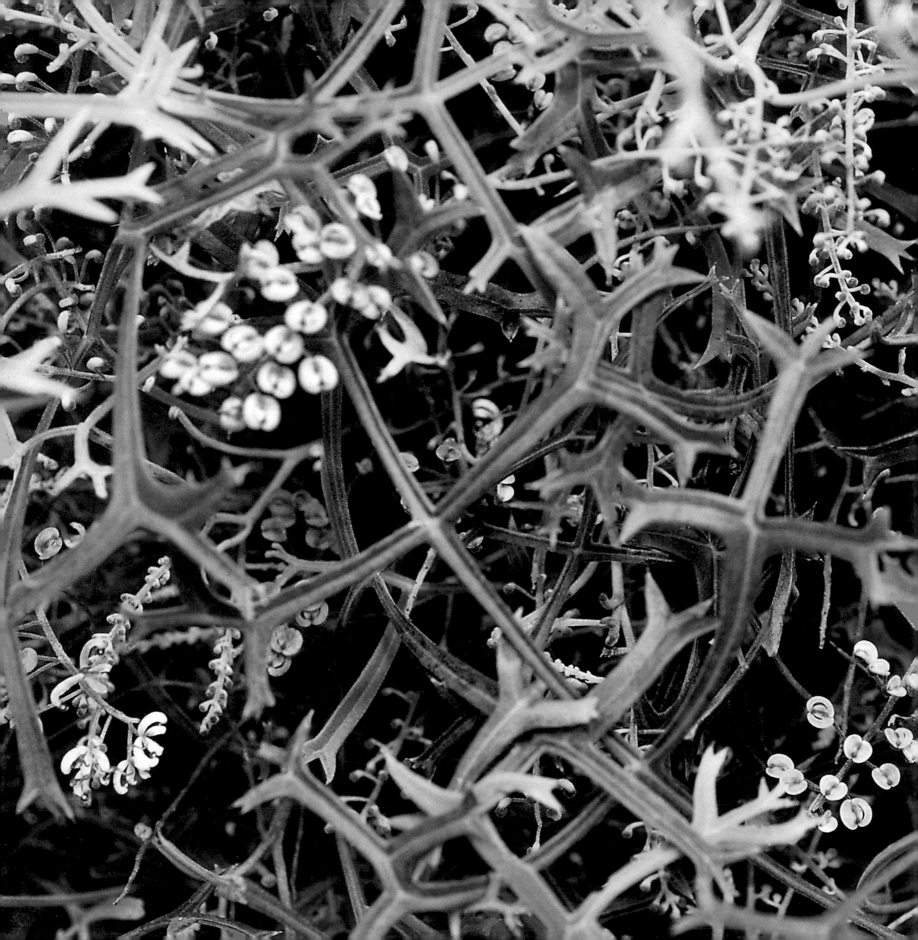

Putting it on paper

Begin your garden planning by applying design principles to the hard landscape, the garden layout, then types, sizes and forms of plants, before thinking about the actual plant species. What will you require in terms of trees and/or large shrubs for the boundaries, groundcover plants, and different plants to suit the varying microclimates in your garden? The choice of species to fill niches will come much later.

A second approach is to select the plants you would like to enjoy in the garden, trying not to include too many 'impulse buys' of numerous irresistible offerings, and prepare a detailed list; sort them into various categories (trees, large shrubs, ground-covers); then work out the conditions they require in terms of soil, sunlight, temperature and water, how these can be provided and how the plants can all be arranged into a garden. This can be more difficult than it seems!

Most gardeners probably combine these two approaches. Drawing (or just sketching) a plan can help immensely whether you are working on a whole garden, a single bed, or redesigning an area. If you plot the spread of plants fairly accurately, according to size guidelines in handbooks or reference books, the spacing will be more correct than if you just guess. A sketch will indicate which plants may be too big for a small garden – often hard to believe while they are still tiny plants. Moving large Australian plants usually kills them, so it pays to plan well.

Design concept

Line is the first element in design. Take into account the shapes in your setting. You might decide on a quite formal layout of garden beds with straight lines, circles and squares carefully measured and arranged in symmetrical fashion. For a more informal design, you can lay out a long hose to establish pleasing shapes for edges of areas you plan to plant. You can be adventurous and start a garden design with an abstract design concept – like the painter Klee, you can 'take a line for a walk', not in a painting but on your garden plan. Perhaps experiment with a freehand drawing of cross-hatched or swirling lines on paper, or clusters of shapes, and then simplify it to a satisfying layout pattern.

Sketching bubble diagrams

Start with a plan of your block on tracing paper, showing the position of the house and other structures, including neighbouring houses. Bubble diagrams are an easy way to sketch general areas and their possible uses. Initial measurements can be rough – pacing distances to find approximate lengths in metres. Rough sketches on layers of tracing paper will increase your confidence. These early drawings can be overlaid, analysed and refined until you and the family are happy. You can then begin to design the site in detail, including the planting plan.

Photographs both within the garden and from outside can be extremely useful. Plot on the plan where these photographs are taken.

PREVIOUS PAGE: The intricate pattern of stems, foliage, buds and flowers of *Grevillea leptobotrys* (Tangled Grevillea).
PHOTOGRAPH BRIAN SNAPE

OPPOSITE: Royal Botanic Gardens, Mount Annan NSW. Designed by Peter Cuneo. Multiple plantings of the Paper Daisies *Rhodanthe chlorocephala* ssp *rosea* (pink), *Schoenia filifolia* ssp *subulifolia* (yellow) and *Rhodanthe manglesii* (white) build these very small plants into large and significant components of the landscape.
PHOTOGRAPH PETER CUNEO

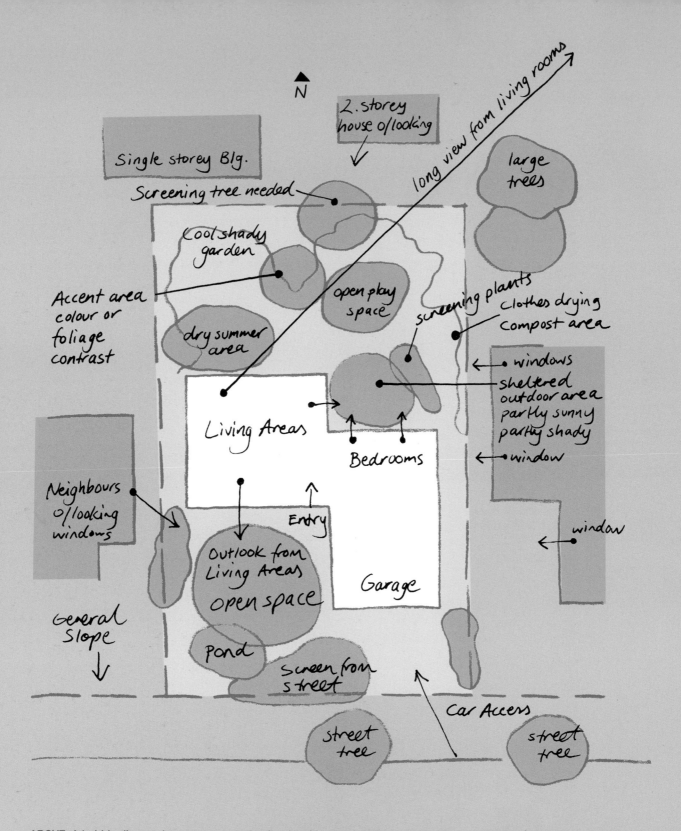

ABOVE: A bubble diagram is an easy way to begin, sketching general areas and their possible uses. ILLUSTRATION JOHN ARMSTRONG

Plants on the plan

A plan can become a record of your plants and their situation in the garden. Show positions of tree trunks and the extent of their canopy and those from trees next door. Note any spectacular plants – a few of these will create drama, but do not crowd them together. Star performers need quiet companions to show them off. Remember that the best overall effect is one of simplicity, even though it may consist of dozens of interesting plants. Look at massing plants and creating layers of foliage. Where space will allow, plants generally look better planted in groups of odd numbers rather than dotted about singly or in pairs.

ABOVE: Rowland garden NSW. Designed by Gordon Rowland. A tall wall becomes a splendid backdrop and its height is scaled down by a group of architectural Bangalow Palms (*Archontophoenix cunninghamiana*) and attractive plants with foliage interest such as Black Wattle (*Callicoma serratifolia*) and Long-leaved Tuckeroo (*Cupaniopsis newmanii*).

PHOTOGRAPH DIANA SNAPE

Avoiding mistakes

Mistakes made on paper are much easier and less costly to correct than those made on the ground. Your plan may help you respond to the following warnings.

· Don't divide up your block in a complicated and fussy way.

· Make sure differences in ground level are visually significant, not just liable to trip you.

· Be careful that repetition doesn't become tedious; for example, plants of distinct form (such as small conifers) just scattered throughout a garden.

· Avoid straight lines unless in a very formal garden – but also avoid sinuous wavy edges to garden borders, especially exaggerated by a stark outline of broken rocks, unsoftened by plants.

· Make sure arches and pairs of plants to frame views look or lead somewhere in particular.

· Avoid losing valuable views by choosing plants that grow too large.

· Don't create a fire hazard in fire-prone areas, especially close to the house.

· Check positions and eventual sizes of plants near windows and adjacent to paths.

· Plant some prickly bushes to cater for wildlife but not right beside pathways.

· Don't plant ferns on mounds or place ponds on the high side of the garden.

On the other hand, if your instinct is good and you have confidence in it, as Andrew Pfeiffer, landscape architect, says: 'Almost any rule that you care to devise about the design of gardens is capable of being deliberately broken with dazzling success.'

Garden styles

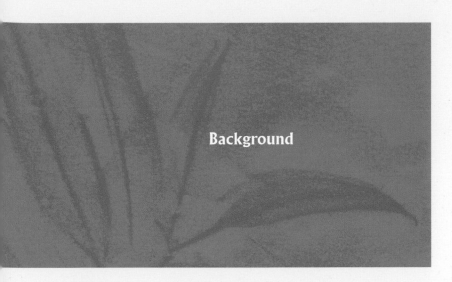

Background

You may already be an experienced gardener who has thought carefully about garden styles or you may be a beginner with a lifetime's delights and challenges ahead. The concept of style may seem elusive.

Over the centuries and in different countries garden styles have changed and evolved. At times the emphasis has been on individual plants. For example, when intrepid Victorian explorers and botanists returned to England with collections of plant specimens from Asia and the New World, gardens became places to display flowers and demonstrate one's skill in raising novelties. At other times the form of the garden became more important.

Formal styles have tended to alternate with naturalistic styles. In the Baroque gardens of Italy, for example, plants became subordinate to architectural devices. The regularity of the designs contrasted with nature's seeming haphazardness and illustrated man's domination over nature. In the great open-air rooms of the gardens of Le Notre in France, with their regimented style, plants were used as green walls to set off the peacock clothes of the courtiers. The naturalistic, classically inspired Arcadian landscapes of Capability Brown in England involved control but contrasted with the drama of the Baroque. Again the beauty of individual plants was less important than the overall composition, and the grounds were primarily intended to display the wealth and taste of the owner.

The 'Picturesque' style of massed beds of colour and single species of trees can still be seen around Australian buildings of the nineteenth century and in Australia's older botanic gardens and parks. Quite apart from the grand gardens, cottage gardens have long provided working men and women with culinary and medicinal plants and decorative flowers.

The greater wealth and improved technology of the twentieth century brought many more gardens and more widespread experimentation. A bewildering range of styles is now available.

When my husband, Brian, and I first started to plan our garden in Melbourne, our aim was to achieve a very natural style. However, we were soon tempted to grow some special Australian plants which, though not indigenous, brought us great joy. Gradually the garden evolved and became more controlled. This attempt at a 'natural' composition has proved, in practice, to require considerable contrivance, pruning and management.

Gardens reflect facets of our culture, imprinted with the creator's personality. The experiences and memories of a lifetime will influence each person's response to gardens and to gardening. A garden with satisfying consistency of style is long remembered, but so too is one of dramatic contrasts. With growing awareness of our unique Australian environment and its rapid degradation, garden styles are likely to emerge that reflect the nation's natural heritage.

PREVIOUS PAGE: Fern Garden, National Gallery ACT. Designed by Fiona Hall. Decorative gates open to a secluded courtyard garden in which a path, curled like a new fern frond, passes between Soft Tree-ferns (*Dicksonia antarctica*) used in a simple but highly effective formal design. Here a section of the Fern Garden shows the canopy of fronds and patterning of paths. PHOTOGRAPH DIANA SNAPE

OPPOSITE: Snape garden Vic. A pathway of woodchips and prostrate *Lobelia pedunculata* leads to *Eucalyptus rupicola* (Cliff Mallee Ash) as a focal point in the middle distance. On the left, the trunks of *Melaleuca lateritia* (Robin Redbreast Bush) rise from foliage of smaller shrubs, including *Correa reflexa* var. *nummulariifolia*. On the right, beneath *Hakea obtusa*, strap-leaved *Orthrosanthus multiflorus* echoes the other linear elements of trunks and branches. PHOTOGRAPH SIMON GRIFFITHS

Indigenous Gardens

Every great locality has its own pure daimon (spirit) and ... expresses itself perfectly, in its own flowers, its own birds and beasts ...

D.H. Lawrence, *The Spirit of Place*,

Studies in Classic American Literature, 1923

An indigenous garden is one created with only local flora. Wherever possible, consider including such plants in your garden as they have many advantages. Indigenous species have evolved to suit the local soil and climate. They don't demand extravagant use of water or fertiliser and many will recover rapidly from fire and drought. Unless conditions in your area have been profoundly altered, most local plants should prove hardy and reliable and less prone to pests and disease. Local species are more likely to regenerate naturally and you can welcome the unexpected appearance of their seedlings. If you already have some local natural vegetation, you may experience the thrill of discovering a new orchid or some other small treasure amongst your indigenous flora.

Edna Walling was an early advocate for retaining local flora, for example in roadside verges. Noted Sydney landscape architect, Bruce Mackenzie, has designed with indigenous plants for many years. More recently the conservation movement has raised general awareness of the importance of indigenous plants.

Marked regional differences in flora throughout Australia can enable a garden to be quite distinctive, with a unique sense of place. Using a variety of local plants as a framework heightens the special identity of a neighbourhood. If selected and placed carefully, even a scattering of indigenous plants in a garden will 'look right' and provide a little local flavour. Repeating chosen species helps to achieve a feeling of unity and tranquillity.

In urban and suburban areas, the 'sense of place' is often a complex issue, as the original 'place' may no longer be evident. You may wish to reflect the landscape of nearby natural areas but also 'fit in' with surrounding gardens. There is always a solution to such problems through design and the careful choice of plants so that some at least are compatible with those of neighbouring gardens.

In outer regions, indigenous plants can provide a framework linking the garden to the surrounding natural vegetation. Nearby areas such as heathland and grassland invite the gardener to create a garden that melds the house into its environment. However, in forested regions, to re-introduce tall forest trees into cleared garden space is often inappropriate because the trees will become too large, not on a human scale, and may possibly be dangerous through dropping branches or uprooting in storms. They will also create heavy shade. One possible solution is to use smaller but compatible trees, so the canopy is harmonious but its scale less imposing. With sparser planting, sunlight can penetrate and this will increase the range of suitable plants.

The diversity among Australian plants is vast – large and small, subtle and bold. A gardener in England would envy our

OPPOSITE: Appealing Flannel Flowers (*Actinotus helianthi*) are indigenous to areas of NSW and Qld. Related species occur in Tasmania and WA.
PHOTOGRAPH BRIAN SNAPE

wealth of local species. In each area, a great variety of species grows (or once grew) naturally, though the range and proportions of different types vary greatly. Growing a selection of lower-, middle- and upperstorey species provides a number of benefits. It embraces biological diversity, provides better habitat and greater visual impact. Covering the ground well can also reduce the need for weeding. Even an isolated local specimen (the token local eucalypt) has an impact, but a cluster of indigenous plants is more exciting. Plants look more effective in groups, with an appealing mix of, for example, understorey shrubs, tufted plants, grasses, scramblers and ferns contributing to the total picture. Clumps of a local 'signature' plant will highlight its beauty. Try letting a light climber such as Common Apple-berry (*Billardiera scandens*) or Small-leaved Clematis (*C. microphylla*) weave its way through taller shrubs.

Every garden is an ecosystem comprising a balance of plant and animal life. Indigenous plants are the basis of the natural ecosystem, providing for the needs of embattled native wildlife – food, shelter and habitat. It is true that possums,

kangaroos and even koalas are not struggling in places where they have adapted to use the food, shelter and habitat we provide. However, loss of natural habitat through land clearing continues to threaten a great many species. Local plants encourage local animals such as lizards, frogs, small mammals, butterflies and indigenous birds, which are such effective consumers of 'pests' that chemical pesticides are unnecessary. Gardeners often forget the existence of wildlife food chains, pollination by insects, and soil microflora and microfauna. There are many beneficial fungi, either visible and often fascinating or hidden but important, such as mycorrhizal fungi. Fungi help by decomposing dead plant material or by their partnership with living plants. Designing in harmony with nature by using local plants will benefit the total environment.

The balance of plants chosen by gardeners and the range of wildlife species attracted are often not representative of any natural environment; for example, many gardeners concentrate on shrubs. If popular banksias and hybrid grevilleas are too dominant in a garden, they can attract disproportionate

numbers of aggressive honeyeaters like Brush Wattlebirds, Noisy Miners or New Holland Honeyeaters, which tend to drive out smaller birds. Many butterflies and other insects benefit from specific host sedges or grasses.

Knowledge and availability of indigenous plants

As knowledge of their beauty and potential application in garden design grows, it is becoming easier to make local plants the first choice in establishing a garden, followed by plants from elsewhere in Australia. The Appendix lists a small range of indigenous plants from each state capital, providing a glimpse of the variety of species from which to choose.

Books or pamphlets are now available, or being written, about the indigenous flora of many areas of Australia. Fortunately some plant nurseries, municipal and forest service nurseries are now growing local plants. You may be lucky to find a local nursery that specialises in indigenous flora. Often you will need to hunt for indigenous plants in a general nursery where they are inconspicuous, with no colourful label

to highlight a new form or a selected flower colour.

Conservation-minded gardeners are concerned about provenance – just how 'local' the plant source is – and use seed of plants collected nearby rather than further afield. The same species occurring across a range of habitats may have slightly different characteristics. Planting local forms ensures that they are the most appropriate and hopefully the most successful. It also means that the genetic integrity of the species in adjacent or nearby bushland is not compromised through interbreeding.

ABOVE LEFT: Stony Range Flora Reserve NSW. A natural shrubby woodland garden embellished with the dark-green, sturdy leaves and lace-like texture of flowers of *Thelychiton speciosus* (Rock Orchid) in an appropriate setting among rocks. Slim trunks and a tracery of fine branches give a pattern of dappled light and shade.
PHOTOGRAPH DIANA SNAPE

ABOVE RIGHT: Morton garden NSW. A house built (cave-like) into a mountain slope has a sandstone shelf providing a no-maintenance area for outdoor living. The indigenous garden retained on the roof includes a self-sown Tree Fern, with a few special small plants introduced.
PHOTOGRAPH CHERYL MADDOCKS

Designing with indigenous plants

To date, most indigenous planting has been for the purpose of revegetation using direct seeding, often on a broad scale. In this case, 'design' is often limited to the choice of local species available. On a smaller scale, some indigenous gardens have been created in a similar way. However, the principles of garden design can still be applied when using local plants. It's a matter of selection and placement, of proportion and balance – of design.

Indigenous gardens naturally tend to reflect the natural landscape. Only recently has interest been shown in using indigenous plants in formal gardens; it will be fascinating to see what is achieved. Among the spectrum of local plants, determine which could fill the various design roles in your garden – trees, groundcovers, framework, feature, ornamental and infill plants. You can introduce exciting plants from other places to blend against a framework of local plants. For example, with good fortune a magnificent Scarlet Banksia (*B. coccinea*) from Western Australia might grow in the east against a background group of the local, modest (but attractive) Dusty Miller (*Spyridium parvifolium*). The scarlet and pale-grey flowers and bold leaves of the superb banksia could be highlights against the pretty, pale-grey floral leaves and small, neat oval foliage of the hardy spyridium.

In any locality, there is potential for different selections of its plants to be combined in a myriad of ways. You may wish to follow a certain design concept as well as give indigenous plants a 'fair go'. In considering design roles, the following approach is recommended:

· Look first at indigenous plants from a source as close to home as possible.
· If no suitable local plant can be found, look to plants from further afield, first in the general region, then the state or Australia-wide and, finally, overseas.

OPPOSITE: Don & Marea Burke's garden NSW. In any area, indigenous plants can be chosen to add colour. In this garden of plants indigenous to the Hawkesbury sandstone, a group of NSW Christmas Bush (*Ceratopetalum gummiferum*) provides a beautiful, colourful summer screen. This is in harmonious balance with the garden of small trees and lowerstorey plants on the other side of the lawn, which receives minimum watering.

PHOTOGRAPH DIANA SNAPE

ABOVE: Morton garden NSW. A large square space built into the roof as a light well allows for a small courtyard garden below, in which a retained *Angophora costata* (Smooth-barked Apple) continues to flourish. Local Flannel Flowers (*Actinotus helianthi*) grow on the roof among a variety of low plants.

PHOTOGRAPH CHERYL MADDOCKS

Blended Gardens

Most gardeners will not only choose plants from their own locale but also explore the wonderful treasure-trove of Australian plants or the myriad from overseas. In this book, all gardens that include non-indigenous plants are 'blended' gardens, even those growing all Australian plants. Plants from coastal Queensland and inland Western Australia share little in common! However, the term 'blended garden' is more commonly used for gardens combining Australian and exotic plants.

Many blended gardens with predominantly Australian plants include a few exotics, either retained from earlier gardens on the site, or possibly grown for sentimental value or sound design reasons. Among conspicuous exotic plants may be mature deciduous trees, which will provide summer shade and winter sun. In the suburbs such trees might help link the garden with its neighbours, but they can also present problems, with extensive root systems and a blanket of leaves in autumn. In a bush setting they will look even more incongruous, although they may add a measure of fire-resistance. Clusters of native evergreens can provide a backdrop for a deciduous exotic (or Australian) tree – a claret ash against the grey-green of allocasuarinas or melaleucas; a golden elm against the blue-grey of eucalypts. These trees complement each other and Australian evergreens maintain their green framework throughout the year, avoiding that bare look in winter.

Most blended gardens start with the introduction of Australian plants into existing exotic gardens. Neighbouring plants need to be compatible in both appearance and growing requirements, especially for water and fertiliser. If the exotic plants have been appropriately chosen to suit local conditions, it will be much easier to establish Australian plants among them. Australian plants can blend beautifully with each other or with exotics as long as care is taken in selection. Leaf size, shape and colour are important factors in blending the appearance of plants and there are countless possible combinations. Among small plants, croweas, correas and daisies will mix happily, while the flamboyant grevillea hybrids will provide a spectacular display among larger shrubs. Many climbers blend particularly well, for example *Clematis aristata* (Austral Clematis) and *Passiflora cinnabarina* (Red Passionflower). A garden based on the concept of choosing plants that will flourish in the existing conditions, rather than attempting to modify these conditions to grow less suitable plants, will necessarily include indigenous and other Australian plants. A garden dependent on heavy inputs of water and fertiliser (let alone pesticides) will be more difficult to maintain – and justify – in the future.

Australian rainforest plants are very popular in blended gardens because of their handsome form, glossy leaves and attractive flowers and fruits, for example any Lilly Pilly. *Elaeocarpus reticulatus* (Blueberry Ash) is a handsome tree with red new growth, white or pink-fringed bell flowers and shiny blue fruit carried on the tree till the following year's fruiting.

OPPOSITE: Tozer garden Vic. Variegated, strappy leaves of Tasman Flax-lily (*Dianella tasmanica*) are an unusual feature in an Australian plant and, in this garden, link visually to the pale-green foliage of exotic trees on the left and to the lawn beyond. Reddish-brown foliage tones are complementary.
PHOTOGRAPH DIANA SNAPE

Other plants to consider for blended gardens are Australian gardenias and closely related randias with sweetly scented white flowers, as well as many Australian hibiscus and the native Murraya (*Murraya ovatifoliolata*). Some hardy, showy hakeas blend well, for example *H. elliptica* (Oval-leafed Hakea) with its shapely form and elegant, bright-green foliage and bronze new growth. Colour contrasts are provided by the attractive dark-green toothed leaves of *Callicoma serratifolia* (Black Wattle), a bushy small tree with upright growth and clustered pale-yellow flowers. Other elegant species with distinctive foliage are the polyscias – *Polyscias elegans*

(Celerywood) is usually a medium-sized tree and *P. sambucifolia* (Elderberry Panax) a tall shrub.

Australian plants appropriate for formal gardens (see lists in 'Formal Gardens') will also suit blended gardens. Many more are now available in both general and specialist nurseries – hardy, attractive and reliable plants, needing only modest amounts of water and fertiliser. As horticulture of Australian plants develops, their availability will increase.

Styles of blended gardens

A blended garden is not restricted to any one style. However, gardens with mainly exotic plants tend to be more formal, while those including mostly Australian plants are likely to be more naturalistic – often due to the gardener's preferences and the 'look' of the plants. Even when plants are mainly exotic, a garden can be naturalistic in style if exotic plants are chosen with sensitivity. Many Australian plants from the Proteaceae family (for example, banksias, grevilleas and waratahs) will mix happily with Gondwanan plants from New Zealand, South America or South Africa. (Many florists still think South African proteas and leucadendrons are Australian.) These Gondwanan plants are often closely related and have forms and foliage in sympathy with Australian plants. Nowadays a number of Gondwanan gardens are being established.

MEDITERRANEAN GARDENS

The possibility of introducing Australian plants into Mediterranean-style gardens will be obvious. Mediterranean gardens are those with plants suited to the hot dry summers and cool wet winters of the typical Mediterranean climate. Such gardens are essentially dormant in summer in contrast with a typical English garden. The aim is to find plants that look fresh and green while dormant. Lawns are minimal, if present at all, and should be allowed to brown off in summer. Gravel is often used as mulch and for paths. Shade is an essential feature. Sometimes there is a patio for relaxing, with a small water feature to cool and humidify the air.

In much of southern Australia, Australian sclerophyll plants will grow seamlessly in largely exotic gardens of this style because they come from similar climates and have similar needs. The one requirement for most is good drainage. Some of the prostantheras and small myrtaceous plants thrive with added fertiliser and water but may then need more regular pruning. Australian plants are increasingly being included in the palette of plants used in Mediterranean gardens overseas. Plants like rosemary, lavender, sages and many bulbs mix easily with Australian plants. There is, however, a potential danger in introducing new plants from similar Mediterranean climates into our gardens: some grow too successfully and their seeds may escape over the garden fence and become weeds in the natural environment.

A Mediterranean-style garden can draw from an enormous range of Australian plants though not those from Tasmania or from Queensland rainforests. Some suggestions include acacias, lomandras, olearias, phebaliums, philothecas and westringias.

TOP: 'Peach blossom' flower of *Grevillea insignis*.
PHOTOGRAPH BRIAN SNAPE

BOTTOM: Silver Plectranthus (*P. argentatus*) with softly textured foliage is suitable for a Mediterranean or cottage garden and responds well to a semi-shaded position.
PHOTOGRAPH DIANA SNAPE

Natural Gardens

Everybody needs beauty as well as bread, places to play and pray in, where Nature may heal and cheer and give strength to body and soul alike.

John Muir, *Our Natural Parks*, 1901

In Australia we are fortunate to have natural gardens to inspire us – in National Parks and other reserves, in coastal areas and arid areas, in the high country, heathlands, grasslands and wetlands. These gardens are fashioned and shaped by nature. For many, the local natural landscape is usually the first source for ideas to assist in designing a garden. We can also find inspiration in beautiful natural gardens elsewhere – a dainty plant against a rock; reeds and rushes beside a pool; massed flowering shrubs colouring the landscape; or a grand forest scene with an expanse of vertical trunks.

The conservation of these natural gardens is by no means straightforward. Wilderness areas were once managed by Aborigines. However, few are now. Tragically, extensive areas are still being cleared and the remainder is increasingly precious. It is important that examples of all types of ecosystems be conserved – and ample areas, not small patches where disturbance created by activity at the edge nibbles away at their conservation value.

Compared with the average domestic garden, natural gardens normally have a greater diversity of plants, more random in their spacing and more varied in age, height and density. For example, in woodlands there might be, for each single tree species, two species of large shrubs, several small shrubs and many understorey plants, with several species of daisies, orchids or lilies, and more species again of grasses and sedges. There are much larger numbers of the smaller plants. There will be a succession of flowering times so, through the seasons, different species are visually dominant. After disturbance by storm, fire or clearing, regeneration will occur. Local pioneer species, for example wattles, cassinias and members of the nitrogen-fixing Fabaceae (Pea family), reappear first, then other plants in succession.

With a sufficiently large area, and minimal disturbance, a natural garden might be retained on much of the land. On cleared land, the romantic ideal of reproducing a completely natural landscape within a contrived, planted garden and limited space is probably impossible to achieve. However, we can aim to reproduce some of the qualities of the natural areas we most admire. Gardens can provide a glimpse of the beauty and calm of those areas; their patterns, rhythms and vivid contrasts; and celebrate the effects of light, space and, of course, the wonderful plants. Our gardens can symbolise the essence of our natural heritage.

OPPOSITE: A natural arid area garden SA. Sturts Desert Pea (*Swainsona formosa*) at home and exuberant in its arid environment. Seeds germinate quickly after rain and plants fix nitrogen to enrich the soil.
PHOTOGRAPH DIANA SNAPE

Naturalistic Gardens

If you want to convert your lawn to a woodland, you are trying to compress a long evolutionary process into a few short years. You will have to make some compromises.

Rosalind Creasy, *Earthly Delights*, 1985

Naturalistic gardens are informal gardens strongly influenced by nature. Most lovers of Australian plants create gardens in the range of styles this term embraces. Natural communities of plants require relatively low maintenance, relying largely on rainfall and nutrients recycled from fallen leaves and twigs. In recent years there has been an acknowledged trend towards such naturalistic gardens in Europe and the United States.

The first recognised Australian style was the 'bush garden', a term coined in the 1960s and 1970s and still used for virtually any garden composed of Australian plants. The trendsetter was Betty Maloney's Sydney garden and, in Melbourne, a key designer was Gordon Ford. Today we recognise many possible styles of 'bush garden', varying with place and environment. They include rainforests, woodlands and mallee, largely distinguished by the nature of the trees and the extent of their canopy.

Whatever style is chosen, the successful garden often looks so natural that it appears to have just happened without design. The spacing, balance and display of plants, the interplay of foliage and colour, the creation of vistas and special places are just as important in the naturalistic garden as in other styles of garden.

In a naturalistic garden, each plant has its own sphere of influence in terms of horticulture and design. These spheres interact as individual plants compete for light and space above ground, nutrients and water underground. However, they benefit from each other's shelter, shade and support. Letting plants 'do their own thing' ensures a more fluid and spontaneous garden. Cooperating with nature makes our task easier. Sustainable plant communities have a natural succession of plants that depends on the longevity of each and its ability to self-propagate. However, change will occur over time in the number of species present and their proportions. To maintain a satisfying visual balance, restrict dominant species by pruning or occasionally removing them. You can always plant subsidiary ones where necessary. This prevents the mix of plants in a garden becoming less interesting, with fewer species.

Some exotic gardens in Australia have been developed and tended by generations of keen gardeners. However, I know of only one garden of Australian plants where such care has continued. In 1982 Rodger and Gwen Elliot began their lovely garden in Melbourne, which is now being further developed and nurtured by Elspeth and Gary Jacobs. Such gardens are rare.

OPPOSITE 'Offshore' Vic. Designed by Jane Burke. This garden includes wonderful forms and textures of indigenous, low-growing coastal plants including Knobby Club-rush (*Ficinia* [*Isolepis*] *nodosa*), silvery Cushion Bush (*Leucophyta brownii*) and a Spear Grass (*austrostipa*), with a middlestorey of shrubs. Close to the house, Willow Myrtle (*Agonis flexuosa*) from WA gives good shade.
PHOTOGRAPH SIMON GRIFFITHS

Naturalistic Australian plant gardens are far more intricate than many formal gardens, which use a limited number of plant species (usually exotic) and rely on traditional European layouts. In a garden, the characteristic repetition and distribution of plants, as in nature, help to create a peaceful, serene environment. You can soften edges in transitional areas by gentle sculpturing of layered plant heights. One area can merge into another with a loose drift of plants – a few trees in a tall drift projecting out into the open, or a greater number of groundcover plants intermingling with trees. You can balance extensive repetition by introducing a little contrast, and consider including formal elements in a naturalistic garden to give it more structure.

The spontaneity or seeming disorder of nature in such a garden has an underlying order that is deeply satisfying. A unique ambience will permeate each naturalistic garden, creating a sanctuary for nourishing the soul.

WALKABOUT GARDENS

A naturalistic style especially appropriate to large gardens in Australia can be called the 'walkabout garden'. This is an Australian version of the Japanese 'stroll garden', which was adapted by French Impressionists including the painter Monet. They developed somewhat formal stroll gardens around the borders of lakes, with paths partially enclosed by trees, and occasional viewing places and spaces with seats to observe special features.

Walkabout is an expressive word that reminds us of the lifestyle of Australia's original inhabitants. The diverse and widely dispersed Australian flora provided Aborigines with food and other resources throughout the different seasons of the year. Walkabout suggests an indirect path but also a purposeful pursuit of a journey, as it was for Aborigines.

Many gardens are not designed to be viewed from one fixed position (or even several), as formal gardens are, but to 'be in' rather than 'be looked at'. Owners and visitors alike go for a wander in the garden at any time of day or year to enjoy what it has to offer, including unexpected or rare delights. Changes probably occur daily and certainly weekly. The walkabout garden suggests a relaxed and intimate approach. In a large garden, a network of pathways can develop through the landscape, each presenting different vistas and offering new pleasures. This concept can be based on any natural area of Australia and can even be followed in a 0.1 hectare garden in the suburbs. 'Bush tucker' plants can be included as a bonus. While going 'walkabout' in the garden, there should still be sheltered areas to pause and sit in – we do not have to keep moving on.

GRASSY WOODLAND GARDENS

Two hundred years ago, Australia possessed vast areas of grassy woodlands and grasslands that contained a variety of Australian grasses, dotted with colour in spring by delightful herbs. Increasingly graziers introduced pasture grasses, resulting in the destruction of much of the indigenous grassland. The small areas that remain are still under threat as are the ground flora of natural grassy woodlands, important for maintaining the health of the remaining trees.

In many areas of Australia you can design a beautiful garden based on a grassy or shrubby woodland. In the country or outer suburbs, or even on a large suburban block,

OPPOSITE LEFT: Taylor garden NSW. Coolness and moisture of a coastal gully garden with a rainforest feel – tall, slender trunks of Scaly Tree-ferns (*Cyathea cooperi*), other ferns and beautiful tree trunks create a serene and peaceful atmosphere.
PHOTOGRAPH DIANA SNAPE

OPPOSITE RIGHT: Brindley garden Vic. Designed by Tony Brindley. Even in a dry season when the water level is low, a created wetland garden with Water-ribbon (*Triglochin procerum*) trailing on the water's surface introduces a natural beauty and serenity that restore the soul. For the construction of a large wetland area, professional help is strongly advised.
PHOTOGRAPH DIANA SNAPE

you can include all three levels of vegetation and interweave a wonderfully diverse range of plants. Depending on the size of your garden, you might plant a sparse upperstorey of indigenous eucalypts, allocasuarinas, callitris or large acacias, for example Black Wattle (*A. mearnsii*), Silver Wattle (*A. dealbata*) or, in moister situations, Blackwood (*A. melanoxylon*). Consider including a framework of trees and shrubs in rows, clumps or drifts, or scattered individually. For the shrub layer, choose plants from a very broad palette – smaller acacias, callistemons, grevilleas, pea-plants and many more, preferably local. A few feature plants could include banksias or Grass Trees (xanthorrhoeas), or saw sedges (gahnias) in moist areas. Treed areas can contrast with open grassy areas, described later. A number of small ornamental plants close to the ground will add another delightful dimension. Attractive plants with strap-like leaves including dianellas, lomandras and the superb Nodding Blue-lily (*Stypandra glauca*) are abundant in natural areas. Exquisite ground orchids belonging to this layer are unfortunately, in suburban gardens, a magnet for snails and slugs.

COASTAL GARDENS

Gardeners living within earshot of the ocean have the opportunity to create a distinctive style of naturalistic garden. Sandy soil and fierce salt winds may have shrivelled the plants you attempted to grow. However, these failures will ultimately help your coastal garden develop its own character – limits are the stuff of design. In an exposed site, the selection of plants will be restricted until there is some shelter. Once this is established, the microclimate changes and your choice becomes much wider. Look at the local scene and consider plants with salt-tolerant characteristics. You may not want to make a garden with these alone, though this can be beautiful, but they will create a durable screen and framework.

Plants for coastal gardens

Acacias, banksias or distinctive casuarinas, for example *C. equisetifolia* (Coast She-oak), can provide the upperstorey. *Banksia integrifolia* (Coast Banksia) flaunts the contrasting silvery-white underside of its foliage in coastal breezes. Middlestorey screens provide valuable shelter from salt winds – *Atriplex cinerea* (Coast Saltbush) and *A. paludosa* (Marsh Saltbush) have attractive silver-grey foliage, Coast Rosemary (*Westringia fruticosa*) and multi-trunked Coast Tea-tree (*Leptospermum laevigatum*) are grey-green. Dwarf She-oak (*Allocasuarina pusilla*) and *Rhagodia candolleana* (Seaberry Saltbush) add variety. Once screens are substantial you can introduce plants from elsewhere either to blend or to feature. For example, beautiful coastal plants from the south coast of Western Australia often thrive on the south coast of Victoria. The Red-flowering Gum (*Corymbia ficifolia*), weeping Willow Myrtle (*Agonis flexuosa*), Showy Honey-myrtle (*Melaleuca nesophila*) and colourful Kangaroo Paws (anigozanthos) are just a few examples.

Coastal areas display many strap-leaved plants, for example *Dianella revoluta* (Spreading Flax-lily), *Ficinia nodosa* (Knobby Club-rush), lomandras and splendid *Lepidosperma gladiatum* (Coast Sword-sedge). Other key species among ground flora are Tussock Grasses –

OPPOSITE: Tribe garden Vic. In difficult conditions, a coastal garden is protected by a hedge of plants such as Coast Saltbush (*Atriplex cinerea*) which allows a number of other coastal plants to thrive in its shelter – Cushion Bush (*Leucophyta brownii*) and Tussock Grasses (poas) among them.
PHOTOGRAPH DIANA SNAPE

FOLLOWING PAGE: 'Karkalla' Vic. Designed by Fiona Brockhoff. An outside eating area, just the place to sit for a drink after a swim. The shaped forms of several small to medium shrubs and topiary allocasuarinas add definition to the garden and are in pleasing contrast with more relaxed forms. Shells, shell grit and subtle colours reflect the coastal location.
PHOTOGRAPH SIMON GRIFFITHS

Poa poiformis (Coast Tussock-grass) and *P. labillardierei* (Common Tussock-grass); daisies – the unique silvery *Leucophyta brownii* (Cushion Bush); brachyscomes, for example *B. parvula* (Coast Daisy); xerochrysums, for example *X. viscosum* (Sticky Everlasting); calocephalus and chrysocephalums; and *Rhodanthe anthemoides* (Chamomile Sunray). Textures and a beautiful combination of subtle foliage colours can be featured. Against these, the contrasting colours of fleshy groundcovers look brilliant – lipstick pink *Disphyma crassifolium* subsp. *clavellatum* (Rounded Noon-flower), yellow *Hibbertia scandens* (Climbing Guinea-flower) and bright-green, succulent and delicious *Tetragonia implexicoma* (Warrigal Spinach).

Acaena novaezelandiae (Bidgee Widgee) is an attractive and effective groundcover, but it can over-run paths. Sea grasses such as eel-grass can be useful for mulching, in addition to natural mulch from on-site vegetation. Shell grit may serve as mulch and an appropriate surface for paths and spaces in the garden, 'framing' the plants. With their distinctive forms and foliage, many coastal plants function very effectively in a formal garden.

ARID AREA GARDENS

Arid areas have low rainfall and are prone to drought. In extreme conditions, in a hot Australian summer, temperatures can exceed 40 degrees Celsius every day for weeks on end. Here, plants space themselves for living room. If thunderstorms or cyclones provide most of the rain, water-harvesting techniques and drainage are important. Limited rainfall over a short period influences the life cycles of plants; some have short but rapid growth periods. In these arid areas, choosing indigenous plants for garden design makes good sense. You can link them with the colours, textures and forms of the natural surroundings. Retaining existing vegetation will maintain microclimates and stabilise soils.

Larger trees can provide shade while smaller, sparser mallee species may be used more generally. If you have vast space, plants of different heights and forms could provide an attractive arrangement of foreground, midground and background views. Groundcovers in the foreground help achieve human scale or, planted in masses, can be a substitute for large areas of lawn. The rocks, pebbles and gravel of arid areas often add interesting texture and colour.

The striking Arid Lands Botanic Gardens at Port Augusta, South Australia, and the younger Alice Springs Desert Garden in Central Australia provide inspiration. Even in a more benign climate you can design for a low-water regime. One example is the Hoffman Walk in Victoria, created by Kevin Hoffman. Red scoria or gravel can replace inland red sand as a background for foliage of grey and silver tones – the completely different colours encourage a different way of seeing. A small patch of green can become a vibrant foreground colour.

Plants for arid area gardens

Inland vegetation has adapted to harsher (or more selective) conditions than the relatively lush vegetation of the coastal fringe, yet many arid area plants can thrive in conditions nearer the coast or be replaced by other similar plants. For example, the exquisite silver-grey and lilac-mauve tonings of popular *Eremophila nivea* (Emu Bush) can be duplicated by those of *Prostanthera nivea* (Snowy Mint-bush) or *Prostanthera baxteri* var. *sericea* (Silky Mint-bush).

Eucalypts or acacias provide shade in an arid area garden, especially *Acacia aneura* (Mulga), *A. pendula* (Weeping Myall)

OPPOSITE: Scotia Sanctuary NSW. An arid area garden in far western NSW features Bluebushes (maireanas) and eremophilas, including forms of *E. glabra* (Common Emu-bush). These present blue-greys and grey-greens against a background of red sand – a different and distinctive colour scheme.
PHOTOGRAPH DIANA SNAPE

and *A. iteaphylla* (Flinders Range Wattle). There is the silver-grey foliage of maireanas, for example *M. sedifolia* (Pearl Bluebush) and *atriplex* (Saltbush). In the Botanic Gardens at Port Augusta, eremophilas are conspicuous with amazing variations in size and shape, leaves and flowers. Silver-grey foliage contrasts with bright greens; the colour of flowers varies, but deep purple and pink often feature. Some wonderful colour changes can be introduced with showy species like *Eremophila racemosa*, *E. mirabilis* and *E. platycalyx* (Granite Poverty Bush). Selected species are now available in eastern nurseries, some made more reliable by grafting.

Eremophila glabra (Common Emu-bush) and *E. gilesii* (Desert Fuchsia) will provide a massed groundcover (*E. glabra* can be a rich green). Prostrate, spreading *Myoporum parvifolium* 'Purpurea' (Creeping Myoporum) forms a purplish mat in winter. Annual and perennial daisies add charm, for example minurias, especially the floriferous *M. leptophylla* (Minnie Daisy) or *Rhodanthe anthemoides* (Chamomile Sunray). Where available, ptilotus (Foxtails), for example *P. obovatus* (Silver-tails), add appealing and unusual forms with their upright, woolly flower heads. Many other plants are capable of coping with minimal water, including *Adenanthos sericeus* (Woollybush), *Einadia nutans*, lasiopetalums and swainsonas. Even some melaleucas tolerate dry conditions, for example *M. armillaris* 'Green Globe' can be bright green all year while *M. incana* 'Nana' provides a contrast with its silver-grey foliage and mauve flowers. *Guichenotia macrantha* (Large-flowered Guichenotia) has similar attractive tonings and a delicate appearance.

HEATHLAND GARDENS

Heathland can be defined as soil desert, poor in nutrients rather than water. In natural heathlands there is likely to be

subsoil moisture and even occasional flooding. Heathland communities exist in the Wallum of coastal Queensland and near the coast, in some inland areas or in the high country of other states. The name Wallum is derived from the Aboriginal name for *Banksia aemula* (Wallum Banksia), dominant in these areas with its characteristic woody gnarled look. In the Wallum area there are few trees but abundant smaller plants, while the somewhat similar Kwongan of Western Australia has no trees and the small plants are more closely packed. In coastal heaths, plants are often kept low by wind pruning.

The exciting flora of an Australian heathland garden could thrive on infertile, mineral-deficient soils yet languish in fertile, well-watered gardens. Heathland gardens are visually open and uncluttered with a background of sparse, fine-foliaged vegetation, including acacias, baeckeas, epacris, hibbertias and grasses. There is a wide choice of ornamental species with a variety of leaves, flowers and bark. A framework of paperbarks (melaleucas and callistemons) will use subsurface moisture, or one or two could serve as feature plants. Australian conifers will contribute a brighter shade of green to contrast with grey-green foliage of the heathland plants. With low soil fertility, if you choose appropriate plants and use groundcovers or gravel as mulch, you will have a garden with minimal weeding. Gaps between plants can become sandy wallaby tracks.

OPPOSITE: Little Desert Lodge Vic. In an arid area garden, water has a special significance. A dam with a central island and a 'transplanted' dead tree for nest hollows can become a haven for birds and other wildlife.
PHOTOGRAPH DIANA SNAPE

Special arid area plants:
ABOVE LEFT: Minnie Daisy (*Minuria leptophylla*)
ABOVE RIGHT: Crimson Foxtail (*Ptilotus atriplicifolius*)
PHOTOGRAPHS DIANA SNAPE

Formal Gardens

In the last analysis there is only one common factor between all gardens, and that is control of nature by man. Control, that is, for aesthetic reasons.

Hugh Johnson, *The Principles of Gardening*, 1996

We are so accustomed to Australian gardens influenced by 'the bush' that a formal garden of Australian plants may sound like a contradiction in terms. Most gardeners do not set out to make a particular style of garden but try to create something that suits the site, pleases the eye and fulfils its expected uses. The style emerges. However, the creation of a formal garden requires clear objectives and thorough planning.

The design of a formal garden is disciplined and strong, and frequently complements architectural structures. Characteristics include the repetition of forms, with definite patterns in both plan and detail. Such gardens are best appreciated from particular vantage points. In earlier days, formal gardens were generally planned in a flat, decorative design to be viewed from above, for example the first-floor windows of the mansion. This is the case especially for knot and parterre gardens with their intricate patterns. Traditionally a formal garden has a central axis along a path leading to a focal point, with side paths meeting at right angles. It is relatively static; plants are selected for their form and colour to complement the design, trimmed to shape and constantly maintained; balance and symmetry are always obvious. Lawns and paving, terraces rather than slopes, ornaments such as fountains and statues can all be part of a formal garden. With a lot of hard landscaping and with plants almost as accessories, formal gardens express strong control over nature. Such gardens can be created with Australian plants, though to date this is rare. One striking example is the large formal garden at Horse Island, near Bodalla, New South Wales, designed and created by Christina Kennedy.

Generally Australian gardens contain elements of both formal and naturalistic styles. There are places where a degree of formality is particularly appropriate, for example in public spaces and around large buildings. On a much smaller scale, modern formal gardens can provide a decorative living area in a courtyard or close to a suburban home, frequently functioning as an outdoor room for entertaining guests. Around the world many informal gardens are now being designed in styles scattered along a continuum from strictly formal at one end to completely naturalistic at the other. Some must be regarded as formal even though there are no straight lines, regular symmetry or much hard landscaping. One example is a wonderful garden in Holland with clipped hedges in sinuous sweeps and billows. There is a marked degree of control over layout and spacing, suggesting that conspicuous control is the essence of formality.

Today many Australian gardeners may choose to exercise rather more control than in the 'bush garden' of thirty years

OPPOSITE: Horse Island NSW. Designed by Christina Kennedy. A formal circular lake surrounded by paving and lawn has a strong central axis, with asymmetrical positioning in relation to the building. Beyond the extensive lawn is an enclosing screen of shrubs and eucalypts. *Pandorea jasminoides* (Bower Vine) flowers are visible left foreground.
PHOTOGRAPH CHRISTINA KENNEDY

ago, even if only in part of the garden. An overall naturalistic impression might include some formal elements. A spectrum of styles may exist within a garden, with linked elements providing continuity. Consistent maintenance is required for any formal garden – continual clipping and tidying – but this is more straightforward than the work needed for a more naturalistic and less predictable garden.

You can introduce formality into a garden of Australian plants in three different ways.

A regular ground plan

During the last half-century famous gardens were built on 'good bones', the lines of a firm basic plan that were then partly, or even largely, obscured by exuberant planting. One way to introduce formality is to use this approach, with a regular ground plan based on geometric lines imposed by the size, shape and uses of the space. If your ground plan is conspicuous and formal, for example with straight lines and circles, your planting can follow a more naturalistic style. Natural plant shapes and combinations flourish freely, yet are defined by the regular, geometric garden beds – a 'controlled wildness'. If beds are matched, you can vary the type, size and placement of the plants within them. You might concentrate on soft rounded shapes, using for example different tea-tree

ABOVE: Kings Park Botanic Garden WA. The colourful display of annual Australian plants in the centre of the Floral Clock (seen here in Summer) is changed, with the seasons, five times during the year. The Roman numerals in green foliage stand out against a contrasting background of silver-grey foliage.
PHOTOGRAPH DAVE BLUMER

OPPOSITE: Horse Island NSW. Designed by Christina Kennedy. Attractive, mounded forms of *Leptospermum scoparium* 'Pink Cascade' and the lower *Melaleuca thymifolia* (Thyme Honey-myrtle) border steps on the eastern approach to the house. NSW Waratahs (*Telopea speciosissima*) and *T.* 'Shady Lady' give a stunning display, additional drainage having been provided for them along the base of the bank. Plants of *Lepidozamia peroffskyana* (Pineapple Zamia) are sculptural and striking against the wall.
PHOTOGRAPH CHRISTINA KENNEDY

BOX 1 PLANTS THAT CAN BE CLIPPED TO GIVEN SIZES

Small shrubs (1 metre or less)

- *Austromyrtus dulcis* (Midgen Berry)

- *Babingtonia pluriflora* dwarf forms

- *Correa reflexa* (Common Correa) forms

- *Darwinia citriodora* (Lemon-scented Myrtle) dwarf form

- *Einadia nutans*

- eremophilas, for example *E. maculata* (Spotted Fuchsia), *E. aurea*

- grevilleas, for example *G. baueri*, *G. diminuta*

- *Leptospermum scoparium* ' Nanum', *L. polygalifolium* 'Pacific Beauty'

- melaleucas, for example *M. decussata* (Totem Poles) dwarf form, *M. holosericea*, *M. thymifolia* (Thyme Honey-myrtle)

- *Rhagodia spinescens* (Hedge Saltbush), *R. crassifolia,*

- *Syzygium australe* selected forms

- *Westringia fruticosa* 'Smokie', 'Wynyabbie Gem', 'Jervis Gem'

Medium shrubs (1–3 metres)

- *Acacia boormanii* (Snowy River Wattle), *A. iteaphylla* (Flinders Range Wattle)

- *Acmena hemilampra* (Broad-leaved Lilly-pilly)

- *Backhousia citriodora* (Lemon Ironwood)

- *Bauera rubioides* (Wiry Bauera)

- *Bursaria spinosa* (Sweet Bursaria)

- callistemons (bottlebrushes)

- *Calothamnus quadrifidus* (Common Net-bush)

- *Pittosporum (Citriobatus) spinescens*

- correas, for example *C. baeuerlenii* (Chef's Cap Correa)

- *Darwinia citriodora* (Lemon-Scented Myrtle)

- eremophilas, for example *E. youngii*, *E. oppositifolia* (Twin-leaf Emu-bush)

- grevilleas, for example *G. buxifolia* (Hairy Spider-flower), *G. endlicheriana*, *G. lavandulacea* (Lavender Grevillea)

- leptospermums, for example *L. polygalifolium* (Tantoon), *L. obovatum*, *L. myrsinoides* (Heath Tea-tree)

- melaleucas, for example *M. hypericifolia* (Red Honey-myrtle), *M. huegelii* (Chenille Honey-myrtle)

- prostantheras, for example *P. ovalifolia* (Mint Bush)

Tall shrubs and trees (above 3 metres)

- *Acmena hemilampra* (Broad-leaved Lilly-pilly), *A. smithii* (Lilly Pilly)

- callitris, for example *C. macleayana* (Stringybark Cypress-pine)

- callistemons (bottlebrushes)

- *Graptophyllum excelsum* (Scarlet Fuchsia)

- melaleucas, for example *M. alternifolia*, *M. quinquenervia* (Broad-leaved Paperbark)

- *Podocarpus elatus* (Plum Pine)

- syzygiums, for example *S. australe*, *S. luehmannii* (Riberry)

- *Waterhousea floribunda* (Weeping Lilly-pilly)

(leptospermum) forms. If the planting of garden beds forms a mirror image, the effect is formal. You could fill small beds with a random mix of Fan Flowers (scaevolas), daisies and other small, easily propagated plants; or arrange these in definite patterns to increase the formality. Similarly a straight or curved hedge can be either strictly regimented or a little relaxed. You can prune it severely or lightly, if at all. For example, an unpruned hedge of *Grevillea endlicheriana* in the Newcastle Grevillea Garden in New South Wales is lovely, with the soft effect of silvery foliage and sprays of dainty white flowers.

At the entrance to the Royal Botanic Gardens at Cranbourne, Victoria, are striking massed blocks of small plants in long straight rows, each of just one species. These are enclosed by curving hedges of handsome, tall, dark-green callitris (Cypress Pine). There is no strict symmetry but the design is certainly formal. The Botanic Gardens at Mount Annan in New South Wales regularly have spectacular displays of annual daisies and, for the Olympics, Sydney Botanic Gardens grew marvellous formal display beds. At Kings Park Botanic Gardens in Perth, a floral clock celebrates the seasonal changes with segments of massed colourful annuals. There are also dazzling beds elsewhere in the gardens. It is not easy for amateur gardeners to grow large beds of annuals as in public parks, simply because few Australian plants are yet commercially available in punnets in the quantities required. Their availability will improve with demand.

Control of plant shapes

In the past, few Australian gardeners controlled their plants by clipping, but there is a growing interest in plants that respond well to the more formal effect of regular shaping. In this regard, one area in suburban gardens that has stimulated interest is the narrow strip often found between a driveway and the side fence. To be successfully clipped, a plant usually

TOP: Japanese Garden Cowra NSW. A formal landscape is made more so by the pruned hedges, with *Westringia fruticosa* (Coast Rosemary) in the foreground.
PHOTOGRAPH DIANA SNAPE

BOTTOM: National Gallery ACT. Unadorned white containers display the unique, sculptural character of Grass Trees (xanthorrhoeas) in a formal setting near the entrance to the National Gallery.
PHOTOGRAPH DIANA SNAPE

BOX 2 PLANTS WITH NATURAL REGULAR SHAPE

- *Acacia cognata* 'Green Mist'

- *Actinostrobus pyramidalis* (Swamp Cypress)

- allocasuarinas, for example *A. verticillata* (Coast She-oak), *A. torulosa* (Rose She-oak)

- *Banksia spinulosa* (Hairpin Banksia) dwarf forms

- callitris especially when young, for example *C. columellaris* (Coastal Cypress-pine), *C. gracilis* (Slender Cypress-pine)

- *Crinum* lilies

- cyatheas (Tree Ferns)

- *Cycas media* (Zamia Palm)

- *Dicksonia antarctica* (Soft Tree-fern)

- *Dietes robinsoniana* (Wedding Lily)

- *Doryanthes excelsa* (Gymea Lily)

- *Homoranthus papillatus, H. flavescens* (Mouse and Honey Plant)

- *Lophostemon confertus* (Brush Box)

- macrozamias, for example *M. communis* (Burrawang)

- *Melaleuca armillaris* (Bracelet Honey-myrtle) 'Green Globe', *M. incana* (Grey Honey-myrtle) 'Velvet Cushion'

- *Phyllocladus aspleniifolius* (Celery-top Pine)

- *Pittosporum bicolor* (Banyalla)

- *Polyscias murrayi* (Pencil Cedar)

- *Rhodosphaera rhodanthema* (Deep Yellowwood)

- syzygiums

- *Westringia fruticosa* (Coast Rosemary)

- xanthorrhoeas (Grass Trees)

requires small leaves, short internodes, slow growth (so you do not need to cut it too often) and a suitable growth habit, depending on the ultimate height required and whether you want leaf cover to ground level. Many small Myrtaceae, melaleucas, callistemons, baeckeas and chamelauciums are suitable, but are by no means the only candidates. Gardeners are using the obliging westringias, rhagodias, dwarf syzygiums and Midgen Berry (*Austromyrtus dulcis*) among others as replacements for English Box in parterres.

Plants that respond well to clipping can be used as screens, hedges and topiary. In Linda and John Floyd's garden in Melbourne, a 'Stairway to the Stars' has a series of shrubs clipped flat at increasing heights forming a series of steps. Although romantically named, this feature is functional as a divider in the garden. Controlled plant shapes are typical of Japanese-style gardens. As well as rather attractive bird or animal shapes, topiary can take on bizarre forms, but simple geometric shapes are the most popular choice in Australian gardens. It can be very satisfying to create a smooth rounded curve forming a globe, cone or hemisphere.

Clipped Australian plants in more naturalistic gardens can serve as features in key positions, or add solidity to an area of less substantial shrubs. Often clipping (not too regular) will encourage flowering. Limited repetition of a shape, placed with care, adds continuity through a garden. Any degree of pruning exercises some control over the sizes and shapes of plants. In nature fire, frost, wind and animals have always done the pruning – but not as carefully. Some examples of plants that can be clipped to a given size are included in Box 1, but there are many more.

OPPOSITE: Brown garden WA. Established banksias in a naturalistic garden grow in clearly defined beds, surrounded and framed by contrasting green lawn. The intriguing blend of formality and informality has its own appeal.
PHOTOGRAPH DIANA SNAPE

Using plants with a natural formality

Formality may be introduced to a garden by using Australian plants that have a natural regular shape and need minimum control. If their shape is not too eye-catching, they can make good framework plants in the garden, lending form to the design and setting the mood. However, many of these plants are so striking and dramatic that they may better serve as feature plants against a plainer background. Tree Ferns, Grass Trees, Gymea Lilies, Bangalow Palms and cycads all have stunning regular and predictable forms.

Soft Tree-ferns (*Dicksonia antarctica*) feature in a courtyard Fern Garden at the Australian National Gallery, Canberra, where they are planted on either side of a path curled like a new fern frond. The path leads to a small central fountain, passing several secluded seating areas. Ultimately the view from windows above will be the patterned canopy of circles of fern fronds. This is a simple balanced plan of soft lines carried through with regular repeated shapes – definite dark trunks contrasting with a soft fuzziness in the foliage outlines. Its exact position on the formal/naturalistic continuum is irrelevant to its tranquil beauty.

A plain formal background of plants with regular shapes such as a row of callitris, melaleucas or westringias can be used to display other more quirky feature plants with irregular growth habits, for instance members of the Proteaceae family, such as dryandras, isopogons and banksias. The standard, grafted weeping grevilleas now available have tremendous potential for providing a long-flowering, arching or pendent pillar of colour suitable for any formal garden. They can also be used as specimen plants or as focal points in front of less formal shrubs, increasing the sense of order in the composition. The range of such weeping standards will extend as more species are grafted and experimented with. Potted topiary specimens are also available for similar uses.

Examples of plants with a naturally regular shape, needing little or no clipping, are included in Box 2.

Formal and informal gardens can benefit from the expanding range of Australian plants becoming available and the growing confidence of gardeners to prune and shape them. There is great scope for designing a fascinating garden anywhere along the continuum between formal and naturalistic.

THEME GARDENS

A garden may be based around one overall theme that dominates the design, linking its elements together. You can combine two themes, for example a particular colour scheme and perfumed plants. Some theme gardens are quite formal – those imitating the style of a historical period (for example, Edwardian) or culture (for example, Oriental). A naturalistic garden might also develop a theme. A design may aim to produce 'bush tucker' plants or cut flowers; or a garden that caters for children or disabled people. An idiosyncratic garden can reflect the owner's passion and artistic flair; it can be surreal, dramatic, or even kitsch.

COLLECTORS' GARDENS

Many gardeners collect a wide variety of individual Australian plants to study and enjoy – for them, the interest and fascination lie in the plants. Other gardeners collect a single genus or family of plants, for example grevilleas, banksias, eremophilas or ferns, as a hobby, for research or as an educational resource (for example, members of the Ornamental Plant Collection Association). If you include only one or two plants of each species and do not take care to visually link them, the garden will tend to look uncoordinated and lack harmony, however appealing the individual plants may be. Repeating certain species and carefully grouping the plants will enhance both the unity of the garden and its beauty.

ABOVE: A group of waratah flowers (*Telopea speciosissima* and *T.* 'Shady Lady') have rich colour well complemented by green foliage. Their distinctive, strong forms have a certain formality.

PHOTOGRAPH CHRISTINA KENNEDY

Small Gardens

Praise the large estate, but cultivate a small one.

Virgil

If you live in a city, suburb or country town, you will probably have a relatively small area of 0.1 hectare or less in which to create your garden. For a city or suburban block, the surrounding environment is likely to be quite artificial, with no 'sense of place'. You may want to screen it off completely, or you may like to adapt ideas from neighbouring gardens and enjoy their borrowed landscape.

The area is frequently rectangular and one obvious style choice is the formal garden. However, this is certainly not the only possibility. You can round square corners and disguise straight walls. You can create a cottage garden, or a more naturalistic wildflower garden; a grassland or a tapestry style influenced by heathlands or alpine herbfields. Another approach is to create a miniature tropical paradise crammed with large-leafed plants, including ferns, and penetrated only by narrow tracks that invite exploration and discovery. With a closed canopy, horticultural knowledge and care are needed to maintain foliage at all levels. Develop your own personal style – but try to keep it simple.

Repetition of linking plants will give the garden unity. To create surprises, you can bend a pathway, build up a mound, or place rocks or shrubs so that new areas are at first concealed. You could plant a light creeper such as a dainty billardiera (Apple Berry) in the same hole as a shrub, so that it grows up through the bush to delight you later with bouquets of flowers. The range of small Australian plants available in nurseries has widened dramatically over the past forty years, due to the work of the Australian Plant Society and the horticultural industry.

Low plants are likely to occupy much of the garden space but fence screens and groups or borders of larger shrubs are important for structure and variety. An area of 0.1 hectare can accommodate several small or even medium trees. A rainforest tree, for example *Davidsonia pruriens* (Davidson's Plum), provides a stunning effect in a small garden with its fernlike crown of spreading leaves, pink new growth and narrow shape.

Consider keeping the longest axis of the garden open and emphasising its length by large dark leaves close to the main viewpoint gradually leading to small silvery leaves in the distance. A dramatic focal point, such as a sculpture, planted chimney-pot, or special feature plant, arrests the eye and terminates the vista. While keeping the sight line open, divide the length with partial screens on either side, slender shrubs or trellises with creepers. You can create different 'rooms' with plantings concealed behind these screens. As long as the screens are in balance, they need not be symmetrical. Asymmetry is often more intriguing; the vital thing is the invitation to explore.

Around the boundary the screen can have a variety of heights and solidity to cater for successive vistas. Heights of

OPPOSITE: Bates garden NSW. Designed by Michael Bates. Colour and form in the hard landscape dominate this modern courtyard garden, softened by the sound of water and the green foliage of tufted plants and Elderberry Panax (*Polyscias sambucifolia*). It is a much-used outdoor living room. PHOTOGRAPH DIANA SNAPE

fences or walls do not all have to be the same. If you are unlucky enough to look at and be overlooked by an adjacent building, you may need a tall screen. A dense screen could block the view completely, or you may prefer sparse foliage to break the lines of the building and distract from it. Only solid walls will significantly reduce noise from outside – trees or shrubs will not, though they will improve air quality and add to your enjoyment of the garden.

A small garden on a slope provides interesting opportunities for special effects. If the land slopes down away from the house, the feeling of space is enhanced. Worthwhile views can be retained without the garden being overlooked. This could mean dense perimeter planting (not too tall) which draws the eye to the view beyond. Foreground planting needs to be low, except for framing tree trunks. Land sloping up from the house gives a more closed-in, intimate feel. There is scope for planting small treasures close by where they can be seen and enjoyed, for example delicate *Stylidium armeria* (Grass Triggerplant), orchids, tetrathecas (Pink Bells) including *T. ciliata* and *T. thymifolia*, blue-flowered *Cheiranthera cyanea* (Finger Flower), tufted *Conostylis setigera* or matting *C. seorsiflora*. Much depends on the orientation and degree of slope. You can build mini rock terraces for planting.

COURTYARD GARDENS

In a courtyard garden, as in any really small garden (25 square metres or less), every square metre is precious – the smaller the garden, the more surely each plant must deserve its place. You may choose to focus on the hard landscape – paving, rocks or pebbles – and introduce a pool, with very few plants. You may prefer a flamboyant approach, with rainforest and tropical plants, cycads or zamias, Bird's-nest Ferns, cordylines or palms. Or create a more subtle and tranquil atmosphere with Grass Trees, pimeleas and hibbertias. Your favourite plants could combine fittingly with rocks, providing a pleasing contrast of soft and hard textures. Australian daisies, tufted grasses and *Scleranthus biflorus* (Knawel) will complement the definite outlines of rocks. Try grouping small phebaliums, spyridiums or correas with versatile Mat Rushes (lomandras) or Flax Lilies (dianellas); or a Tree Fern surrounded by an area of native ferns, violets and mulch. These can be framed by geometrically shaped beds with well-defined edges or irregular soft-edged shapes. Consider introducing contrasts between formality and nature's exuberance, for example by letting groundcovers spill over edges of regular raised beds – a prostrate grevillea, banksia or acacia, or the delightful prostrate conifer *Microcachrys tetragona* (Creeping Pine) with its little red cones.

Using few varieties will avoid a cluttered appearance. Dwarf forms can substitute for their larger parents, for example dwarf acacias, Lilly Pillies, *Banksia spinulosa* (Hairpin Banksia) or *Babingtonia pluriflora* (Tall Baeckea). Perhaps plant a slender tree (or train a tall shrub as a tree) to lift the eyes and the spirits. Not only will it act as a focal point and a magnet for birds, but it will also contribute a strong vertical accent and extend the space of the garden upwards. If all plants are less than fence height, the garden seems very limited. The choice of style and plants will affect the amount of on-going work required but no worthwhile garden, however small, is entirely maintenance-free.

To achieve the harmony we now associate with a Japanese garden, study the form and foliage of plants and make sure these are well suited to the hard landscape in the

OPPOSITE: McAllister garden Vic. Knowledge and horticultural expertise have resulted in the creation of a lovely garden of western wildflowers in a small garden in Eastern Australia. A great variety of small shrubs, herbs and tufted plants produce a wonderful array of spring colour. These include lechenaultias, tetrathecas, pimeleas, stylidiums (Triggerplants), *Micromyrtus leptocalyx* (in the foreground) and boronias such as floriferous pink *B. microphylla*.
PHOTOGRAPH SIMON GRIFFITHS

background. Walls and paving will probably occupy a significant proportion of the available space, making them relatively more conspicuous. Colours can be neutral and unobtrusive or bold and exciting – burnt orange, rusty red, deep blue. A pool can be colourful too. A mirror or other reflecting surface on one wall can increase the light and extend the visible space. One or two decorative features will add a personal touch – a sculpture, mosaic work or 'found object'; a pool, fountain or birdbath; all add character to a small garden.

Walls can be pleasant to look at but are often more attractive when partially screened by foliage. Climbers excel here, requiring very little 'foot space'. They can grow in small narrow beds or in containers beside walls and be trained on widely patterned, fixed wires or firmly attached lattices. Pruning may be necessary. A north-facing wall is most easily covered, a south-facing wall the most difficult, forcing climbers to head for the sky and sunlight. Beautiful climbers include the light billardieras (Apple Berries) and clematis, *Hibbertia scandens* (Climbing Guinea-flower) showing its 'olympic gold' for much of the year, *Hardenbergia violacea* (Native Sarsaparilla) forms and *H. comptoniana* (Native Lilac). Vigorous kennedias, *Cissus antarctica* (Kangaroo Vine) and *Aphanopetalum resinosum* (Gum Vine) might better tolerate a south-facing wall. You can also espalier hardy shrubs such as melaleucas and westringias.

A limited space enclosed on three or four sides has advantages and constraints. It is easy to water and weed and it will be protected from wind, but you will find that some plants need good air circulation. Shade from adjacent buildings and walls will be present for much of the year but will vanish in mid-summer, just when the sun is hottest and

highest in the sky. You can minimise the effects of such constraints by designing with foresight and choosing appropriate hardy plants. Containers provide a flexible garden which can be moved at different times of the year to benefit from sun or shade. Designing mini-gardens in containers is a whole world of delight, using small infill gems as well as tried and true ornamentals.

AUSTRALIAN COTTAGE GARDENS

Cottage gardens in Europe belonged to the ordinary person with a small plot of land to grow vegetables, fruit, herbs and flowers. Subsistence gardening led to the essential characteristics of practicality, lack of pretension, intimacy of scale and a quality of 'organised disarray'. Cottagers could not afford to buy plants or follow garden fashions; they swapped cuttings and collected local plants. Europeans brought favourite plants to set up gardens in a new and foreign land and, after two hundred years, such English cottage gardens are still popular, using plants exotic to Australia.

An Australian (or blended) cottage garden is equally possible, though the gardening conditions are very different from those in the northern hemisphere. The colourful offerings from traditional English gardens depend on substantial resources of water, fertiliser, time and maintenance. However,

OPPOSITE: Sullivan garden NSW. A sloping bank of Australian orchids enables these exquisite plants to be seen close up and, in a very small garden, their delicate beauty can be enjoyed from the house.
PHOTOGRAPH DIANA SNAPE

ABOVE: Harper garden WA. This wildflower garden, filled with light and colour, draws on the wealth of Western Australian shrubs. Tall stems of Kangaroo Paws (anigozanthos) provide a vertical accent in the foreground.
PHOTOGRAPH DIANA SNAPE

there are a number of soft-stemmed Australian herbaceous perennials, annuals and biennials with a 'cottagey' look, which will blend happily in this style of garden and do not require much upkeep. Traditionally a cottage garden will cover all the available space, except for formally laid-out paths.

Australian plants for cottage gardens

Soft, low groundcovers include scaevolas, now widely used in Europe too, for example *S.* 'Mauve Clusters', *S. aemula, S. albida*; dampieras, for example *D. linearis, D. rosmarinifolia*; goodenias, violas, Austral Stork's-bill (*Pelargonium australe*) and isotomas – starry white *I. anethifolia* and blue *I. axillaris* (Rock Isotome). There are numerous lilies and hundreds of daisies, for example Showy Podolepis (*P. jaceoides*) with lovely fringed golden flower heads; and Golden Billy-Buttons (*Pycnosorus* (Craspedia) *chrysanthus*) with silvery leaves and tall globular flower heads.

Small tufted plants include conostylis (for example *C. candicans*), orthrosanthus, Grass Triggerplant (*Stylidium armeria*) and patersonias (Purple Flags). Other small plants include delicate bluebells (wahlenbergias), *Pimelea humilis*, hibbertias (Guinea Flowers), for example *H. riparia*, and exquisite twining plants, for example *Thysanotus patersonii* (Twining Fringe-lily) and *Comesperma volubile* (Love Creeper). Treasures such as lechenaultias (*L. formosa* in red or orange, and *L. biloba* in sky or royal blue) can grow at focal points such as the intersection of two pathways. Ground-hugging herbs for edging include *Isotoma fluviatilis* (Swamp Isotome) for moist areas, and *Dichondra repens* (Kidney Weed) for shady dry areas.

Taller plants will add variety – showy *Lythrum salicaria* (Purple Loosestrife), silver-foliaged *Plectranthus argentatus* and *Derwentia (Veronica) arenaria* 'Cottage Blue'. Stiff blue-grey rosettes of leaves of *Ammobium alatum* produce unexpected tall stems of white everlastings. Sculptural strap-leaved plants can add height in addition to the interest of their colour, leaf shapes and plant forms.

WILDFLOWER GARDENS

The Australian flora excels in its diverse and fascinating range of small ornamental, woody-stemmed shrubs. Often these have interesting foliage, usually sclerophyll rather than soft. Their individual flowers are frequently small, becoming conspicuous and showy when massed in clusters. An Australian wildflower garden can draw from this enormous range. As in a cottage garden, size, showiness and colours of flowers should be considered carefully, as large splashes of bold colours can overpower small delicately coloured flowers.

The word 'wildflower' invokes various images. Anyone from the east coast who has visited Western Australia in spring will recall with delight the brilliance of natural wildflower gardens there, generally growing in sandy soil. To reproduce a vivid Western Australian wildflower garden in the east requires knowledge of plant cultivation and flowering time, plus 'green thumbs' – Peg McAllister in Melbourne has this talent. In the east, sandstone areas provide different natural wildflower gardens, with exciting combinations of small shrubs and ground flora. The gardener can choose a marvellous combination of plants – 'woody' shrubs (including prostrate or low forms of larger ones), tufted plants, groundcovers, herbs, creepers; there can be annuals or perennials, small flowers or large. Picture these plants as they grow in many natural areas – generally a metre or less in height and often growing quite close together.

Most areas of Australia, including deserts, support a variety of smaller indigenous plants suitable for the wildflower garden. Each garden can have its own proportions of variety and repetition, its own mix of colours, foliage and perfume. You can plan the colour scheme of flowers carefully for each season of the year, or it can be quite serendipitous.

Some plants are long-flowering, others inconspicuous for much of the year until they burst into bloom. The wildflower garden can either be mulched and left to look after itself quite well in terms of watering and weeding, or given frequent attention. Plants such as stylidiums (Triggerplants), daisies, croweas and *Actinotus helianthi* (Flannel Flower) may self-seed, especially in sand or gravel, which will make the design increasingly random if you let them stay.

Forms of plants

Low plants have a variety of pleasing forms, sometimes enhanced by pruning, which you can combine to great effect by repeating similar shapes and selectively using contrasts. There are arching shapes, like *Astartea fascicularis* 'Winter Pink', thryptomenes, *Micromyrtus ciliata* (Fringed Heath-myrtle) and sparse *Hypocalymma angustifolium* (White Myrtle), a delicate beauty when it flowers. Some low plants like

the blue-grey *Derwentia perfoliata* sprawl rather than arch. There are many spheres or ovoids, most with small leaves, some with dainty pale flowers, like *Boronia muelleri* 'Sunset Serenade' and *Chamelaucium ciliatum* (Small Wax-plant); or deeper colours – pink *Crowea exalata* (Small Crowea), coral or pink *Correa pulchella* and deep purple-pink tetrathecas.

Low mounds include mauve *Thomasia pygmaea* (Dwarf Paper-flower), Guinea Flowers *Hibbertia vestita* and *H. serpyllifolia*, low forms of *Correa alba* and *C. reflexa*, *Grevillea diminuta* and *Acacia cardiophylla* (Wyalong Wattle) 'Gold Lace'. Upright or vertical accents can be introduced by epacris (Heaths), for example *E. impressa* (Common Heath) and *E. longiflora* (Fuchsia Heath), or by *Dampiera purpurea* and *Halgania preissiana* to add blue.

ABOVE: *Epacris longiflora* (Fuchsia Heath) is long-flowering and colourful. It could find a place in many small gardens and benefits from pruning. PHOTOGRAPH DIANA SNAPE

Homoranthus flavescens, *Melaleuca violacea* or *Rulingia hermanniifolia* (Wrinkled Kerrawang) will introduce distinctive horizontal strata. With less distinctive but still structural profiles are *Pseudanthus pimeleoides* – another unfortunate name – the inverted cone of its green foliage a foil for bright white flowers, and soft-leaved thomasias with their mauve flowers.

The small suburban garden can include other layers of medium-sized ornamental shrubs – reliable *Philotheca myoporoides* (Long-leaf Wax-flower) and *Darwinia citriodora* (Lemon-scented Myrtle), *Calytrix tetragona* (Fringe Myrtle) and *Grevillea dimorpha* (Flame Grevillea). The bushy purple, pink and white forms of *Hardenbergia violacea* are lovely planted in combination. *Hovea lanceolata* (Lance-leaf Hovea), the hardier boronias, for example *B. denticulata* or *B. pinnata* (Pinnate Boronia), and beautiful *Pimelea nivea* all grow well in semi-shade. Taller species can provide a backdrop – colourful *Ceratopetalum gummiferum* (NSW Christmas Bush) and telopeas (Waratahs), white *Kunzea ambigua* and *K. ericoides* (Burgan) and a choice of many acacias. In a restricted space, *Acacia boormanii* (Snowy River Wattle) can be pruned to attractive multiple trunks with foliage above head height. The range of small to medium shrubs is so wide that it is best to investigate those from your local area.

TAPESTRY GARDENS

Van Gogh reputedly introduced the idea of a tapestry garden, relying on the hue and texture, size and shape of foliage creating a tapestry-like mosaic. With this permanent display, a garden can be beautiful all year. The Impressionists also used ornamental grasses in their tapestries. There are hundreds of different species of low-spreading Australian plants, each with distinctive foliage, with which you can create a pattern of subtle harmonies and contrasts. Leaves can be simple or ornate, tiny or spectacular, shiny or dull, smooth-surfaced or crinkled. There are inspiring natural tapestry gardens in coastal heathlands and in alpine herbfields in the high country. Foliage in gardens and nurseries will suggest ideas.

An area of low shrubs provides an open and spacious feel to a garden, with several fine trunks to provide vertical elements. Heights of a metre or less can be maintained with pruning. A vantage point is an asset – a tapestry garden can be designed to be observed from a first-floor terrace. For a more prostrate 'carpet garden', arrange low groundcover plants (100 mm or so) similarly in patterns of contrasting colours, forms and textures. You can design a lovely tapestry to be viewed from ground level by repeating three or four different groundcover species, with sections of white or coloured gravel for contrast.

There are many shades of green but foliage can show other colours too. Silvers and greys are abundant in coastal and arid area plants, for example eremophilas, poas, saltbushes and *Senna (Cassia) artemisioides*, as well as *Plectranthus argentatus* (Silver Plectranthus) and *Adenanthos cuneatus* 'Coral Drift'. As a contrast, *Brachysema praemorsum* 'Bronze Butterfly' has attractive purple-bronze foliage. Selected leptospermums have superb plum or copper-coloured foliage, as do cultivars *L.* 'Copper Glow', *L.* 'Copper Sheen', some forms of *L. obovatum* and *L. brevipes* (Slender Tea-tree). A few low allocasuarinas, for example *A. paludosa* (Scrub She-oak) forms and *A. humilis*, offer wonderful texture and colours. Many Australian plants have colourful growth flushes, especially rainforest plants. New forms of *Austromyrtus dulcis* (Midgen Berry) are being developed for more vivid leaf colour. Prostrate *Banksia petiolaris*,

OPPOSITE: Suburban garden Vic. You can position grasses to catch late afternoon light. It is wise to use locally indigenous grasses where possible and check that any introduced grasses are not invasive.
PHOTOGRAPH DIANA SNAPE

B. blechnifolia (Fern-leaf Banksia) and low forms of some other banksias have attractive, rusty-bronze new growth.

GRASSLAND GARDENS

Clumps or drifts of grasses in a small garden give the wonderful effect of grasses rippling in the wind. A natural grassland will have fifty or more different species of perennial flowering plants and grasses. *Themeda triandra* (Kangaroo Grass) is widespread throughout Australia and looks superb, with green-tinged purplish flower heads turning russet at maturity. A themeda grassland might contain other grasses such as Wallaby Grass (austrodanthonias and joyceas) or Plume Grass (dichelachnes) displaying showy panicles. Consider planting daisies, lilies, brunonias, convolvulus, wahlenbergias, bulbines and fascinating *Eryngium rostratum* (Blue Devil). If you want to alter the framework species, select strap-leaved plants such as dianellas (Flax Lilies), diplarrenas (Native Iris) or lepidospermas (Sword Sedges).

In nature, 'bare' ground between the grass clumps, with its binding crust of lichens, mosses and liverworts, is home to small reptiles and seed-eating birds. In a created grassland garden this can be replaced initially by organic mulch. A driveway can be an Australian grassland – cars will cause little damage even when the grasses are flowering and you are enjoying the seedheads.

Weeds should be cleared before planting grasses in winter or early spring. A very occasional deep watering in spring will help plants establish and prolong the flowering of most species over spring and summer. A grassland garden needs little water but regular weeding if there is a source of weed grass seeds nearby.

Decorative tufted grasses are especially attractive in close-planted clumps. There are many species of poa (Tussock Grass) and several are widely used. Austrostipas (Spear Grass), for example *A. elegantissima*, are inconspicuous when not in flower but have spectacular feathery flowering stems. Two grasses with blue-green foliage are *Cymbopogon ambiguus* (Lemon Grass), with scented foliage and attractive silvery-green flower heads, and beautiful *Dichanthium sericeum* (Silky Blue-grass), with purple-tinged foliage. After setting seed, tufted grasses can be renewed between mid-winter and early spring by neatly cutting back with hedging shears. Cutting back close to ground level has a similar effect to burning – fire can be a useful management tool but is not always practicable. A three-yearly burning and varying the timing of maintenance in a mosaic pattern will help protect the grassland garden's diversity. Alternatively, poas can be 'cleaned up' by raking out old dead sections, which will come away easily. Once established, plantings become self-sustaining with seeds and runners.

In addition to those flowering herbs already mentioned in 'Cottage gardens', there are white candles (*Stackhousia monogyna*), goodenias, tetrathecas (Black-eyed Susan), subtle pink *Convolvulus angustissimus* and fascinating soft pussytails (*Ptilotus spathulatus*). There are also numerous peas - pultenaeas (Bush Peas), bossiaeas or dillwynias, for example *D. cinerascens* (Grey Parrot-pea). The choice is yours.

OPPOSITE: Thomlinson garden Vic. This small front garden, with mainly low planting, features a Hairpin Banksia *(B. spinulosa)* as a dramatic small tree. If required, its lower branches could be pruned away to give a more pronounced trunk.

PHOTOGRAPH DIANA SNAPE

Large Gardens

It has always been my aim to have as large a garden as possible, to be tended with the least work, and to provide interest and beauty of flower and foliage throughout the year.

Graham Stuart Thomas, *Three Gardens of Pleasant Flowers*, 1983

Being responsible for a hectare or more of land in the outer suburbs, semi-rural or country areas can be quite overwhelming. The scale will be much grander than in the suburbs and the designer will need to 'think big'. Such a garden needs to be in balance and harmony with the natural forms, lines, colours, textures and scale of the existing landscape and vegetation. If there has been little clearing, the 'sense of place' will be evident and respect for this will help guide your garden design. If you enjoy views from the site, your planting and the personal environment you create will ideally merge into the surrounding landscape, providing an attractive extension of the garden. This is truly a fortunate situation.

If you can afford to, consult a professional designer at the start, especially if you plan to move earth. The experienced eye can quickly see the possibilities and problems of the area, and it need not be costly. If you are an enthusiastic gardener, you will still want to be largely responsible for the garden. Starting with professional advice will let you carry on with confidence. You can seek further professional help if necessary, or use friends, fellow gardeners and books – unexpected and helpful ideas will emerge.

While large gardens are generally naturalistic in style, a more formal approach can lead to a stunning result, though the regular maintenance required places greater demands on the time and energy of the gardener.

Perimeter planting

Whatever style you choose to follow in a large garden, establishing trees and shrubs around the perimeter is a good start to the framework, on paper and on the ground. If you experience strong winds, perimeter planting will provide shelter belts and may be the beginnings of internal garden 'rooms'. If all boundary plantings and those visible from outside the property are as local as possible, they will blend seamlessly with the surroundings. When non-indigenous flora in a garden looks out of place, a buffer of indigenous species will help retain the intrinsic natural character of an area. Allow a generous width of trees or shrubs, not just a single line, for practical as well as aesthetic reasons. The internal boundary of the perimeter plantings need not be straight but can curve at appropriate intervals.

An indigenous screen also protects nearby bushland against potential spread of seed or pollen from non-local Australian or exotic plants grown closer to the house and from weeds. Local plants will help protect any nearby bushland against invasion from exotic weeds. Birds, people

OPPOSITE: Roberts garden Vic. On a large, steeply sloping block, a garden of colourful small plants is visible from the kitchen window, with a distant view down the slope to a dam and eucalypts along the boundary and then to the far hill beyond.
PHOTOGRAPH DIANA SNAPE

and machines distribute seeds widely. Even ants can spread plant seeds. Avoid planting anything likely to become an environmental weed, as *Acacia baileyana* (Cootamundra Wattle), *A. saligna* (Golden Wreath Wattle) and *Pittosporum undulatum* (Sweet Pittosporum) have become in many areas of southern Australia. If tough *Grevillea rosmarinifolia* (Rosemary Grevillea) hybridises with indigenous species such as *G. alpina* (Mountain Grevillea), it will eventually destroy all pure *G. alpina* in the area.

On land that has been cleared and farmed, it is usually easy to re-establish indigenous trees and larger shrubs. Smaller understorey shrubs can be more difficult, mainly because of competition from weeds, especially introduced pasture grasses. Fortunately there are now many nurseries supplying plants from their local areas, but you may still have problems in persuading the plants to grow in the altered environment. You may have to wait for trees to grow sufficiently to reduce competition from weeds and provide

frost protection, dappled shade and a carpet of fallen leaves as mulch. Deep penetration of tree roots also restores drainage patterns.

Nibbling herbivores, native and introduced, can also make establishing small plants difficult. Satin Bower Birds can be forgiven for eating the leaves of a clump of bluebells (wahlenbergias), but regular destruction by rabbits and hares is unforgivable. So planting indigenous is not always easy but is well worth pursuing to achieve something approaching a natural balance of herbs, grasses, shrubs and trees.

How large a garden?

On a farm an early decision is the size of the garden, because of the need to fence it from stock, pest animals such as rabbits, or wildlife. After you have met the practical needs around the house, plan the remaining area for intensive gardening, including vegetables and herbs. The extent of beds will depend on the water supply and how much time

and effort you are prepared to expend. Here in prepared beds is the place for small treasures that a gardener can watch over and enjoy. The area may be distinct and different with a more formal style than that beyond the regular waterings.

In the extended garden, which will be more relaxed and need less intensive care, you will often be planting into holes in old pasture rather than prepared beds. Placing larger plants wide apart will allow easy mowing which is the simplest way of controlling weeds until they are suppressed by trees and shrubs. If you have been used to the confines of a city garden, you may find it difficult to adjust to the space needed by larger mature trees – at least 6 metres or, where they are in a small close copse, 3 to 4 metres. Planting in recognisable lines makes mowing much simpler but lines do not have to be straight – gentle curves are just as easy to manage and will avoid a regimented orchard look. Essential in getting trees and shrubs off to a good start is the need to prepare the hole well and to control weeds. In large areas, carefully spraying

with a non-residual herbicide around the planting site can save hours of weeding.

The greater the urge to plant trees, the more space you can allocate to the extended garden because, once established, trees require little maintenance. Expansive areas are best kept simple, not just because fussy detailed treatment requires additional maintenance, but because big bold sweeps suit big bold spaces.

OPPOSITE: Stewart garden Vic. Easy care treatment for a garden 'room' or glade, with 'mushrooms' for a touch of fantasy on a moonlit night.
PHOTOGRAPH DIANA SNAPE

ABOVE: Wicksteed garden NSW. A dam on a country property need not be square and can have sloping edges with different inclines for the benefit of wildlife. Water levels vary with the seasons and plants such as melaleucas cope well. A vegetated island provides further protection for waterbirds.
PHOTOGRAPH DIANA SNAPE

Planting for views and vistas

Making the most of views is another major starting point that cannot be overstressed. Each window of the house should have a pleasant outlook, even if limited in depth. With any luck kitchen and living areas will face the wider landscape where plantings in front need to be kept low. Northern aspects are usually protected from summer sun by verandahs or wide eaves but, on eastern and particularly western sides, you may need to compromise between the view and the need for shade. One solution is to use trees (or closer to the house, shrubs trained as trees) with clean trunks and spreading canopies. Many eucalypts have this profile, for example the Salmon Gum (*E. salmonophloia*) and some rainforest species. Carefully sited away from the house, the trunks will frame the view but there will be an inevitable stage of growth when branches will partly block it. As the trunks gain height, the view will reappear and be all the more appreciated. You can accelerate the process by pruning the lower limbs as the tree or shrub grows.

Pergolas offer an alternative, providing a pool of shade through which you can capture the view beyond. When there is no extended view, the circle of vision from a window should be designed to offer a self-contained picture, placing small treasures in front for full enjoyment. If you have enough water, you can keep these close areas green throughout summer. Shrubs planted quite close to blank walls of the house will frame the vistas from nearby windows through to the outer garden.

Vehicle access

On a large property it is usually essential to provide a drive, turning circle and parking spots for visitors, so vehicle access is another obvious consideration in dividing up available space. Surrounding areas can all display eye-catching plants. The choice will depend on location but plants should provide a framework with a floral display as a bonus. If the approach is through open paddocks, resist the temptation to try to create a stately avenue with a single row of trees on either side. The risk of uneven growth and odd losses is too great. Assuming the area is fenced from stock, a wide mixed belt of indigenous plants similar to those in the perimeter is the most natural relaxed solution. A slightly more formal effect can be achieved by planting several species of trees in two rows, or separate small clumps and copses with no understorey. You can carefully select the species for rises and hollows, with a mix of types and occasional gaps in the screen to allow glimpses of the house ahead and other vistas. Such planting reduces the potential of the avenue to act as a wind tunnel during a fire, especially if the drive is straight. A curved drive is attractive and will reduce erosion on a slope. The drive garden deserves special attention as you have to look at it frequently and it greets visitors. Bold clumps or informal hedges are seen more easily from a car than are small individual plants. Understorey plants with silver foliage reflect light at night and help to delineate the driveway.

A turning circle provides an opportunity for spectacular feature planting, with perhaps a tree for shade. The Firewheel Tree (*Stenocarpus sinuatus*) has large glossy green leaves and dazzling red flowers and buds for many months. It will recover well from pruning and there are few places where it will not grow, given care. Golden Penda (*Xanthostemon chrysanthus*) is another outstandingly attractive rainforest tree. Perhaps the turning circle could highlight some Grass Trees (xanthorrhoeas) or other feature plants, or a collection of some of the new cultivars that grow as low rounded cushions – *Melaleuca incana* 'Velvet Cushion', *M. armillaris* 'Green Globe', *Acacia cognata* 'Green Mist' or *A. fimbriata* (Fringed Wattle dwarf form), with an *Acacia spectabilis* (Mudgee Wattle) for height and spring drama. Be sure not to plant too close to wheel tracks as even these dwarf forms will spread in time and hinder access. This is a chance to display something special, with more to offer than just a brief burst of colour.

From these starting points (perimeter planting, consideration of size, views and vehicle access) the garden's masses and voids should begin to take shape. Ways to develop the remaining space will gradually become obvious. Look for areas that lend themselves to making 'rooms', or separate spaces with their own identity. Several 'walls' are probably already planned (or planted) to hide outbuildings or to create surprises – a few more could be established, leaving 'doors' or 'windows' as vistas develop. 'Windows' can often be made by simply pruning the trees or shrubs already there. See where paths develop – the paths made by animals (domestic or wild) on a large property can often be used to the garden designer's advantage.

The original design will probably alter as the garden develops, changing the microclimate as it does so. Progress may seem slow, even imperceptible; then you will suddenly realise that your garden is beginning to develop. At this stage you may need to re-assess your strategy.

Minimising fire risk

In many areas gardeners should plan for the possibility of bushfire. Contradictions still exist in advice on the best way to minimise fire risk, because every fire is unique in its combination of factors. While the local fire authority has booklets offering advice, there is still some prejudice in rural areas against using Australian plants. Selection of plants is the

TOP RIGHT: Thomlinson garden Vic. In a country garden, a screened loggia shaded by pruned *Omalanthus nutans (populifolius)* (Bleeding Heart) provides refreshing summer shade and a transition between house and garden.
PHOTOGRAPH DIANA SNAPE

RIGHT: Gunn garden Vic. A handsome, sturdy avenue of mixed corymbias and eucalypts, planted in informal rather than formal rows.
PHOTOGRAPH DIANA SNAPE

key. Eucalypt foliage contains flammable oils and plants that accumulate a lot of dry twiggy matter should be kept pruned and well away from the house. What is generally accepted is that an Australian garden will recover far better from a fire. This may be little consolation if the worst happens and you lose the house but, if it has survived through a combination of luck and your sensible forethought, your morale will be greatly restored when the first rains stimulate green regrowth and new seedlings.

Every family living in a fire-risk area ultimately has to find its own compromise between the needs and pleasures of daily life and protection against fire. Open space near the house, especially against the walls, acts as a firebreak but there are alternatives to being tied to regular lawn mowing. Nothing is safe in a holocaust but the more probable grass fires can be halted by hard landscaping such as gravel or paving, or softer treatments such as low-growing, fire-retardant plants. These include *Carpobrotus glaucescens* (Coastal Noonflower), *Eremophila debilis* (*Myoporum debile*) and *Myoporum parvifolium* (Creeping Myoporum). Organic mulches will burn and should be used sparingly, if at all, in a fire-risk area. Shade in summer is often a necessity but trees overhanging the house are a recipe for disaster. Green plants can provide a shield against radiant heat, which is a major killer in advance of a fire front. Resist the temptation to plant right against the house but keep the area around the house as green as possible. A row of acacias reportedly performs very well, in one case preventing paint from blistering on a weatherboard house while its brick neighbour was destroyed.

Water availablilty

Another factor influencing design is the water supply. This may be mains water but more often rainfall has to be conserved in tanks and dams. Whatever the source, water is becoming increasingly precious everywhere, so irrigating a hectare or so of land is hard to justify and also unnecessary with the right selection of plants. Australian gardens can be beautiful with only a very small area watered (or none at all). A dam or lake not far from the house can store water for the garden and in case of fire and also be a source of beauty and pleasure. It is beneficial to include one wherever possible, depending on neighbourhood considerations and shire permits. However, the quantity of water stored is always finite, especially in dry years.

There is a widely shared vision of the ideal homestead garden being a lush and green oasis, offering relief from dry yellow paddocks in the heat of summer. This does not necessarily mean lawns and soft perennials. There are many plants such as cycads, Lilly Pillies, zamias, green-leaved acacias, eremophilas and hakeas, which look surprisingly lush with a minimum of water. Apart from those close to the house, plants really need to cope without watering after their first year. If plants are not pampered, growth will be slower but the need to prune and shape will be much reduced. It is a matter of trial and error for each garden.

The most suitable plants for country gardens are from areas with similar rainfall patterns – not just the total annual rainfall, but also the time of year in which it falls. In Mediterranean climate areas such as the south-west of Western Australia, cool wet winters are followed by long hot

FAR LEFT: Davidson garden Vic. A pleasing balance of mass and void (or open space), with a bed of low daisies for foreground interest. Open grassed areas between banks of medium to large shrubs in the midground keep the distant view open.
PHOTOGRAPH DIANA SNAPE

LEFT: Cockburn garden NSW. Designed by Bruce Mackenzie. A large, indigenous garden can develop a park-like feel. Here a path bordered by trees and low plants curves out of view – an invitation to explore the contours of the garden and the distant, rounded bank with their large shrubs and trees.
PHOTOGRAPH JO HAMBRETT

dry summers. Autumn, not spring, is the season of reviving life and growth. Many hakeas, banksias and grevilleas begin to flower in autumn and to put out new roots and fresh leaves. They spend the summer in a resting dormant stage during which watering can be detrimental to their health. Some summer-dormant plants will drop many of their leaves and look miserable during the heat while others stay green, having evolved to reduce water loss in different ways. Ideal plants for gardens with this climate are wax-flowers (philothecas) and the small Couch Honeypot (*Dryandra nivea*); medium-sized prickly, floriferous shrubs *Hakea ceratophylla* and two colourful grevilleas, *G. dielsiana* and *G. wilsonii*; and the large Bull Banksia (*B. grandis*).

Most of the eastern seaboard experiences summer rain and growth slows with the cold of winter, so many showy Western Australian plants perform poorly there. Sydney sandstone plants grown away from their natural habitat require summer water. The inland is completely different, with extreme temperatures and erratic rainfall at any time of

year. Annual averages hide the reality of several years of drought balanced by years in which there are repeated floods. Local plants use rain whenever it falls, hence the sheets of annual daisies or Sturts Desert Pea (*Swainsona formosa*) in good seasons. These plants germinate, grow, flower and seed before the water is exhausted – they can provide spectacular infill colour in gardens well away from their inland home.

There is less precise information available for inland or arid zone gardeners than for those on the coastal fringe, because the inland is vaster and more varied and because, with its much sparser population, fewer gardeners have recorded their experiences. One way to tap into existing information is to join the nearest group of the Australian Plant Society (formerly Society for Growing Australian Plants), as members freely share their knowledge and propagation materials. As the development of Australian plants for the horticultural and cut-flower trades expands, hardy forms and hybrids that can cope with weather extremes will further extend the range of plants available for large gardens.

OPPOSITE: Geale garden Tas. A simple but dramatic view from inside the house, kept open with mulch close to the house and an extensive area of tufted grass beyond, in a district of low fire risk. Eucalypts in the distance put this spacious scene at home in Australia.

PHOTOGRAPH DIANA SNAPE

ABOVE: Lindner property Vic. A magnificent Bunya Pine (*Araucaria bidwillii*) matches its companion building in age, if not in stature. A definite statement in a large garden – not appropriate for a suburban backyard!

PHOTOGRAPH DIANA SNAPE

The role of plants

Australian trees

To plant trees is to give body and life
to one's dreams of a better world.

Russell Page, *The Education of a Gardener*, 1962

Gardeners have scarcely begun to do justice to the role of Australian plants in designing gardens. In the words of Tommy Garnett, plantsman and author:

'In no field is a self-imposed inferiority complex more conspicuous than in that of gardening: none have fuelled it so assiduously as some gardening historians ... By reason of our climates, we have a far wider palette [of plants] on which to draw than anywhere else in the world except those few places like California, parts of South Africa and the Mediterranean Riviera similarly blessed. What we seem to lack is confidence and imagination.'

The largest, most significant and permanent plants in any garden are trees. They act as focal points, habitats for wildlife and screens; they establish essential windbreaks; they provide protective canopies for shade and shelter; and, as living sculptures, they give structure and height to the overall design. A tree defines its own area and also extends the 'feel' of a garden upwards. Each tree is a specimen of beauty with many decorative features – form, texture, colour and scent. Trees cannot easily be replaced in the fabric of a garden and Australian trees give a garden a quintessentially Australian look.

In groups, trees are important components of the larger garden picture. Shifting patterns of shade create a changing scene throughout the day as areas light up or recede into shadow. A vista that includes patches of sunlight and shade has increased depth and interest. The sizes of gaps in the canopy are linked to the total garden size, your needs for summer shade and winter sun, and the requirements of the types of plants grown underneath. The amount of sunlight penetrating to the ground will depend on the height of surrounding vegetation, so tall trees need a larger gap than shrubs to allow sun onto the same area of ground.

In 1975 landscape designer Glen Wilson named five Australian genera as basic landscaping plants – acacia, callistemon, eucalyptus (including corymbia), grevillea and melaleuca. His next six genera were angophora, banksia, casuarina (including allocasuarina), hakea, leptospermum and prostanthera. Today there are many more Australian plants available in nurseries than in 1975. However, these genera retain a central place in garden design, especially in south-eastern Australia where Glen Wilson worked, because of their reliability and the wide range of plants they offer. Eucalypts, angophoras and casuarinas are nearly all trees as are a significant number of species of the others, though many are shrubs. In the north and north-east, rainforest genera such as

PREVIOUS PAGE: Clustered buds and fruit of *Corymbia ptychocarpa* (Swamp Bloodwood) PHOTOGRAPH BRIAN SNAPE

OPPOSITE: Glen Wilson's garden ACT. The garden of a pioneering designer is a minimum maintenance, water-saving garden of trees with indigenous Red Spotted Gum (*Eucalytpus mannifera* ssp. *maculosa*) and River Peppermint (*E. elata*). These shade the western side of the suburban house and screen it lightly from the street. Their natural appearance reflects careful placement. Rainwater is retained in shallow gravel scoops and natural mulch is provided by the trees. PHOTOGRAPH DIANA SNAPE

acmenas, elaeocarpus and syzygiums could be added to these lists. Indigenous trees are hardy and reliable in creating a garden framework; they also reinforce the sense of place, linking the garden to the natural environment

Individual trees

Trees already established in a garden may form a basic part of the design and save many years of waiting for new ones to grow. However, because trees play such a crucial role in the overall design, it is important to choose wisely. Is the tree healthy and attractive? Is its position suitable? Is the tree already too large and spreading, or will it be in the future? Will its shade be too dominant? Always try to retain a mature tree wherever possible, especially an indigenous one, as it is helpful to see its mature size and the extent of its shade. However, if a particular tree presents a problem or if it does

not fit the design criteria, it is better to remove it early. Otherwise it will have a major influence on design and planting; removal later will be both difficult and costly.

When planting trees, picture their future size and shape, many years ahead. Their full size should be appropriate for the garden space and the house. An individual tree can be planted alone in an open space as a specimen tree for its form and decorative features. Edna Walling advocated the use of Australian plants long before they became of general interest for gardeners and nurseries. Many of her plans showed areas of lawn or rough grass with occasional trees scattered at random, emphasising the openness of the space. In an inland landscape a lone tree increases the 'wide open space' look of the countryside.

A single tree in the foreground frames a garden and gives it depth. A tree can be a vertical focus at a bend in a path, the end of a path, or right at the back of the garden. In a narrow space a small

tree espaliered along a wall distracts from or softens its hardness. Similarly the texture of a tree provides contrast with rocks.

Groups of trees

Create informal spaces such as groves and enclosures with trees, or plant trees closely to form a copse. The repetition of one species looks natural and there will usually be some interesting variations between individual trees. At eye level, trunks and types of bark create visual interest. A collection of different trees integrates well against a background composed of one or two main species. Trees of the same species at different ages look natural and remind us of the fourth dimension of time. Irregular spacing between scattered plantings increases the natural appearance and allows meandering pathways in a 'walkabout' garden. Spacing may be horizontal as well as vertical – a layered effect of taller

OPPOSITE LEFT: Foliage and male flowers of *Allocasuarina littoralis* (Black She-oak)
PHOTOGRAPH BRIAN SNAPE

OPPOSITE RIGHT: Hambrett garden NSW. Attractive trunk of White Cedar (*Melia azedarach*) and crinkled new foliage of Long-leaved Tuckeroo (*Cupaniopsis newmanii*) blend well with trunks and foliage of many exotic trees.
PHOTOGRAPH JO HAMBRETT

ABOVE LEFT: A natural garden NSW. The shapely and distinctive forms of Cypress Pines (callitris) can be incorporated in the design of a formal or a naturalistic garden.
PHOTOGRAPH DIANA SNAPE

ABOVE RIGHT: 'Ferns Hideaway' Qld. Marvellous contrasts in form and foliage of three tall trees – an Alexandra Palm (*Archontophoenix alexandrae*) with its unique and evocative silhouette, a melaleuca (Paperbark) and a rainforest tree.
PHOTOGRAPH DIANA SNAPE

trees behind more shrub-like ones.

Tree trunks may interrupt space but do not trap it – vertical spaces appear between neighbouring trunks. The edges of open areas are valuable, providing semi-shade or open-shade positions for other plants, with a great range of micro-environments. If you plant around a level space with trees, the northern edge of the space will be shaded all day while the southern edge will be sunny. Slope will affect the extent of a tree's shade. In a small garden where sun is precious, if open areas run north-south, they will remain more open and unshaded than those running east-west.

Trees can be planted in formal straight or curved lines, or can create formal spaces such as circles, squares or avenues. Formal planting of tall trees with straight trunks can be striking, for example *Corymbia maculata* (Spotted Gum) in a quadrangle at Macquarie University in Sydney. However, each tree has its own subtle variations in form, density of foliage, bark colours and patterns.

Evergreen and deciduous

A characteristic of Australian vegetation is the evergreen nature of most of its flora. However, Australian trees delight us with changes in their bark, foliage and blossoms throughout the year. In Sydney the beautiful *Angophora costata* (Smooth-barked Apple) sheds bark to reveal a glistening pearly, salmon-pink torso just in time for Christmas. Many rainforest species have new leaf growth that is brilliant in colour and form, especially in autumn and winter.

Beautiful deciduous Australian trees include hardy *Melia azedarach* (White Cedar) with a shady rounded canopy and lacy fernlike foliage; its chocolate-scented mauve flowers are followed by yellow fruit hanging from the tree after leaf-fall. Other examples include *Toona ciliata* (Red Cedar), glowing *Brachychiton acerifolius* (Illawarra Flame Tree), *Nothofagus gunnii* (Deciduous Beech) and *Ficus virens* (Deciduous Fig).

In the north of Australia, a number of trees, including some indigenous eucalypts, lose their leaves in response to the dry, not the cold.

Eucalypts – eucalyptus, corymbia and angophora

These three genera of trees are closely related, so the term 'eucalypt' can be used to include all of them. Eucalypts are wonderful Australian trees and most of us want at least one in our garden, however small. For many years, eucalypts planted in suburban gardens were too large for their positions – trees in gardens still sometimes grow bigger than expected. The Garden Design Study Group now defines a small tree as one whose height is limited to 6 metres. This restricts the selection of small eucalypts to shrub-like trees or slender, often multiple-trunked, trees such as mallees. Several small eucalypts planted in one hole can simulate this effect. Many mallees will grow a single trunk in garden conditions and you can train them to do so or, if you want a solid definite trunk, you can plant a medium tree (6-12 metres). These can still be appropriate for even a small garden because of their slender form, taking little space near ground level.

A whole garden can consist of eucalypts, with a limited understorey of low plants, even on a small block. An ideal position is on the western side of a house, between house and street, to shade the house from strong western sun and partially screen it from the street. In such a location the self-mulching and partial shade of eucalypts help inhibit weeds. A spacious garden in the country or outer suburbs will have room for large trees and also the inclusion of a tree garden. There are hundreds of magnificent large eucalypts to choose from, and at least some locally indigenous species should be desirable.

OPPOSITE: Floyd garden Vic. A partly deciduous Australian tree that does not lose all its leaves nor flower consistently, the Illawarra Flame Tree (*Brachychiton acerifolius*) is breath-taking in full flower.
PHOTOGRAPH JOHN FLOYD

Small eucalypts recommended (6m or less)

All come from Western Australia and all are very beautiful.

E. preissiana (Bell-fruited Mallee); E. kruseana (Book-leaf Mallee); E. websteriana (Webster's Mallee); E. pluricaulis ssp. porphyrea ; E. forrestiana (Fuchsia Gum); E. torquata (Coral Gum); and the outstanding but 'fussy' E. caesia (especially ssp. magna 'Silver Princess') with weeping habit, pendulous pink blossoms, white stems and bell-shaped fruits.

Medium eucalypts recommended (6-12m)

From different states as indicated. (N = NSW; Q = Qld; S = SA; T = Tas; V = Vic; W = WA; nt = Northern Territory)

E. multicaulis (N) (Whipstick Mallee Ash); E. gregsoniana (N) (Wolgan Snow Gum); E. lansdowneana (S) (Crimson Mallee); E. curtisii (Q) (Plunkett Mallee); E. viridis (NQSV) (Green Mallee); E. calycogona (NSVW) (Gooseberry Mallee); E. leucoxylon (NSV) (Yellow Gum); E. fasciculosa (SV) (Pink Gum).

Acacias

Australia has more than 950 different species of wattles ranging from groundcovers to medium trees. Brilliant flowers, superb foliage, different shapes, landscaping adaptability, low maintenance and quick growth are some of the reasons why acacias are such popular garden plants. As well as the plants providing protective cover for birds, their seeds are an important food source for rosellas, other parrots and pigeons. Wattles are very hardy. Most are frost-resistant,

TOP: Coastal garden Vic. *Allocasuarina verticillata (Casuarina stricta)* (Coast She-oak), indigenous to this area, is used as a street tree for its shapely form. With no need to attract birds or bees, the wind-pollinated flowers still flaunt their pollen colour – male plant only. The female plant has tiny red flowers.
PHOTOGRAPH DIANA SNAPE

BOTTOM: Autumn foliage of deciduous White Cedar (*Melia azedarach*) is brilliant against an evergreen backgound.
PHOTOGRAPH JO HAMBRETT

will grow in any well-drained soil and do not require fertiliser because they are leguminous, nitrogen-fixing plants. Trimming them regularly after flowering should improve the production of blooms and prolong their life (one-third of one-third of the branches each year is a useful guide). Many wattles live for a long time but others are quick-growing and shorter-lived. They are useful 'nurse plants' for the slower-growing, more permanent plants such as banksias which can be grown nearby. Borers and galls are two pests to watch out for in wattles. Again the locally indigenous species are most appropriate, especially of large wattles.

Acacias recommended as small trees (6m or less)

These are showy in form and foliage with masses of golden blossom.

A. spectabilis (QN) (Mudgee Wattle); A. pendula (QNV) (Weeping Myall); A. howittii (V) (Sticky Wattle) and A. pycnantha (NSV) (Golden Wattle) – our floral emblem with eucalypt-like foliage, racemes of golden flower heads.

Acacias recommended as small to medium trees (6-12m)

Each has its own special features and attractions.

A. binervia (NV) (Coast Myall); A. cognata (NV) (Bower Wattle); A. covenyi (N) (Blue-bush); A. fimbriata (QN) (Fringed Wattle); A. prominens (N) (Golden Rain Wattle). A. baileyana (N) (Cootamundra Wattle) has been popular but it can self-sow and be a threat to natural environments.

Acacias and eucalypts can flower in succession and, in many places, bear flowers in the garden throughout the year, providing essential food for insects and for both insect- and nectar-eating birds.

Rainforest trees

Rainforest trees comprise 50 per cent of all Australian tree species. They have become increasingly popular over recent years as gardeners discover this vast range of spectacular ornamental plants. They come in such a variety of form, colour, size and appearance that their design applications seem limitless. Blossoms and fruit are striking and unusual; new foliage growth is decorative and flamboyant. When grown away from their natural habitat they frequently become smaller, denser and rounder and so more suitable for use in gardens. Their colourful foliage and striking fruit grow closer to the ground where you can better appreciate them. Many of these trees are superb in formal gardens and can be used with or in place of exotic species. Many also make highly ornamental plants in containers.

It is possible to establish and maintain a rainforest garden based on these trees in a broad range of climates from Tasmania to Queensland. Some rainforest trees will even tolerate moderate frosts once established. The closed canopy of a rainforest garden creates the shade and tranquillity of a forest as well as, on hot summer days, a cool microclimate where a spectrum of shade-loving plants thrive. The dry summers of south-eastern Australia signal the need for a protected microclimate and extra water, however plants from dry rainforests (a verbal contradiction) will grow without such protection. Rainforest plants have shallow roots and should not be planted too deeply – they do best on top of a mound of well-dug and composted soil. One pioneer plant that provides quick cover and shade for new plantings is *Omalanthus nutans* (*O. populifolius*) (Bleeding Heart), with a rounded canopy, large heart-shaped leaves ageing to red, and purple fruit.

Small to medium rainforest trees recommended (6-12m)

There is a wonderful variety of distinctive trees.

Acmena smithii (QNVnt) (Lilly Pilly); *Atherosperma moschatum* (NVT) (Southern Sassafras); *Anetholea anisata* (N) (Aniseed Tree); *Backhousia citriodora* (Q) (Lemon Ironwood); *Buckinghamia celsissima* (Q) (Ivory Curl); *Callicoma serratifolia* (QN) (Black Wattle); *Cupaniopsis*

newmanii (QN) (Long-leafed Tuckeroo); *Davidsonia pruriens* (QN) (Davidson's Plum); *Diploglottis campbellii* (QN) (Small-leafed Tamarind); *Elaeocarpus reticulatus* (QNVT) (Blueberry Ash); *Melia azadarach* (White Cedar) (QNW); *Pullea stutzeri* (Q) (Hard Alder).

Banksias

Though gardeners seldom choose them as small trees, banksias have great character and interest. Generally slower-growing than popular eucalypts and wattles, they maintain a more modest size than many of the speedy growers and, comfortingly, live for a long time. Banksias have a solid presence with shapely trunks, often gnarled, and characteristic foliage interspersed with intriguing cones at different stages of maturity. Flower spikes can be gold, orange or red or many shades of green and brown. Banksias tolerate pruning and you can shape them to a form of your choice. Western Australia has a tremendous variety of banksias, so gardeners there or in South Australia have a wide choice.

Banksias recommended for eastern states as small to medium trees (6-12m)

B. aemula (Wallum Banksia); *B. integrifolia* (Coast Banksia); *B. ericifolia* (Heath Banksia) and *B.* 'Giant Candles' (a hybrid between *B. ericifolia* and *B. spinulosa*); *B. conferta*; *B. marginata* (Silver Banksia); *B. serrata* (Saw Banksia).

Callistemons

Callistemons and melaleucas have been widely grown for many years and both adapt to a range of different conditions,

LEFT: Hoffman Walk Vic. Designed by Kevin Hoffman. *Eucalyptus scoparia* (Wallangarra White Gum) is a magnificent tree of medium height. Here the white trunks stand sentinel over low, silver-white Cushion Bushes (*Leucophyta brownii*) and green foliage against a background of red scoria, colours reminiscent of arid areas.
PHOTOGRAPH DIANA SNAPE

with a particular liking for wet spots. You can prune both to suit your garden design. A number of callistemons have papery trunks and you can prune to display this feature and to encourage a tree form. Alternatively, pruning after flowering will create a compact rounded form and increase future flowering. Bottlebrush flowers in a variety of hues (often in two seasons a year), colourful new leaves and bird-attracting qualities make callistemons very popular and reliable garden plants.

Callistemons recommended as small trees (6m or less)

C. rugulosus (*C. macropunctatus*) (Scarlet Bottlebrush) and *C.* 'Harkness'; *C. citrinus* (Crimson Bottlebrush); *C. sieberi* (*C. paludosus*) (River Bottlebrush); *C. viminalis* (Weeping Bottlebrush). Numerous natural and cultivated forms of *C. viminalis* offer variations in form, leaf colour and flower colour, from the original bright-red brushes to salmon-pink, rose or dark red. Other callistemon cultivars or hybrids have lemon, white, pink, burgundy, mauve, lilac or purple brushes – a rainbow of colours, some dotted with golden anthers. They all may grow to medium height (6-12 metres).

Melaleucas

Most melaleuca trees are striking when they begin to age and the paperbark trunks become conspicuous. Older specimens are frequently gnarled and full of character. They are often quite formal stately trees, their rounded green canopies covered with blossoms in season.

Melaleucas recommended as small to medium trees (6-12m)

M. cuticularis (SW) (Saltwater Paperbark); *M. linariifolia* (QN) (Snow-in-Summer); *M. alternifolia* (QN); *M. ericifolia* (NVT) (Swamp Paperbark) can colonise by suckering; *M. armillaris* (NVT) (Bracelet Honey-myrtle) – has been widely used for screens and hedges; fast-growing, attractive and adaptable but prone to wind damage when aged, especially if multi-trunked and isolated.

Melaleucas recommended as medium to large trees (12m or taller)

M. quinquenervia (QN) (Broad-leaved Paperbark); *M. leucadendra* (QWnt) (Northern Paperbark).

Hakeas

Hakeas are good, reliable plants that require only sunshine and drainage to flourish in a garden. Most are medium shrubs to small trees with attractive form and often superb foliage and flowers. Their flowers have various colours and, unlike their close relatives, grevilleas, they produce hard fruit. A significant number have prickly foliage, ideal for protecting small birds and deterring unwanted animals.

Hakeas recommended as small trees

H. elliptica (W) (Oval-leafed Hakea); *H. laurina* (W) (Pincushion Hakea); *H. petiolaris* (W) (Sea Urchin Hakea); *H. eriantha* (QNV) (Tree Hakea); *H. coriacea* (W) (Pink Spike Hakea) and *H. francisiana* (SW) (Narukalja) – in eastern states the last two are frequently grafted on *H. salicifolia* (Willow-leaved Hakea).

Allocasuarinas and casuarinas

Allocasuarinas and casuarinas are small to large evergreen trees and shrubs that adapt to a variety of conditions and purposes. You can grow them for their beautiful form and foliage or for their interesting textured trunks. Female trees bear tiny red flowers that glow when lit from behind. Then follow attractive cones loved by many birds. Male allocasuarinas look magnificent when their branchlets are laden with pollen. The 'leaves' are needle-like but soft and vary in colour from green through to brown, rust or purple, depending on the season. Areas under allocasuarinas need little care, as their fallen needles form a distinctive mulch which, with their shade, inhibits most growth. A grove of these lovely trees is very attractive and, on a windy day, their soft whispering and sighing add a new dimension to a garden.

Small to medium trees recommended

Allocasuarina littoralis (QNVT) (Black She-oak); *A. verticillata* (*C. stricta*) (NVTS) (Drooping She-oak).

Medium to large trees recommended

A. torulosa (QN) (Rose She-oak) with slender drooping branchlets, often purple or copper in colour; *Casuarina cunninghamiana* (QNnt) (River Oak); *A. huegeliana* (W) (Rock She-oak).

Conifers

Conifers team well with casuarinas as their forms and foliage blend appealingly and conifers grow happily where the casuarina needles have been brushed aside. Conifers differ greatly from flowering shrubs or trees and have a distinct place in the garden. Their definite pleasing forms make them ideal focal points or feature trees in a large garden or equally successful as boundary delineators, windbreaks, screens or hedges. Some are small but most are medium to very large trees, hardy, shapely and slow-growing. The larger conifers are suitable only for spacious gardens and parks. However, young plants of many large species are valued as container plants because of their attractive foliage and slow rate of growth. In fact, they may grow happily in containers for many years.

Conifers recommended

Callitris species (Cypress Pines) – handsome, elegant trees whether used alone or in groups; you can shape them to form a magnificent tall hedge.

Small to medium: *C. rhomboidea* (QNVTS) (Port Jackson Pine); *C. oblonga* (NT) (Tasmanian Cypress-pine).

Medium to large: *C. endlicheri* (QNV) (Black Cypress-pine); *C. macleayana* (QN) (Stringybark Cypress-pine); *C. gracilis* (NVS) (Slender Cypress-pine).

SPECIES OTHER THAN CALLITRIS

Small to medium: *Actinostrobus pyramidalis* (W) (Swamp Cypress-pine); *Podocarpus elatus* (QN) (Plum Pine)

Medium to large: *Athrotaxis cupressoides* (T) (Tasmanian Pencil-pine); *Lagarostrobus franklinii* (T) (Huon Pine); *Phyllocladus aspleniifolius* (T) (Celery-top Pine).

Large: all are handsome and distinctive trees: *Athrotaxis selaginoides* (T) (King Billy Pine); *Araucaria bidwillii* (Q) (Bunya Pine), with threateningly heavy cones; *A. cunninghamii* (QN) (Hoop Pine); *A. heterophylla* (Norfolk Island Pine), widely regarded as Australian; *Agathis robusta* (Q) (Queensland Kauri).

Conclusion

The environment and design of every garden are enhanced by at least one tree. Among small Australian trees are also some tall species of popular genera of shrubs. These include *Leptospermum petersonii* (Lemon-scented Tea-tree), *Prostanthera lasianthos* (Victorian Christmas Bush) and *Eremophila longifolia* (Berrigan), all small; *Hibiscus tiliaceus* (Cottonwood) is small to medium, and *Grevillea robusta* (Silky Oak) can grow quite tall. Popular *Ceratopetalum gummiferum* (NSW Christmas Bush) is the smallest member of a genus of larger trees. In a large garden, the main problem will be restricting the selection of trees from the vast range available. In a small garden, there is no need to forgo the pleasure of these beautiful plants, as there are so many appropriate species. There is a suitable Australian tree for every Australian garden

ABOVE LEFT: Ford garden, Fülling, Vic. Designed by Gordon Ford. A path meanders between low, groundcover plants to reach the house. Tall eucalypts are elegant in the background and both define the garden and extend its space upwards. Their presence would be missed. Linear elements of tree trunks and house are a satisfying contrast to rounded forms of foliage.

PHOTOGRAPH TRISHA DIXON

ABOVE RIGHT: Densley garden Vic. A single tree beside a pathway can be a sign enticing further exploration of the garden.

PHOTOGRAPH DIANA SNAPE

Groundcover plants

Australian groundcover plants are extremely popular and widely used in gardens for a number of reasons. First, a marvellous range of these attractive plants is now available. A second reason is the practical value of having these plants as a living or green mulch, shading the soil and reducing weed growth. They also reduce loss of moisture from the soil (though using some water themselves) and act as insulators, helping to maintain an even soil temperature. There is an appropriate groundcover plant for every garden situation, no matter how difficult. They vary from low prostrate, ground-hugging plants to spreading plants up to 30 centimetres high, covering areas from many square metres to less than 1 square metre. Some are compact and provide dense cover; others are more sparse.

Groundcovers provide a layer of plants in addition to the recognised lower-, middle- and upperstoreys, adding interest to the gardenscape. The designer can have fun decorating the ground with living patterns and textures.

Open areas or garden beds

Many gardeners are looking for ways to treat open spaces other than with lawn. For an open area without foot traffic, an enormous variety of Australian groundcover plants are available for use individually, or grouped together to form a carpet. Some may act as a substitute for lawn, with a formal or trodden pathway through them. A selection of the same species can suit a garden bed. The choice of species will depend on the size and style of the garden and the situation or microclimate, which will also influence how much the plant spreads.

Prostrate

Low prostrate, close-knit plants include grevilleas such as *G. 'Poorinda Royal Mantle'*, magnificent with serrated green foliage and abundant deep-red flowers. It spreads easily (one plant can readily cover more than 4 square metres) and is dense enough to inhibit all weeds. Many ground-hugging plants will cover a smaller area and generally inhibit weeds. These can be used in combination to create a wonderful patchwork or tapestry. The following all have very small leaves. *Pultenaea pedunculata* (Mat Bush-pea) usually has red and yellow flowers but there are yellow, orange and pink forms. Less dense, blue *Dampiera diversifolia* combines well with yellow *Hibbertia pedunculata* (Stalked Guinea-flower) or *H. procumbens* (Spreading Guinea-flower). *Lobelia (Pratia) pedunculata* (Matted Pratia) forms a completely flat lawn, dotted with pale starry flowers that attract butterflies, but it may tend to 'wander' a little unless kept in its place.

Kennedia microphylla is a very close-knit, small ground-hugging plant. Trailers can be very decorative in a garden bed or enhancing a wall or bank. *Kennedia prostrata* (Running Postman) has neat foliage and bright red flowers. There are cheerful hibbertias. For example, *H. dentata* (Trailing Guinea-

OPPOSITE: Blake garden Vic. Two Australian grasses *Microlaena stipoides* (Weeping Grass) and the local danthonia (Wallaby Grass) combine to make an excellent lawn, which remains green throughout the year with no watering. It requires mowing only four or five times during the year.
PHOTOGRAPH DIANA SNAPE

flower) is not dense but is very beautiful with large yellow flowers and reddish stems and foliage – there is also an exquisite cream-flowered form.

Ankle high

Growing slightly higher, 100 mm or so above the ground, suckering *Viola hederacea* (Native Violet) can form a dense and wide-spreading lawn. It is an excellent groundcover for a semi-shaded moist area, but in a garden bed it can overgrow small plants; blue and white forms are less vigorous. You can tread a path through this versatile groundcover. Brachysemas have neat foliage – both *B. latifolium* (Broad-leaved Brachysema) and *B. praemorsum* 'Bronze Butterfly' have cream pea flowers, the latter ageing to red and accompanied by unusual foliage colour. The green of reliable Fan Flower *Scaevola aemula* is liberally sprinkled with mauve or purple, and *S. albida* with sparkling white or sky blue. In a moist area, a relaxing and attractive green space can be provided with *Mazus pumilio* (Swamp Mazus) and *Goodenia humilis* (Swamp Goodenia). These plants can cope with light foot traffic and will flower in purple and gold for many months. The purple-blues of *Scaevola* 'Mauve Clusters' and the less dense *Dampiera linearis* (Common Dampiera) complement the yellow hues of *Hibbertia serpyllifolia*.

Above ankle high

Slightly higher-growing are the spreading dwarf forms of a number of popular acacias, including *A. howittii* (Sticky Wattle) and *A. cultriformis* (Knife-leaf wattle). *Correa decumbens* and prostrate forms of *C. alba* (White Correa) and *C. reflexa* (Common Correa) are also favourites. Both *Pultenaea capitellata* and *P. subternata* prostrate form have distinctive foliage and colourful pea flowers. *Persoonia chamaepitys* (Prostrate Geebung) has superb bright-green, pine-like foliage and small deep-yellow flowers; *P. chamaepeuce* is also lovely. In moist areas, blechnums (Water

Ferns) or adiantums (Maidenhair Ferns) look luxurious.

Creepers or scramblers can be attractive and spread well on the ground though they don't entirely suppress weeds. *Jasminum suavissimum* (Sweet Jasmine) has fragrant starry flowers and can produce quite dense green foliage – its stems develop roots at intervals. The jasmine (or vigorous *Pandorea jasminoides* 'Lady Di') looks magnificent interspersed with trailing *Abelmoschus moschatus* (Creeping Hibiscus), its large pinkish-red flowers contrasting well with the smaller white flowers.

The following three groups of groundcovers deserve a special mention.

Groundcover grevilleas

There are numerous attractive prostrate grevilleas but the following six species are beautiful dense groundcovers for carpeting level ground or cascading down a slope.

Grevillea humifusa – vibrant contrast between ashy grey-green, soft foliage and masses of vivid red flowers.

G. lanigera (Woolly Grevillea) – dense grey leaves contrasting delightfully with pink and cream flowers.

G. laurifolia (Laurel-leaf Grevillea) – red toothbrush flowers; a probable parent of G. 'Poorinda Royal Mantle'.

G. microstegia – deeply divided green leaves, colourful new growth and dark-red toothbrush flowers.

G. nudiflora – variable – the 'curly leaf' form is best; massed red and yellow flowers on long trailing stems.

G. repens (Creeping Grevillea) – attractive holly leaves colour in winter; burgundy-red toothbrush flowers.

Prostrate banksias

Creeping Banksia (*B. repens*), *Banksia blechnifolia* and *B. petiolaris* can all spread vigorously to provide groundcover on quite a grand scale. These plants are excellent on slopes or banks and, with their distinctive foliage (beautifully coloured when new) and upright flower spikes and cones, their ornate

texture is fascinating. Remove all weeds (especially grasses) from the area before planting, as it is much more difficult to weed afterwards.

Beautiful prostrate forms of *B. integrifolia* (Coast Banksia), *B. spinulosa* (Hairpin Banksia) and *B. serrata* (Saw Banksia) are now available from nurseries. These combine well with paving or rock shelves and other distinctive foliage such as the horizontal strata of *Homoranthus* species. They also blend attractively with extensive areas of softer groundcovers in similar tonings. These prostrate banksias are conspicuous low features in the garden, so selecting their position requires a little thought. The same applies to the new vigorous prostrate acacias, for example *A. cardiophylla* 'Gold Lace'.

Daisies

Daisies serve many functions in garden design and are invaluable groundcovers. They may act as linking plants, used in a number of garden beds. *Brachyscome multifida* (Cut-leaf Daisy) and *B. angustifolia* (Stiff Daisy) are excellent for this

and, once established, need little watering. With different forms of *B. multifida*, you can create an appealing patchwork of mauves and purples accented with pink, white or cream. Flower sizes vary and colours intermingle at the edges. Brachyscomes are easy to propagate from cuttings. Other delightful species include *B. formosa* (Pillaga Daisy), *B. nivalis* (Snow Daisy) and *B. segmentosa* (from Lord Howe Island). You can soften borders by using daisies as small edging plants.

Daisies add welcome colour to a depleted summer garden. In open bushland and along roadside corridors, *Chrysocephalum (Helichrysum)* species grow naturally as spreading groundcovers. Beautiful *C. apiculatum* (Common Everlasting) has a hundred local variations of grey foliage and gold flowers for many months of the year – the excellent

ABOVE: Closs garden Tas. An unusual and attractive lawn of Swamp Mazus (*M. pumilio*) between two garden beds is protected by stepping 'stones' of timber roundels. Preferring moist conditions, the mazus flowers for many months of the year.
PHOTOGRAPH DIANA SNAPE

C. ramosissimum (Yellow Buttons) is one such variation. With similar appeal is *C. semipapposum* (Clustered Everlasting), also hardy in sunshine or partial shade. Some popular daisies such as these chrysocephalums and also *Brachyscome multifida* need to be pruned when new growth at the base of the plant is well established, not after flowering. Yellow, blue and white are summer colours – beach colours – sand and sun, water and sky, surf and clouds. Add small bluebells (wahlenbergias), halganias or *Derwentia arenaria* 'Cottage Blue' to the garden for shades of blue. Scaevolas and dampieras are lovely but, like daisies, tend more to mauve or purple-blue.

Sloping areas

There is a wealth of soil-binding plants for use on sloping sites. Many plants that sucker and layer will stabilise banks and prevent soil erosion. One excellent plant for a sloping site is *Myoporum parvifolium* (Creeping Myoporum) which has several forms with very attractive foliage; each spreads quickly, putting down sturdy roots that help stabilise the ground. Other possibilities include some with rounded foliage and pea-flowers – *Brachysema latifolium* (Broad-leaved Brachysema) (orange-red), *Kennedia beckxiana* (large scarlet flowers) and *Platylobium formosum* (Handsome Flat-pea)

PREVIOUS PAGE: Hanson garden Vic. Designed by Bev Hanson. In many gardens a conventional lawn is used to provide an extensive open area, here bordered largely by Australian plants. It requires consistent but straightforward maintenance. *Melaleuca wilsonii* (Wilson's Honey-myrtle) splashes pink across the foreground.
PHOTOGRAPH SIMON GRIFFITHS

LEFT: Jacobs garden Vic. Purple-blue dampieras are colourful and popular groundcover plants. Here a gravel path leads towards a Bower Wattle (*Acacia cognata*) between almost prostrate plants of Common Dampiera (*D. linearis*) on the left and low, pink-flowering shrubs on the right including *Astartea fascicularis* 'Winter Pink'. The groundcovers help give a spacious feel to the garden.
PHOTOGRAPH DIANA SNAPE

(yellow and red). Two yellow-flowered plants are hardy *Goodenia ovata* (Hop Goodenia) prostrate form and *Hibbertia scandens* (Climbing Guinea-flower), with showy large leaves and flowers. *Melaleuca wilsonii* prostrate form (Wilson's Honey-myrtle) has pale stems, fine foliage and deep mauve-pink flowers. *Grevillea* 'Poorinda Royal Mantle' is another groundcover that looks magnificent cascading over steep banks or walls.

Grassed areas

Whilst a lawn may be difficult to maintain or wasteful of water in parts of Australia, many people enjoy an area of green grass for lying out in the garden, or as a children's play area (no grazed knees or elbows). Grass doesn't have to be green all year; autumn rains will soon revive a seemingly dead, brown lawn. Grasses have evolved annual life cycles to suit their natural environment. Some are dormant in summer and some in winter, no matter what rain they receive; others respond to any reasonable fall regardless of season. Sometimes the parent dies and the species is renewed only by seed germination; other grasses maintain a dormant growing tip underground. These characteristics determine the usefulness of any species in a lawn.

A grassed area can be less formal than a conventional manicured lawn. In a larger garden, in particular, the green (or bronze-golden in summer) is a means of linking garden 'compartments'. Many people enjoy the varying shapes, sizes and colours of tufted Australian grasses, as they present an interesting contrast to the bushy forms of herbaceous plants and shrubs. *Microlaena stipoides* (Weeping Grass) is a soft, green perennial grass with spreading rhizomes, a good plant for both sunny and shaded areas. It offers an excellent alternative to a traditional lawn and requires mowing only two or three times a year. Another native grass with similar potential is

Eragrostis brownii (Common Love-grass). Both these grasses can invade cultivated garden beds if planted nearby. Wallaby Grass (austrodanthonias, joyceas and their relatives) can be successfully combined with microlaena in a lawn.

ABOVE: Larkin garden Vic. Prostrate groundcovers Mat Bush-pea (*Pultenaea pedunculata*), Cut-leaf Daisy (*Brachyscome multifida*) and a brachysema species blend to form a low, tapestry garden.
PHOTOGRAPH DIANA SNAPE

129

Framework plants

The best advice I ever received about gardening was to plant the 'bones' early and not to worry about the details; they could adapt and change as inclination and experience allowed.

Montagu Don, *The Sensuous Garden*, 1997

The wonderful kaleidoscope of Australian plants mirrors the enormous range of their natural habitats. In the garden, those plants of different origins will require different conditions, which need to be studied just as carefully as do those for any exotic plant. The plants mentioned in this book are generally hardy and reliable, providing that the soil, climate and position are suitable. Over time, Australian plants have adapted to poor, relatively shallow soils, low in elements such as phosphorus, by the development of narrow, leathery leaves and prickles or spikes (sclerophylly). Low rainfall in a large part of the continent has encouraged many plants to further accentuate such adaptations to also conserve water within their tissues. Some acacias, hakeas and grevilleas exemplify these devices. Research continues on many aspects of the characteristics of Australian plants, such as associations with soil micro-organisms.

Gardeners can learn from books, catalogues or nurseries (ideally local ones) as to whether their garden can provide appropriate conditions for a particular plant. The *Encyclopaedia of Australian Plants Suitable for Cultivation* now extends to volume 7 and books have been written about the flora of a single region and individual genera or families.

After trees and groundcovers, it is helpful to think in terms of four design roles for Australian plants – framework, feature, ornamental and infill. Many plants may be used in more than one role, depending on the size of the garden and the number of plants, their position and treatment (such as pruning). After trees, framework and then feature plants will be the most permanent occupants and should be chosen and planted next.

In this book, small shrubs are 1 metre or less in height; medium shrubs are between 1 and 3 metres; large shrubs 3 metres or more. Most gardeners include a selection of shrub sizes to add interest and diversity.

Framework plants define the shape of a whole garden and its various sections. They can also provide the essential unity to bind the whole together. Important characteristics of framework plants are reliability, long life and green foliage that maintains its attractiveness throughout the year, in scorching summers and freezing winters alike. Some suitable indigenous plants in this role will provide a link with the local environment as well as shelter and sustenance for local wildlife. Framework plants act as windbreaks and block unsightly views. They can be positioned to create a private enclosure or frame an attractive view from the house. Used as a backdrop, they can highlight a feature plant or sculpture. In a large garden, trees will be important components of framework planting.

OPPOSITE: Snape garden. Many callistemons grow as small, bushy trees and make excellent framework plants. Here a bank of different, large callistemons on the right provides a substantial screen to give privacy in an area for relaxation. Small to medium shrubs include *Grevillea* 'Robyn Gordon' and G. 'Superb' in the foreground.
PHOTOGRAPH SIMON GRIFFITHS

Repetition provides a strong framework, for example creating a screen of one or similar species, or using plants with the same or similar types of foliage. A row of plants of similar height is more effective than one of different sizes. Plants with similar foliage colour can also define a curve, as the eye will follow the line of colour standing out from other greens. Feature plants with elaborate form or distinctive foliage do not make good framework plants because they capture too much attention. Many framework plants may have beautiful flowers as a bonus. Shrubs recommended for shaping as a formal hedge will also be suitable as informal framework plants.

Callistemons

Few callistemons (bottlebrushes) are naturally small or medium shrubs but there are some hybrids, cultivars and selected dwarf forms of larger species. Callistemons are particularly hardy and reliable plants. They benefit from pruning to retain a dense compact form with abundant flowers, unless space allows a more open, exuberant plant. Some forms are compact; others have a weeping appearance. They can have many roles in garden design and show brilliant colour in full flower.

Small: *C. pinifolius* dwarf form; *C.* 'Little John'; *C. citrinus* 'Anzac'.

Medium: *C. sieberi* (*C. paludosus*) (River Bottlebrush) dwarf form; *C. viminalis* (Weeping Bottlebrush) 'Captain Cook'

Large: *C. pallidus* (Lemon Bottlebrush); *C.* 'Burgundy', *C.* 'Mauve Mist', *C.* 'Perth Pink', *C.* 'Violaceus' – all selected for their appealing flower colours.

Leptospermums

Groups of leptospermums (tea-trees) produce a natural massed effect. Many are suitable as screens or for pruned hedges and some respond to coppicing. They all have characteristic and appealing open-petalled flowers, usually white but sometimes delicately coloured with pink.

Small: *L. macrocarpum* 'Copper Sheen'; *L. rupestre* – attractive in cold regions among rocks, or in a container; *L. scoparium* 'Pink Cascade' and 'Crimson Cascade'.

Medium: *L. polygalifolium* (*flavescens*) (Swamp Tea-tree) small forms, for example 'Pacific Beauty', 'Pink Cascade' and 'Cardwell'; *L. rotundifolium* (Round-leaf Tea-tree).

Large: *L. brachyandrum*; *L. laevigatum* (Coast Tea-tree); *L. luehmannii*; *L. myrsinoides* (Heath Tea-tree); *L. trinervium* (*attenuatum*).

Melaleucas

This genus includes a number of splendid shrubs that usually appreciate moisture but also like good drainage. They are excellent framework plants which erupt into showy flowers in season and benefit from pruning. Melaleucas are noted for the beautiful paperbark that gives the trunks of many species a distinctive, rather majestic look.

Small: *M. incana* 'Velvet Cushion'; *M. thymifolia* (Thyme Honey-myrtle); *M. violacea* prostrate form.

Medium: *M. armillaris* 'Green Globe'; *M. bracteata* 'Golden Gem'; *M. decussata* (Totem Poles); *M. elliptica* (Granite Honey-myrtle); *M. lateritia* (Robin Red-breast Bush); *M. megacephala*.

Large: *M. bracteata* (River Tea-tree); *M. bracteata* 'Revolution Green' and 'Revolution Gold'; *M. diosmifolia* (Green Honey-myrtle); *M. hypericifolia* (Red Honey-myrtle); *M. nesophila* (Showy Honey-myrtle); *M. nodosa* (Prickly-leaved Paperbark); *M. tamariscina* (Tamarisk Honey-myrtle).

Correas

Correas are attractive dense, leafy shrubs filling framework and ornamental roles in garden design. They are referred to frequently in this book because they are so reliable, particularly in the shady conditions that many plants will not tolerate. Most correas bear colourful bell-shaped flowers from autumn into winter and benefit from tip pruning after flowering. The range is now extended with numerous selected forms and hybrids.

Small: *C. pulchella*; many forms of *C. reflexa* (Common Correa)

Medium: *C. aemula* (Hairy Correa); *C. alba* (White Correa) with starry flowers; *C. backhouseana*; *C. baeuerlenii* (Chef's Cap Correa); *C. calycina*; *C. glabra* (Rock Correa).

Large: handsome *C. lawrenceana* (Mountain Correa).

Other framework plants

Most banksias are feature plants but the smaller leaves of *B. spinulosa* and *B. ericifolia* link well with those of callistemons, melaleucas, some acacias and many other Australian plants. In an informal hedge or screen their foliage creates a wonderful massed display. For a courtyard garden, excellent small forms of *B. spinulosa* include 'Birthday Candles' and 'Coastal Cushion', which become feature plants when they flower.

Westringias, closely related to the prostantheras but lacking the perfumed foliage, are particularly hardy and useful plants – they have white or mauve flowers, for example *W. fruticosa* (Coast Rosemary); *W. glabra* (Violet Westringia); *W. longifolia*, which are all medium shrubs.

Other suitable framework plants include acacias, for example *A. boormanii* (Snowy River Wattle), *A. prominens* (Gosford Wattle) and *A. iteaphylla* (Flinders Range Wattle) (which can self-sow); baeckea, for example *Babingtonia pluriflora* (Tall Baeckea); dodonaea (Hop Bushes); kunzea, for example *K. ambigua* (White Kunzea), *K. ericoides* (Burgan); prostanthera, for example *P. ovalifolia* (Purple Mint-bush), *P. scutellarioides*; and thryptomene, for example *T. saxicola* (Rock Thryptomene).

Smaller framework shrubs with similar characteristics can be used to define paths and edge garden beds, not necessarily in a formal way. Examples include: *Austromyrtus dulcis* (Midgen Berry), neat with lovely coloured foliage; *Darwinia citriodora* (Lemon-scented Myrtle); pomaderris, for example *P. aurea* (Golden Pomaderris); and dwarf forms of many larger shrubs, both hardy and attractive, for example *Babingtonia pluriflora* and *Melaleuca hypericifolia* (Red Honey-myrtle).

ABOVE: Natural garden Vic. Leptospermum (Tea-tree) species can be typically inconspicuous framework plants all year, then surprise with a wash of colour in spring . Some cultivars have deep pink flowers.
PHOTOGRAPH DIANA SNAPE

133

Feature plants

The beauty of a plant lies not just in the vision of a moment, but in what it was and will be, from seed to leaf, from senescence to decay – and renewal.

Derek Toms, 'An Essayist in the Garden:
A Farewell to Gardening?', *Hortus*, spring 1995

Feature plants are eye-catching focal points in a garden's design, dominant all year round and with architectural value. They should be hardy – you do not want a death to leave a 'hole' in a key position in the garden. Even a large garden needs only a few feature plants – just one or a small number in each planting area. An individual specimen tree is inevitably a feature plant because of its size and natural grandeur. Most trees have architectural value, especially eucalypts. In cooler climates the Snow Gum (*Eucalyptus pauciflora*) can be a living sculpture. She-oaks (allocasuarinas), such as beautiful *A. torulosa* (Rose She-oak), are typical of many areas of Australia, both inland and coastal. *Stenocarpus sinuatus* (Fire-wheel Tree) and *Xanthostemon chrysanthus* (Golden Penda) are handsome all year round, with attractive glossy foliage, and both are spectacular in flower. The significant presence and stately appearance of *Brachychiton rupestris* (Bottle Tree) are rivalled only by the majestic

Adansonia gregorii (Boab) in the far north-west.

Feature plants used in designing an Australian garden can be 'signature' plants that are distinctively 'Australian'. Grass Trees (xanthorrhoeas) provide wonderful contrast between their solid dark base (small or large), the graceful fountain of fine grass-like foliage interacting with light, and the occasional tall slender flower spike. These plants look their best with the surrounding plants kept low and simple. Tree Ferns (cyatheas and dicksonias) have elegant sculptural forms and strong, graceful green fronds, immediately suggesting the cool moist gullies of their natural habitat. Dicksonias (Soft Tree-ferns), in particular, suffer when planted in exposed positions in full sun. As the lower fronds of Tree Ferns die, they can be pruned away to expose the attractive trunk. If left, they form a graceful skirt around the trunk which can provide habitat for wildlife.

Three genera of shrubs that offer a number of feature plants are banksias, hakeas and grevilleas.

Banksias

Banksias are quintessential Australian plants of enormous interest and appeal. They are valuable feature plants in garden design, with distinctive form and foliage throughout the year. The substantial leaves of many banksias are similar to the foliage of waratahs and some dryandras, grevilleas and hakeas, contrasting strongly with fine foliage. *Banksia serrata* (Saw Banksia) is the archetype for most Australians, with its serrated foliage and 'Old Man' banksia cones. The fascinating chunky cones follow abundant bird-attracting flower spikes and attractive buds. Flower colours range from bright gold, orange and red to more subtle shades of lime, green, buff and brown.

OPPOSITE: Roberts garden Vic. Grass Trees (xanthorrhoeas) planted in a small group are wonderful feature plants standing proud in a gravel bed, with Running Postman (*Kennedia prostrata*) nearby as a groundcover. Short but substantial trunks support elegant foliage.
PHOTOGRAPH DIANA SNAPE

The following shrubs are reliable in varying soils in eastern states. Others from the west can also be grown successfully in the east but may prove more of a challenge. In Western Australia or South Australia, the choice of suitable western banksias is extensive. Ideally, local banksias will suit your needs and conditions.

Banksias from the east

Small to medium: *B. paludosa* (Marsh Banksia)

Medium: *B. canei* (Mountain Banksia); *B. oblongifolia* (Fern-leaved Banksia); *B. robur* (Swamp Banksia)

Large: *B. conferta*; *B. ericifolia* (Heath Banksia); *B. marginata* (Silver Banksia); *B. saxicola*; *B. spinulosa* (Hairpin Banksia)

Note: *B. ericifolia*, *B. marginata* and *B. spinulosa* are variable in size and versatile – they have medium- and low-growing forms too and the large forms can be treated as trees.

Banksias from the west

Small: *B. dryandroides* (Dryandra-leaved Banksia)

Medium: *B. baueri* (Woolly Banksia)

Large: *B. caleyi*; *B. media* (Southern Plains Banksia); *B. praemorsa* (Cut-leaf Banksia).

Hakeas

Many hakeas with handsome, formal appearance and firm foliage provide an element of solidity in a garden of finer, softer foliage. Most hakeas have attractive flowers, many in 'pincushion' form – white, cream, yellow, pink, cerise, purplish or two-toned. Their leaves are often distinctive and many produce beautiful bronze new foliage. Some are named after their leaf shapes – fans, hoods, shells or daggers; others for the shapes of their woody fruits – beaked, crested, or like swans or cricket balls. Prickly shrubs are often unpopular, but Bushy Needlewood *(Hakea decurrens)* provides valuable habitat for birds and undergoes a fairy-tale transformation in early spring as masses of dainty fragrant, spidery white

flowers (sometimes tinted pink) appear among the prickles.

Small: *H. conchifolia* (Shell-leaved Hakea); *H. flabellifolia* (Wedge Hakea); *H. myrtoides*.

Medium: *H. cinerea* (Ashy Hakea); *H. cristata*; *H. purpurea*; *H. invaginata* (often grafted); *H. undulata*.

Large: *H. cucullata* (Scallops); *H. macraeana* (Willow Needlewood); *H. bucculenta* (Red Pokers) (often grafted so gardeners in eastern states can enjoy their vivid flower spikes).

Grevilleas

Numerous grevilleas are distinctive even when not in flower, for example medium-sized *G. endlicheriana* with its lovely form and fine silvery foliage. Beautiful structure and foliage make the following grevilleas ideal feature plants, or on a large scale as framework screens or background plants. They are unsuitable where space is limited, as they will quickly swamp a small garden or invade paths.

Large: *G. barklyana* (Gully Grevillea); *G. insignis*; the elegant *G. johnsonii*; *G. longifolia*; *G. tetragonoloba*; *G. willisii* (Omeo Grevillea).

Other feature shrubs

Distinctive characteristics such as interesting form or foliage make a number of other plants highly suitable for use as feature plants. There are trees or shrubs with a weeping form, for example *Baeckea linifolia* (Weeping Baeckea), *Leptospermum*

OPPOSITE LEFT: Buchanan garden Vic. One of the excellent dwarf forms of *Banksia spinulosa* (Hairpin Banksia) can find a rewarding role in any style of garden. With its characteristic form and persistent cones, there is year-round interest.
PHOTOGRAPH DIANA SNAPE

OPPOSITE RIGHT: Hall garden Vic. Designed by Jan Hall. The long, vertical flowering spikes of *Xanthorrhoea quadrangulata* draw attention and add another dimension to the plants. The tiny flowers are attractive to insects and birds.
PHOTOGRAPH JAN HALL

brevipes (Slender Tea-tree) and arching cycads or palms. Medium to large feature shrubs include acacias, selected for their enormous variety of form and foliage, for example *A. cognata* (Bower Wattle) and *A. caerulescens. Buckinghamia celsissima* (Ivory Curl) is a tough but beautiful rainforest plant with long, lobed juvenile foliage, producing pendulous racemes of sweetly scented, creamy-white flowers. Other feature shrubs include telopeas (Waratahs), *Alloxylon flammeum* (Queensland Waratah) and persoonias, for example *P. pinifolia* (Pine-leaved Geebung) with its soft light-green foliage, long golden flower spikes and grape-like clusters of fruit. Numerous grevilleas belong in this category, being distinctive even when not in flower, for example the elegant *G. johnsonii* and *G. endlicheriana* with its lovely form and fine silvery foliage.

Lilies and tufted plants

Many lilies and other tufted plants are also suitable as feature plants. The bold appearance and dramatic foliage of *Doryanthes* species lend themselves to landscaping on a grand scale and *D. excelsa* (Gymea Lily) looks superb growing among large sandstone rocks. The strong elements of the thrusting leaves of *D. excelsa* or *D. palmeri* (Spear Lily) add excitement and structure to a design and the occasional red flower spike is stunning. These 'signature' plants and others like Waratahs (telopeas) with unusual or striking shape are eye-catching when planted individually but are also magnificent in large sweeps among trees, as they occur in nature. Palm-like macrozamias are similar in effect, strong and tough but looking almost delicate with their finely patterned foliage.

The robust habit and delicate flowers of *Crinum* species are amazing too, with thin petals contrasting with stout leaves and round stems. *Crinum flaccidum* (Murray Lily) has beautiful aromatic white or yellow flower heads. There are also cordylines (Palm Lilies), helmholtzias, for example the spectacular *H. glaberrima* (Stream Lily), lomandras and *Baloskion tetraphyllum* (Tassel Cord-rush). *Livistona australis* (Cabbage Palm) is an outstanding architectural plant for a large garden, but give it plenty of room and beware of those sharp frond bases.

Small feature plants

To be dominant, feature plants need to be visible, often spaced a little apart from other plants. In a large garden they may stand out because of their sheer size, and may dominate the garden or balance another feature, such as a special low shrub or ornament – a seat, sculpture or birdbath. However, in a limited area feature plants can be quite small. In a courtyard the feature could be a dendrobium, a brilliant group of spectacular orchids not too difficult to cultivate. An example is the Rock Orchid (*Thelychiton speciosus*). A clump of lomandra could also provide a small feature, for example *L. confertifolia* (Slender Mat-rush) – different forms are like lovely small fountains of green or blue-grey.

Dwarf forms of many larger plants can be captivating. Among acacias, *A. cognata* 'Green Mist' is an arresting low shrub with soft foliage and a most graceful form. *Babingtonia pluriflora* (miniature) forms a neat green bun that does not require pruning. Distinctive dryandras have dramatic form and foliage, for example *D. drummondii*, and isopogons, for example *I. anemonifolius* (Broad-leaf Drumstick), have a special appeal. You could feature a climber, for example the sculptural strength of a Parsonsia (Silkpod) vine snaking its way up a tree trunk or post. In recent years many attractive leptospermum varieties have been developed with deeper colour in both foliage and flowers, making them superb feature plants.

OPPOSITE LEFT: Snape garden Vic. The beautiful natural shape of *Leptospermum polygalifolium* (Tantoon) is valuable in a framework plant but can make it a stunning feature when in full flower.
PHOTOGRAPH DIANA SNAPE

ABOVE: Hanson garden Vic. Designed by Bev Hanson. Banksias are quintessentially Australian plants of enormous interest and appeal, with distinctive form and foliage throughout the year. The leaves of Hairpin Banksia (*B. spinulosa*) are finer than the substantial leaves of many others. The fascinating, chunky cones follow abundant, bird-attracting flower-spikes, here orange-gold in colour, and attractive buds. The plant draws the eye as a focal point among lower plants.
PHOTOGRAPH SIMON GRIFFITHS

Ornamental plants

I consider every plant hardy until I have killed it myself.

Sir Peter Smithers, quoted in *The Collector's Garden*,

by Ken Druse

The majority of Australian shrubs are ornamental plants that add interest and beauty to the framework of a garden. They are usually small to medium in size and have attractive form, foliage and flowers. Ideally they live a long time. They may become temporary 'features' when in flower but are not classed as feature plants because, for much of the year, their role is subordinate. They are usually more numerous than true features and, when not flowering, they blend into the framework.

Grevilleas

Grevilleas have long been among the most popular ornamental Australian plants, due to their characteristic intricate flowers and fascinating range of form and foliage. Many outstanding cultivars have been developed and are widely planted – they flower continuously, attract nectar-feeding birds and tolerate hard pruning. Grevilleas come in all shapes and sizes, from groundcovers to large trees, offering something for every requirement. Selections can be made for full sun, full shade, dense screens, 'tall skinnies', heavy or sandy soil. Despite the fact that there is a grevillea for practically every site, as a general rule they do best in an open, sunny, well-drained position. A small selection from this diverse and most beautiful genus follows.

Small: These are ideal for small gardens and courtyards as beautiful ornamentals with masses of showy flowers in season, or as tub plants or low border shrubs in a more formal setting. *G. lavandulacea* (Lavender Grevillea); *G. chrysophaea* (Golden Grevillea); *G. confertifolia* (Grampians Grevillea); *G. maxwellii*.

Medium: These are attractive ornamental or feature plants, also useful for a decorative low screen.

G. bipinnatifida (Grape Grevillea); *G. levis* (*G. paniculata* pink); *G. montis-cole* (Mt Cole Grevillea); *G. preissii* (*G. thelemanniana*); *G. speciosa* (Red Spider-flower).

Prostantheras

Prostanthera ovalifolia (Mint Bush) is a most popular, large shrub with soft perfumed foliage that in spring disappears behind a glorious display of purple flowers. Almost all Mint Bushes are ornamental, with pleasantly aromatic leaves and flowers in hues of white, pink, mauve and purple. Most benefit from annual pruning. Many specially selected forms are now available.

Small: *P. aspalathoides* (Scarlet Mint-bush); *P. cuneata* (Alpine Mint-bush); *P. magnifica*; *P. saxicola* var. *montana*.

Medium: *P. incisa* (Cut-leaved Mint-bush); *P. nivea* (Snowy Mint-bush); *P. rotundifolia* (Round-leaf Mint-bush) and *P. rotundifolia* 'Rosea'; *P. scutellarioides*; *P. sericea* (Silky Mint-bush).

Large: *P. melissifolia* (Balm Mint-bush)

OPPOSITE: Honeysuckle Grevillea (*G. juncifolia*) – warm apricot flowers against cool grey-green foliage.
PHOTOGRAPH BRIAN SNAPE

Eremophilas (Emu Bush or Fuschia Bush)

Many eremophilas have outstanding potential as ornamental shrubs or small trees, and are long-flowering with attractive or interesting foliage. Recently, selected grafted plants have become available (for example, *E.* 'Nivea' with its wonderful, soft, silver foliage and lilac flowers). Although many are 'desert-loving', coming from and flourishing in the drier areas of Australia, reports indicate that they may tolerate, or even like, a reasonable amount of moisture. A good pruning in the early stages of growth encourages a bushy habit.

In a recent survey the following proved to be the ten most commonly grown eremophilas, highly recommended for their appeal and availability.

Small to medium: The first two (way ahead of the others) are variable with some very attractive forms: *E. glabra* (Common Emu-bush or Fuchsia-bush) – for example, *E. glabra* var. *tomentosa* (Murchison River form); *E. maculata* (Native Fuchsia or Spotted Emu-bush) – for example, *E. maculata* var. *brevifolia*. A clear third was *E. polyclada* (Lignum Fuchsia-bush). Also widely cultivated are *E. calorhabdos* (Red Rod); *E. decipiens* (Slender Fuchsia); *E. macdonnellii*; *E. oppositifolia* (Twin-leaf Emu-bush); *E. weldii*; and *E. latrobei* (Crimson Turkey-bush).

Hibiscus

Given the range of size, the variety of habitat, their widespread distribution and 'faunascape' potential, hibiscus and hibiscus-like plants enhance most garden designs. Australian representatives of the Hibiscus family may be trees, shrubs of varying size, or herbs. Most species occur in tropical and subtropical regions, though some can grow quite happily in cooler climates. Flowers are spectacular and may be white or various shades of yellow, pink and purple, often with a contrasting centre. They attract butterflies and other insects, and therefore insect-eating birds as well as nectar-feeders.

Their leaves vary enormously in form, colour and texture and are all decorative. Most benefit from pruning.

Recommended as well suited to conditions in southern states are the following hardy, fast-growing and floriferous hibiscuses and related plants.

Small to medium: *Alyogyne hakeifolia* (SW) (Red-centred Hibiscus); *A. huegelii* (SW).

Medium to large: *Hibiscus heterophyllus* (QN) (Native Rosella); *H. splendens* (QN) (Pink Hibiscus).

Dodonaeas

Dodonaeas vary in size from small trees to prostrate shrubs and have a special role in garden design. They are grown not for their inconspicuous flowers but for their highly decorative fruit capsules, called hops, which remain on the plants for some months and range in colour from green to many shades of pink, red and deep purple. The female plant, in full fruit, appears to glow.

Medium: *D. boroniifolia* (Fern-leaf Hop-bush); *D. viscosa* (Sticky Hop-bush); *D. sinuolata* (Hop-bush).

Medium to large: *D. megazyga* – tallest of the ornamental dodonaeas.

Daisies and other composites

Daisies are small, demure and engaging. They offer a multitude of hues very quickly and flowering can continue for long periods. There are different categories in both habit and

OPPOSITE LEFT: Grevillea Garden NSW. An unusual combination of *Thysanotus multiflorus* (Fringe Lily) and *Homoranthus papillatus* (Mouse & Honey Plant) is successful in its proportions, colours and textures. Fringe Lily is likely to be less easy to grow than the homoranthus.
PHOTOGRAPH DIANA SNAPE

OPPOSITE RIGHT: Pretty flowers of *Hypocalymma angustifolium* (White Myrtle) show colours ranging from white to deep pink.
PHOTOGRAPH BRIAN SNAPE

ABOVE: Carn garden Vic. Ornamental shrubs *Hypocalymma angustifolium* (White Myrtle) (centre back right), *Thomasia pygmaea* (Dwarf Paper-flower) (centre front) and *T. grandiflora* contribute to a pink colour scheme in a wildflower garden.

PHOTOGRAPH DIANA SNAPE

garden use – ornamentals and infills; perennials and annuals; bedding, edging and border plants; groundcovers and shrubs. There are daisies suitable for all types of garden – tropical and subtropical, coastal, bog, alpine and frost-prone. Ornamental daisy shrubs are reminiscent of 'the bush', but pruning will achieve or retain a compact, ordered shape.

Not all composites have the typical daisy flower arrangement comprising a composite head of disc florets surrounded by conspicuous ray florets or showy bracts – *Ozothamnus* species have large clusters of tiny individual flower heads and generally live a long time.

Small to medium shrubs: *Ozothamnus diosmifolius* (Sago Flower); *O. ledifolius* (Kerosene Bush).

Olearia (Daisy Bush) species grow quickly and may be short-lived, so they could be regarded as infill, but they can easily be propagated from cuttings.

Small: *Olearia ramulosa* (Twiggy Daisy-bush); *Ixodia achillaeoides* (Mountain Daisy).

Medium: *Olearia phlogopappa* (Dusty Daisy-bush); *O. tomentosa* (Toothed Daisy-bush).

Other ornamental plants

Correas, which grow well in partial shade, have already been considered as framework plants but could also be classed as ornamental plants.

Long-leaf Wax-flower (*Philotheca (Eriostemon) myoporoides*) is tough, reliable and most attractive when in flower. The leionemas (phebaliums), such as *L. dentatum*, are small to medium shrubs which tolerate shade and bear masses of cream or yellow flowers in spring. Baueras, tctrathecas, thomasias, spyridiums and hardy zierias are all worthy ornamentals. *Pimelea ferruginea* (a Rice Flower) is a neat charming shrub with clusters of tiny flowers in shades of pink.

As well as shrubs, some climbers can be considered in this ornamental category, such as forms of the pandoreas, *P. jasminoides* (Bower Vine) and *P. pandorana* (Wonga Vine), colourful *P. pandorana* 'Golden Showers' and billardieras (Apple Berry). *Sollya heterophylla* (Bluebell Creeper) is pretty but is now regarded as a weed in many natural areas.

Low-growing hibbertias, scaevolas and dampieras add vivid colour to the garden – gold, blue or purple. These and small groundcover plants such as the daisies might be planted with and considered as ornamentals.

Tufted plants

Tufted plants (strap-leaved or with grass-like foliage) include those with bulbs, corms, tubers and rhizomes. Many irises and lilies are small and modest – their advantages include longevity and little maintenance. Orchids are in a special class and a number of books concentrate on them. Members of the iris family have appealing flowers in purples, lilacs, blue and white. These include patersonias (Native Iris), orthrosanthus, for example *O. laxus* (Morning Iris) and *O. multiflorus* (Morning Flag), and diplarrenas, for example *D. latifolia* (Tasmanian Diplarrena) and *D. moraea* (Butterfly Flag).

There is a great range of Australian lilies, mostly small plants but with several marked exceptions, already mentioned as feature plants. Blue flowers characterise *Stypandra glauca* (Nodding Blue-lily), the closely related *Thelionema caespitosum* (Tufted Lily) and dianellas (Flax Lily), which also have colourful berries. Attractive *Calostemma* species (Garland Lily) have bulbs while *Thysanotus* species (Fringe Lilies) have highly decorative, dainty lilac or mauve flowers. Wiry stems and a grass-like habit give *Tricoryne elatior* (Yellow Rush-lily) a delicate and wispy, lace-like appearance.

Lawn Lily (*Murdannia graminea*) is a perennial herb with unusual lilac flowers and tubers, only distantly related to the true lilies.

Horticultural development of Kangaroo Paws (anigozanthos) has resulted in their use in magnificent colourful displays in gardens. Research is also being carried out on blandfordias (the wonderful Christmas Bells). Libertias are attractive tufted plants with white flowers. Lomandras, including the ubiquitous but worthy *L. longifolia* (Spiny-headed Mat-rush), and grasses such as Kangaroo Grass (*Themeda triandra*) or Soft Spear-grass (*Austrostipa mollis*), are ornamentals that quickly give a garden a natural appearance. Drifts of flowering grasses are stunning when lit from behind.

Infill plants

Our final lesson is that now we keep our heads. Plants that die after three repeats are banished.

Mirabel Osler, quoted in *Garden Design*, spring 1988

Infill plants play the least permanent of design roles as they 'come and go'. Their importance lies in adding variation and vitality. Infill planting is usually rather random and includes annuals, biennials, bulbs and self-sowing plants – dainty bluebells (wahlenbergias) and fragrant Chocolate and Vanilla Lilies (*Arthropodium strictum* and *A. milleflorum*) belong to this category. Such plants act as softeners and unifiers, giving ephemeral washes of colour as the seasons change. In new gardens, fast-growing acacias can be used as large gap-fillers and Creeping Myoporum (*M. parvifolium*) and brachyscomes provide quick, temporary groundcover.

Acacias

Acacias can be rather substantial infill plants, generally fast-growing and quick to flower but sometimes short-lived. Many benefit from pruning after flowering, as it keeps them compact and extends their lifespan. Smaller acacias are easy to replace when they begin to grow 'leggy' after a number of years. There are now smaller forms of many larger species – some prostrate forms are spectacular.

Acacias have adapted to climates and soil types all over Australia. The amazing variety of their attractive foliage reflects their diverse origins. Most mature wattles have phyllodes as 'leaves', while some retain the bipinnate ferny foliage that others display only when young. Differences lie in the arrangement of their flowers – in globular heads, spikes, racemes or panicles. Their seed pods can also be a feature. Acacias are excellent screening plants and, in flower, many are highly ornamental – the massed yellow or cream flower heads are spectacular and often sweetly fragrant.

Small: *A. cognata* (Bower Wattle) 'Green Mist'; *A. glaucoptera* (Clay Wattle).

Medium: *A. acinacea* (Gold Dust Wattle); *A. drummondii* (Drummond's Wattle); *A. fimbriata* (Fringed Wattle); *A. myrtifolia* (Myrtle Wattle); *A. plicata*; *A. suaveolens* (Sweet Wattle).

Large: *A. cardiophylla* (Wyalong Wattle); *A. podalyriifolia* (Queensland Silver Wattle).

Two 'pricklies': *A. pulchella* (Western Prickly Moses) (small); *A. verticillata* (Prickly Moses).

Annual daisies

In any garden, an array of reliable and enchanting annual paper daisies can create a spectacular display of colour throughout spring. You can sow seed normally in late winter but, in moderate climates, direct seeding in autumn means seed will germinate as the soil temperature decreases. Plants will grow slowly and develop a strong root system over winter, hardening off before any frosts. As the season warms up, feeding with a good liquid fertiliser helps them along. Direct seeding in beds or tubs adds random drifts of colour. You can create a rainbow display with species from Western Australia such as: *Rhodanthe chlorocephala* ssp. *rosea* (*Helipterum*

OPPOSITE: Flowers of *Thysanotus multiflorus* (Fringe Lily) are exquisite in detail. Little plants with such beautiful flowers are well worth growing even for a relatively short time.

PHOTOGRAPH BRIAN SNAPE

roseum) (Rosy Everlasting) – vivid pink; *R. diffusa* (*Helipterum diffusum*) (Ascending Sunray) – yellow; *R. manglesii* (*Helipterum manglesii*) (Pink Sunray) 'Silver Bells' – nodding, pink paper daisies with a silky appearance; *Schoenia filifolia* ssp. *subulifolia* (*Helichrysum subuli-folium*) (Showy Everlasting) – bright yellow; *S. cassiniana* (*Helichrysum cassinianum*) (Pink Cluster Everlasting); *Brachyscome iberidifolia* (Swan River Daisy) – superb massed displays of blue, purple, pink and white.

Commercial seed of 'Strawflower' annuals has *Xerochrysum bracteatum* (*Helichrysum bracteatum*, *Bracteantha bracteata*) (Golden Everlasting), a cheeky self-seeder, as one parent (the other is exotic) and offers a riot of apricots, oranges and reds. There are also annuals and herbs other than daisies with appeal as bedding plants, for example *Brunonia australis* (Blue Pincushion), *Calandrinia polyandra* (Parakeelya) and *Velleia rosea* (Pink Velleia). *Gomphrena canescens* (Pink Billy Buttons) with its white, pink, mauve or red ovoid or globular flower heads, can be treated as an annual or biennial.

In an empty garden bed, new plants look so tiny in the bare space that the temptation to plant them too close is almost irresistible. Using daisies to fill gaps helps to avoid overplanting with more permanent plants and quickly provides colour and groundcover. Brachyscomes and lovely paper daisies are readily available – 'Paper Baby', 'Paper Cascade' and 'Paper Star', which are different forms of *Rhodanthe anthemoides* (Chamomile Sunray), display soft foliage, grey-green and fragrant. You can trim daisies back as the more permanent plants grow.

Other infill plants

Beautiful small plants such as lechenaultias with their vivid flower colours in seasonal display can be treated as infill. Although they may be short-lived in other than optimum conditions, having these delightful plants for even a year or two is rewarding and they are easily propagated from cuttings. The lifetime of a boronia depends on the species you choose and the conditions in which you grow it. Several years of great pleasure cost less than a bunch of flowers. Two stunning plants, *Hibbertia stellaris* (orange or bronze-gold flowers) and *Platytheca galioides* (*verticillata*) (a beautiful purple-blue), are temperamental but could well be treated as annuals or biennials, or grown in pots for longer life. Pots are extremely handy as infill, accommodating in eastern gardens precious plants like *Swainsona formosa* (*Clianthus form-osus*) (Sturt's Desert Pea) or lovely grafted darwinias and *Pimelea physodes* (Qualup Bell). Lightly suckering plants such as *Pimelea humilis* (Dwarf Rice-flower) may contribute to seasonal groundcover. With infill planting you can experiment a little.

Other genera of infill plants include epacris (heaths) with their characteristic habit of upright stems edged with tiny pointed leaves and decorated with red, pink or white tubular flowers – some species will be longer lasting than others; and grasses such as poas, which may die back annually and spread or self-propagate by seed or rhizomes. Pioneer plants play a valuable role, for example cassinias and the enormous range of beautiful pea-plants (pultenaeas, dillwynias, bossiaeas, chorizemas, mirbelias and indigoferas among many others). Sometimes short-lived, they help colonise degraded areas and fix nitrogen to enrich the soil for other plants. Investigate the local species in your area. Many of these pea-plants include creepers such as hardenbergias, for example *H. violacea* (Native Sarsaparilla), and kennedias, for example *K. rubicunda* (Dusky Coral-pea), which are quite long-lived and could be classed as ornamentals.

Plants that are happy in a garden and self-sow are a delightful bonus. If any appear in the wrong position you can easily transplant or remove them. Flannel-flowers (*Actinotus helianthi*) will often self-sow to produce a wonderful display. Also consider *Enchylaena tomentosa* (Ruby Saltbush), which thrives in difficult conditions and is long-flowering with colourful berries.

OPPOSITE FAR LEFT: Larkin garden Vic. Designed by Roger Stone. On a slope, sufficient level area has been created to allow for decorative pools and surrounding planting. On the far side, *Viminaria juncea* 'Golden Spray' is colourful with pendent sprays of flowers. In a new garden area, this lovely pea-plant quickly becomes significant. It is fast-growing but not always very long-lived.
PHOTOGRAPH DIANA SNAPE

OPPOSITE TOP RIGHT: Snape garden Vic. Hugging the stems, blossoms of Gold Dust Wattle (*Acacia acinacea*) (above) and Bent-leaf Wattle (*A. flexifolia*) catch the spring sunlight. Gold Dust Wattle can grow quickly but then be somewhat short-lived, though tip pruning after flowering can extend its life.
PHOTOGRAPH DIANA SNAPE

OPPOSITE BOTTOM RIGHT: McAllister garden Vic. Unless you have green thumbs, blue and orange lechenaultias may best be regarded as infill plants and replaced every two or three years, or as necessary. They grow well from cuttings. The deep pink tetratheca can also be fussy.
PHOTOGRAPH DIANA SNAPE

Design elements

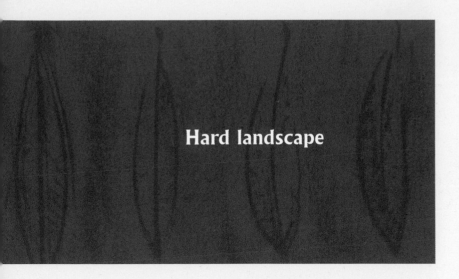

Hard landscape

In situations where Nature has been lavish with her wild charms the signs of the hand of man should be suppressed, so that nothing may appear to compete with effects of a kind that no designer can bring.

Gertrude Jekyll and Lawrence Weaver,

Gardens for Small Country Houses, 1912

The hard landscape is an important visual element that needs to be integrated with the design of the whole garden. The colours and textures of Australian plants harmonise with many different combinations of house materials and hard landscape – red brickwork with matching scoria, bluestone with slates, or painted surfaces with pale-coloured gravel or crushed rock.

For major construction work, obtaining professional help will ensure the right machine is chosen for the size of the job and the accessibility of the site.

Walls, fences and gates

An exposed boundary fence can be part of a garden's design and visually attractive using tea-tree, paperbark, lattice, or weathered timber. Old stone and brick walls are often beautiful and solid walls can lessen external noise in a busy urban area. If the wall is constructed in brick and bagged, on the garden side you may choose to espalier plants, hang a metal artwork or inlay mosaics.

Many fences are sculptures in themselves, for example those made from old bridge timbers. In a rural area, post-and-rail fences blend with the scenery. In the suburbs, most backyard fences are functional but better screened from view by shrubs or climbers that grow dense to the ground and reach the height of the fence. Where there is little or no space at ground level, vertical gardens could provide the solution. Creepers in pots can hang against garden walls or blind facades or drop from tall pipes. Small, spilling plants grow well in raised narrow beds or containers. However watering will be a necessity. A see-through wire fence or plants placed strategically will make the most of attractive landscape in neighbouring parkland or gardens – borrowed landscape.

Low decorative walls within the garden may enclose a patio, serve as informal seating or outline paths. If straight or in a very regular curve, even a low wall is formal and a strong structural line. Grasses and groundcover plants can soften a wall by spilling over the top and, if it is set back from the path, tufted plants or low shrubs could thrive at its base. The height of a wall can vary along its length and it can provide nooks and crannies as homes for skinks and insects.

Often a practical necessity, a gate can also be a decorative feature. There is an extensive choice from timber to wrought iron, or varieties of farm gates. A wide gate is welcoming while a narrow gate creates a feeling of mystery, especially if leading into an enclosed garden.

PREVIOUS PAGE: *Grevillea* 'Marmalade' is a beautifully coloured, long-flowering grevillea. PHOTOGRAPH BRIAN SNAPE

OPPOSITE: Seddon garden WA. In a more formal garden, a regular stone wall marks a change in level between terraces and can also provide seating. Wide, shallow steps cater for easy access to the higher level (and for a pleasant spot to lie). Stone and foliage contrast in texture, emphasised by the effect of sun and shade. A pot plant is a small focal point. PHOTOGRAPH SIMON GRIFFITHS

Ground surfaces

For a hard-surfaced, open area brick pavers or second-hand bricks, stone or slate, treated concrete, gravel or timber are all suitable materials. Paving laid in a random shape, its edges softened with light groundcovers, suits a naturalistic garden. You can intersperse paving with low-growing plants or even dramatic rocks. If materials are well chosen, paving can link the house and garden.

Gravel is a versatile and attractive groundcover, though pale gravel may initially be glary in summer sun unless light is filtered through surrounding trees. If used close to the house, gravel can travel indoors on the soles of shoes.

A timber deck or board-walk has a pleasant, natural look and a board-walk can be an attractive way of crossing areas which become boggy in wet weather.

Paths

Paths give access to a garden and contribute to the patterned horizontal structure at ground level as they are sometimes visible from a high window or other vantage point. Their pattern can be attractive on its own. Once in place, hard paths will probably last a long time so the structural divisions they create will be significant and help determine the evolution of the garden. You can link hard-surfaced, open areas with paths of similar or contrasting surface materials. No paths should threaten walkers with overhanging or prickly plants, or uneven surfaces to trip on.

Soil excavated for paths or other areas is excellent for building up mounds or beds. At a height of 100 to 200 mm the beds will look better and the extra soil will improve their drainage – most Australian plants prefer good drainage. Topsoil is a valuable asset which should always be set aside when building and kept for use in the garden. Although any rocks in the soil will tend to make digging difficult they can provide plant roots with shelter and increased stability.

Much of a garden is viewed from pathways and wandering down a path in an Australian garden can be a delight. A path helps define the garden and gives importance to the areas that border it. As nature uses both curved and straight lines so can garden designers. A curved pathway disappearing out of view gives the impression of 'going on' even if it terminates just around the corner. If you narrow a path or reduce the height of shrubbery on either side as it recedes, you can create a greater feeling of space. Narrow winding paths give the illusion of a bigger garden and curved lines may also suit the topography of the land. However a straight path allows better visibility. Especially in large areas, a straight path allows people to move easily and can provide long views to visually increase apparent space.

Wallaby paths

In bushland where animals such as wallabies wander, narrow paths wind through scrub and trees. Such a feature can be used in Australian garden design. In an extensive area of low plants, access for one person is probably necessary for weeding and narrow wallaby paths can provide this. Wallaby paths both divide and frame sections of the garden, so you can design the shapes of these sections and their layout, like a mosaic.

People tend to move more quickly along narrow paths than wide paths. Along a wallaby path, wider areas between narrow stretches can mark intersections or allow wanderers to pause and enjoy special points. Shrubs spilling over or tree canopies merging above may also be a factor in determining the widths of paths. The same low plants running along either side of a narrow wallaby path looks natural. In contrast, the sides of a wide path or driveway do not need to be linked with similar plants and the plants can be larger.

Steps

Whether a design includes straight or curving steps or ramps depends on the site and personal taste. The material could be bridge timber, stone, brick, or reject concrete sleepers, which are a cost-effective alternative. You can 'age' its appearance

and trailing, prostrate plants will soften outlines. All steps should flow with regular groups or flights of the same proportions, because (as with stepping stones) walkers tend to develop a rhythm. Steps arriving at a door or gate need to have a safe, wide landing. With an informal garden, steps can be varied in length and be offset from one another and landings can be created at random. Rocks may enhance the design.

Use of rocks

Formal gardens may feature regular stone walls but, in naturalistic Australian gardens, rocks placed in a more natural way add interest to the design. This aspect of landscape design has been developed in Melbourne by designers such as Ellis Stones and Gordon Ford. Rocks have long been used more formally in Chinese and Japanese landscapes.

Nature shows us the art of placing rocks. We cannot hope to reproduce the magnificent huge outcrops of wilderness areas but, on a smaller scale and with careful selection and placement, just a few large rocks can look as though they had always been there, creating a wonderful picture. Heavy material can be shifted manually with rollers and levers such as crowbars, but much larger stones need to be moved with a bobcat or crane.

With their shadows and strong forms, sometimes adorned with moss or lichen, any natural rocky outcrops are a special gift for garden design and will complement plantings. Local rock looks best, as using different sorts of rocks tends to fragment the design and destroy the harmony. The local rock of Sydney is usually sandstone while in Melbourne basalt, often decorated with lichen or moss, is the most widely used.

Using rocks successfully in a garden takes skill and professional experience is a distinct advantage. As a general rule, the bigger the better. For a rock to look a reasonable size, it should be heavier than two people can lift unaided. A rock can look disappointingly small once placed in position and one-third (or even half) buried. Rows of small rocks like

ABOVE: Joyce garden Vic. Designed by Paul Thompson. An offset bridge crosses a system of pools in a water-harvesting garden that caters for wildlife. Indigenous water plants have been selected and placed with care in sections around the edges.
PHOTOGRAPH DIANA SNAPE

155

ABOVE: Howes garden NSW. A much-used small paved courtyard garden with a variety of suitably sized plants, including dendrobium orchids and philothecas (eriostemons). White brick walls reflect light and are partly screened by larger shrubs.

PHOTOGRAPH DIANA SNAPE

BOTTOM: Floyd garden Vic. It's wise to watch out for a snake on the path.

PHOTOGRAPH DIANA SNAPE

dragons' teeth along the edge of a path, garden bed or pond look unnatural and usually make weeding difficult. If possible, examine large rocks before they are delivered to the site and earmark the best for the most prominent positions. Keep any strata in the rock horizontal and avoid putting those of the same shape and size together. Most rocks have a definite best side and top. Flatter rocks suit a level site. Some mounds or plants will help them look 'at home', each one belonging to the next. The rocks should look right from all directions. If in small groups, odd numbers will appear more natural.

Rocks in sloping areas

A general slope provides exciting opportunities for design. The traditional treatment of a relatively steep slope in a formal garden is to divide it into terrraces held back by retaining walls. In a naturalistic garden, these are kept to a minimum as walls of sleepers, stone or brick generally add straight lines and detract from a natural, flowing landscape. However curved walls are often suitable and you can soften them with plants. Short walls, one forward of another or ending with a rocky outcrop, look relatively natural. Retaining walls should be sufficiently strong and have good drainage behind them. They can shelter a seat in timber or stone cut into a slope, or curve around a 'sitting well', perhaps a gravelled, circular space large enough for a small table and chairs.

A steep 'cut and fill' slope can be stabilised by the skilful placement of a small number of large boulders. Arranging them creatively with some forward and some back will avoid unnatural straight lines. Extensive planting will further stabilise and beautify the slope.

Artificial rocks

With increased awareness and understanding of the importance of leaving rock in its natural areas, gardeners are being encouraged to use artificial rocks. If done well, these can look natural but an expert touch is needed to achieve a form and finish indistinguishable from the real thing.

Geoff Sitch's rock-making recipe

Geoff Sitch is a Victorian designer who has mastered the art of making artificial rocks. Before you start, study many examples of the type of rock you intend to make. For sandstone 'rocks':

1 Choose site and excavate topsoil to a minimum depth of 0.1m (depending on the amount of rubble you have to bury). Allow for a 'moat' around the rock size you want.

2 Pile rubble randomly to achieve approximate shape of rock, leaving moat clear.

3 Shovel sand to cover rubble and fill any large gaps, leaving moat clear.

4 Mix concrete (4:2:1) with water to suitable consistency then shovel it over sand and trowel or work it from moat up to top of rock.

5 Shape wire netting fairly closely over rock and staple edges together.

6 Repeat 4, then allow to dry a bit until firmish (have a cuppa or a light lunch).

7 Shovel brown-coloured mortar (3:1) over rock and trowel roughly.

8 Scatter yellow and 'marigold' pigments sparsely and unevenly over rock.

9 Mark rock by, for example, shaping flat ledges or drawing parallel lines to simulate cracks.

10 Work surface of rock with a piece of wet lambswool to blend colours and achieve an irregular, natural-looking finish.
   Wait for the 'rock' to dry to see the next stage in the transformation – it will improve as it ages and weathers.

Planting near rocks

Good soil is required around rocks to support your most interesting plants, with good drainage and a cool, secure root run.

It is counter-productive to go to the care and expense of placing rocks correctly, then to plant inappropriately. A slim tree can add vertical emphasis but a bushy grevillea may encroach on the outcrops. Rock orchids (*Thelychiton speciosus*) and small accent plants – grasses, libertias (Grass Flags), orthrosanthus, small lomandras – look just right with rocks. Sometimes a very tight groundcover is required such as Matted Pratia (*Lobelia pedunculata*) squeezing between rocks, or daisies spilling down a slope between outcrops. Some groundcover plants such as Mat Bush-pea (*Pultenaea pedunculata*) spread well over a less attractive rock surface and accentuate its shape. Drifts of the same groundcover taken across to another part of the garden can help unify the total picture. A garden changes with seasons and in time – small plants age, eventually die and need replacing but rocks only improve. They have pleasing form and texture and, if placed well in the first instance, add permanent beauty to a garden.

Colours

When looking into a garden from a window, repetition of the dominant colour inside the room provides a marvellous visual link with the garden outside. Green foliage blends with all colours and it, or brown, is a safe choice to avoid emphasising a feature unduly. However structures such as fences and pergolas can be a more distinctive colour. White was once popular but picture a red seat to enliven a quiet corner and perhaps match a fiery *Kunzea baxteri* (Crimson Kunzea), or blue pergola posts to show off a combination of white and blue-purple Native Lilacs (*Hardenbergia comptoniana*). A garage or shed painted pale green becomes an extension of the shrubs in front and appears to enlarge the area. A pink and pastel garden can benefit from matching furniture. In most gardens just a little of such introduced colour goes a long way, though in a small, modern garden strong colours may be used with flair.

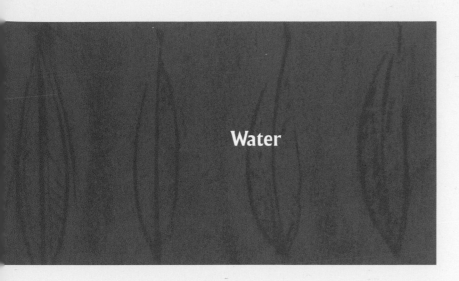

Water

How often it is that a garden, beautiful though it will be, will seem sad and dreary and lacking one of its most gracious features, if it has no water.

Pièrre Husson, *La Théorie et la Pratique Du Jardinage*, 1711

Water in a landscape probably appeals to ancient tribal memories imprinted in our genes. We depend on fresh water for survival, as have our ancestors for countless generations, and its presence is deeply reassuring. We are fascinated by any source of water – a spring, spout, fountain, even a tap or the end of a hose. The pool or water tank in a garden may not be essential for survival now but it's still a potent symbol of security.

Whether in a courtyard garden in town or a spacious country property, water adds another dimension. In a pond, pool or creek it has practical value as it cools and humidifies the atmosphere. Most people love looking at water reflecting the changing colours of sky and garden or adding gentle sound and movement in a waterfall or fountain. Water in a garden adds to its attraction as somewhere for relaxation and contemplation. It also helps entice a variety of fascinating wildlife including birds, frogs and dragonflies.

The location of water, whether a bath or small formal pond or an expansive lake or creek system, is a design priority. Natural surface drainage patterns and the effects of the water table may be used to create a spring or a pond or provide a source of water for a creek. Especially in regard to a large water area, it is worth obtaining professional advice or help. To look part of the local landscape, water will need to lie in low sites as it would naturally, though formal ponds may be raised a little (rarely over 60 centimetres). Appropriate and sensitive siting of water, fitting into the surrounding environment, always produces a harmonious and restful picture. In the natural landscape edges arouse anticipation, so water margins deserve special treatment. If your budget allows, you might even consider mist as a design feature, as in the Sculpture Garden in the Australian National Gallery in Canberra.

Water in a dry country

Most Australians live on the atypical coastal fringe of the continent, where water and green foliage belong in the landscape. However 90 per cent of the country is arid inland where it is often feast or famine – flood or drought. Rivers and pools in the inland areas of Australia are breathtakingly beautiful. Colour schemes are different there – rocks and gravel in strong hues of ochre, orange, terracotta and slate combine with grey or blue foliage tones of plants such as acacias and eremophilas.

Inland rivers are on a grand scale, whether running or waiting for 'the wet' – no garden models here, though a heavy downpour of rain filling a dry creek bed in the garden can be a token reminder. A temporary creek bed, lined with water-worn pebbles, evokes the feel of water and, like a path, carries open space through a garden. Permanent inland pools may be scattered through rocky sections of a river bed or tucked away in

OPPOSITE: Ford garden, Fülling, Vic. Designed by Gordon Ford. The movement of water brings the boulder strewn landscape to life. Weeping Willows, once popular, are now recognized as environmental threats. PHOTOGRAPH RALPH NEALE

sheltered spots among rocky hills, their water either a wonderful blue or mysterious and dark. These scenes and colours might provide inspiration for an oasis – simple yet dramatic – in a dry area garden or a formal garden nearer the coast.

From ancient times, water has played a central role in gardens in arid climates, for example Islamic town gardens in desert areas. In an Australian sandplains garden, without pool or creek, only a small quantity of water in a reflective pool, complemented by green plants, can create a soothing oasis. A reflective pool can even direct sunlight into a room of a house. Water spraying or trickling into a bowl from an outlet or fountain adds gentle, therapeutic splashing or gurgling sounds. You could construct a delightful feature by placing a collection of log stumps of different heights, some with terra cotta trays as birdbaths, in amongst Australian plants. Small birds usually prefer the more hidden lower trays and larger birds like a substantial landing platform before venturing to the higher trays. Apart from adding form to a bed of Australian plants, the birdbaths will give the garden owner hours of pleasure.

Water conservation

Ideally, natural rainfall should provide all (or nearly all) the water for a garden. The garden's design can incorporate and benefit from a number of strategies to conserve water. Designers Glen Wilson and Paul Thompson have long advocated hydrology and water harvesting by the collection, dispersal and use on site of run-off from hard surfaces around the house. This can be based on above-ground drainage, with bogs and soaks as full stops in the system. Low spots can be developed as ephemeral or semi-permanent water areas, shaping saucers (no plastic!) to collect water in swampy areas that dry out seasonally.

In his book John Hunt recommends shaping the soil profile by creating a series of mounds and channels or retention basins. Planting is confined to the mounds, while excess rainfall is retained in the depressions and absorbed by roots through capillary action. This encourages deep rooting so plants are less vulnerable to dry conditions. To prevent erosion in a garden on a steep hillside, you could dig channels to carry water (including that diverted from the street gutter) in a zigzag from top to bottom. The spaces between channels can be planted so that no plant is far from the water-course.

In a water-wise garden, all the water from the house will be directed into underground agricultural pipes for dispersal through the garden. In areas where it is allowed, the 'grey water' from the washing machine (using washing liquid free of phosphate) can be piped separately. Water from wet areas can be directed to dry areas through underground agricultural pipes. You may also need to install some drainage in areas that suffer from flooding during heavy rainfall or experience water run-off from neighbouring blocks, possibly introducing pollution.

Infrequent and deep watering is a good practice. If you are firm-minded enough not to irrigate plants at all after their first summer, then adopt the philosophy that 'if they don't survive, they don't belong'. Plants should be grouped according to their water requirements. A dripper system on the surface of the soil, but concealed by mulch, will waste no water, whereas with above-ground sprinklers most water is lost through evaporation, or falling in areas away from plants' roots. Check dripper systems regularly as they occasionally get blocked.

Large water areas

On a big property, an 0.4 hectare or more, a large water area is an attractive option. Nothing quite matches the effect of a sheet of water in beautifying a garden. An area of water creates a horizontal line to contrast with all the vertical lines of trees and tall shrubs, whose height may seem doubled by

their reflections. It forms the perfect foreground for further views, close or distant. Lakes or extensive pools can replace grass as the major component of the open landscape, offering a serenity that grass cannot really match. Important practical benefits include reduced bushfire risk and low maintenance.

The shape of a large water area can be asymmetric, imitating the complexity of nature. How many square dams with heaped-up ridges of earth on two or three sides could have been transformed with a little thought and planning, and not too much money, into a beautiful lake? You can turn the ridges into wider, more gentle slopes that echo natural landforms; the surrounding land can include depressed areas for inlets and an overflow, and edges with different slopes for different plant and bird habitats. Shallow edges become a dynamic area of plant and bird life and an island with natural vegetation will soon become a valuable bird sanctuary.

If a lake is allowed to follow the seasons its water level will fall over a dry summer to rise again after the autumn 'break'. Exposed muddy edges are not beautiful to many eyes but, as compensation, they often attract hundreds of wading birds. With a large water area, the focus of a garden will change rapidly and in a remarkable way. Sitting contemplating a lake inspires a similar contentment to sitting around an open fireplace in winter. The surrounding landscape could encompass ample open space, usually wide sweeps of grass, carefully planted with trees to provide access and open vistas.

ABOVE: Tondoon Botanic Gardens Qld. The formal effect of the pond's overlapping square shapes is softened by planting – Waterlilies (nymphaeas), a Golden Penda (*Xanthostemon chrysanthus*) on the left, Swamp Banksia (*B. robur*) on the right and Creek Cherry (*Syzygium australe*) behind. The tall light provides a vertical accent linking to taller tree trunks.
PHOTOGRAPH RUTH CROSSON

Small ponds

Even a small pond extends the space of a suburban garden. A generous one might be 4 metres long and 2 metres wide, free form, and dug to a central depth of 80 centimetres. A smaller pond could be 2 metres by 1 metre, and 45 centimetres deep (fish need at least this depth). In still, permanent water, insects such as water boatmen and larvae of dragonflies and mayflies will prey on mosquito larvae. A well-sited and established naturalistic pond will look 'at home', taking advantage of any changes of level in the landforms. It may be a rather secretive, quiet place which blends in naturally with the rest of the garden, separated from open, sunny areas by semi-shade and a mini-marsh. A seasonal pond or marsh is an appealing concept, with appropriate plants that die back when water is lacking, then revive in season. However there is the danger of weeds taking over unless the gardener is ever vigilant.

There are several ways to construct a small informal pond. If possible, a natural clay base is excellent. Otherwise you might use concrete, heavy duty plastic, butyl rubber or a purchased fibreglass shape. The surrounding ground should be level with the water so that the introduced material can be hidden by rocks or plants – tight and ground-hugging or small and arching. If rocks are used to disguise the edges their sizes should vary, as well as the amount protruding over the edge. If ponds are lined with a double layer of plastic, some sand below will cushion the plastic from the soil or rock bed.

A formal pond with a geometric shape, a circle or a square, will integrate well with the hard landscape of buildings, walls or

ABOVE LEFT: Cockburn garden NSW. Designed by Bruce Mackenzie. In an outer suburban block this dam is both useful, collecting and retaining rainwater, and coolly beautiful with its space-extending reflections of indigenous trees. Its formal edging of graded, rounded stones and pebbles helps create an air of mystery.
PHOTOGRAPH DIANA SNAPE

ABOVE RIGHT: Sitch garden Vic. Designed by Geoff Sitch. Water in a small pool gives a silvery backdrop for a selection of delightful little plants, with a handsome Grass Tree (xanthorrhoea) on the right in the foreground as an accent plant. Artificial rocks provide the setting.
PHOTOGRAPH DIANA SNAPE

paved areas. It need not be situated in a particularly low position in the garden. Varying tiling and colours, or including an artificial waterfall or fountain, could add flair.

Plants to enhance water

A major advantage of water is the opportunity to grow some of the multitude of associated plants. A large variety of fine-foliaged, tufted Australian plants look excellent beside water – accent plants such as rushes, sedges and lilies, either upright or weeping. Many act as frog-spawning rafts or poles for dragonflies.

Adjacent to a large pond or wetland area, *Baloskion tetraphyllum* (Tassel Cord-rush) has an extremely attractive weeping form and lovely green and russet colours. Though this may be too dominant for a small pond there is also a dwarf form of the subspecies *meiostachyus*, which is equally appealing, as are other baloskions. If there is space, *Gahnia sieberiana* (Red-fruit Saw-sedge) adds dramatic dark plumes. *Helmholtzia glaberrima* (Stream Lily) is another magnificent plant for a semi-shaded, moist area, giving height to take the eye upwards. Another lovely plant that weeps down into the water and helps blend the pond with its surrounds is the Knobby Club-rush, *Ficinia* (*Isolepis*) *nodosa*. There are various delightful Australian water-loving reeds, such as *Baumea* species. Appropriate rushes such as *Juncus* species may be brought in by water birds to thrive around the borders of large water areas. Smaller plants include hardy sedges like blue-green *Carex gaudichaudiana* or the Black Bristle-rush *Chorizandra enodis*, which add striking form and texture.

Shrubs and small or medium trees with graceful, weeping foliage look very appealing when reflected in water – examples are fine-leaved *Baeckea linifolia* (Weeping Baeckea), elegant *Myoporum bateae* and shapely *Agonis flexuosa* (Willow Myrtle). *Viminaria juncea* (Golden Spray) with pendent flower sprays is beautiful but may be rather short-lived. Textured paperbark trunks of melaleucas provide height and create interesting reflections. Some plants, for example callistemons (bottlebrushes) and *Banksia robur* (Swamp Banksia), flourish in seasonally wet conditions. Ferns suit water areas and small ferns can be tucked into pockets between the rocks. Some Australian ferns are tough and, with shade and protection from wind, demand little water. Ferns generally propagated by division of rhizomes survive drought better than those generally grown from spores. *Pellaea falcata* (Sickle Fern) with its sturdy green fronds, *Doodia* species (Rasp Ferns) with colourful new growth, and delicate Maidenhair Ferns *Adiantum hispidulum* and *A. aethiopicum*, die back during dry periods and flourish again when moisture returns. Around the water edges many small plants will thrive, such as the aromatic *Mentha australis* (River Mint) that spreads readily by suckering.

Plants growing in and on water

Plants growing in water and on its surface add to the enchantment of a pond or lake but, if they cover more than one-third of the surface, they steal too much of the water's magic. In warm climates, waterlilies (*Nymphaea* species) are beautiful and popular. The Giant Waterlily *N. gigantea* is recognised as being one of the most magnificent nymphaeas in the world. However waterlilies need space – one square metre of water per plant, so a domestic pond less than eight square metres is too small. A depth of between a third and one metre is required. Charming *Nymphoides crenata* (Wavy Marshwort), *Villarsia reniformis* (Running Marsh-flower), and *Ottelia ovalifolia* (Swamp Lily) are less demanding and have dainty flowers and a modest habit. Common Nardoo (*Marsilea drummondii*) has most elegant foliage.

Azolla species on the surface, green or reddish in colour, are decorative but spread rapidly and smother a pool so you may need to remove a proportion very regularly. This also applies to Duckweeds, spread and eaten by ducks. If the water is clear and open, free of excessive floating foliage, algae are usually not a problem. Otherwise they should be removed by hand and taken well away from the surrounding area (for example to the compost) to avoid their reappearance. Wind action, water movement and foliage growing beneath the surface all help aerate a pond. Cool water contains more beneficial oxygen than warm water.

Moving water

Lastly there's the joy of moving water in a garden. Whatever the slope of the block, it is a real challenge to create an artificial creek which does not look contrived, even when it follows a natural drainage course. A fall of 1 in 100 is sufficient for water to flow but it looks more exciting on a steeper block. Rocks, real or simulated, seem essential in the design, probably because natural creeks tend to erode soil until they expose rock. To place them effectively requires artistic and scientific skills. In nature, water is slowed down and its flow controlled by stones and fallen logs, which create ponds and dams, and by plants such as tufted reeds, rushes and grasses. The water changes direction and speed; erosion is decreased and wetlands are created for wildlife.

Different-sized rocks and pebbles, sculptured and smoothed by constant water movement, strengthen the illusion of belonging. A bonus is the soothing reassuring sound of moving water. We forget the evaporation and the hidden pump and enjoy lively, tumbling water in rapids or a waterfall. A fountain, with no pretence of being natural, dances with light and lifts the spirits in a similar way. Perhaps with any of these we should turn on the pump only for special occasions. You could consider the exciting combination of sculpture or subtle lighting with your water feature. Imagine the peaceful sound of water trickling gently from a fine pipe (borrowed from Japanese gardens) and the rhythmic croak of a 'pobble-bonk' frog.

Constructions and maintenance

A water feature might include a bridge over a creek, a jetty into a lake, or a short boardwalk adjacent to a pool or over a low, muddy or wet area. Ground surfacing – the areas adjacent to the water feature – may include rocks, pebbles or paving. A pool will need an overflow and possibly drainage, and occasional topping up. For flowing water, practical considerations are complicated a little by the introduction of a water pump (there are various possible types and sizes), with electrical cables and filter screens. Choose pipe materials that resist corrosion. Subtle lighting may enhance a water feature even more.

The chemistry of ponds varies according to growth and season. A pool will always require some limited upkeep and a maintenance program is helpful. Nutrients or pollutants from fertilisers or decaying vegetation such as fallen eucalyptus leaves and twigs, should not run into the water.

Wildlife

Still water introduces a whole new natural ecosystem into a garden. The life that a pool attracts is a constant source of great enjoyment and its balance reflects the health of an area. Insects such as water boatmen, caddis nymphs, water beetles and hovering mayflies and dragonflies are fascinating. Other wildlife includes lizards (skinks) drinking from shallow depressions, water snails, tadpoles and frogs. In the country, a snake may be a less welcome visitor.

Rocks, logs or plants placed carefully in a pool can help protect fish from predators, though stately white-faced herons are patient hunters. Ponds that support tadpoles and frogs are

OPPOSITE: Adams garden Vic. Designed by Gordon Ford. Large rocks shape a 'natural' swimming pool that looks at home close to the house. The components of water, rocks and vegetation are all in easy proportion to one another and to the house, producing a balanced, lovely landscape with a variety of colour and texture.
PHOTOGRAPH TRISHA DIXON

best kept free of fish. A pool can be a magnet for birds. Magpie-larks probe the banks and search for nesting materials while wattle birds dive for insects. Colourful rosellas enjoy a quiet bath. Black ducks and wood ducks weave in amongst the trees to land on a large pond, contrasting with deep swimming cormorants. Magpies pace, willie wagtails flutter nearby and occasional tadpoles provide food for the butcher bird's fledglings.

Safety

Children are attracted to water and its wildlife, so it's essential that any pond can be safely supervised. Fencing is a legal requirement for swimming pools in many regions of Australia. It can be designed to be unobtrusive in the landscape, partly concealed and softened by shrubs or vigorous and attractive creepers such as shiny-leaved *Aphanopetalum resinosum* (Gum Vine).

OPPOSITE: Hanson garden Vic. Designed by Bev Hanson. A naturalistic pool is partly hidden by foliage but the presence of water is confirmed by a variety of ferns, rushes and sedges. It lies naturally in a low area of the garden and gives a sense of peace and serenity. Tassel Cord-rush (*Baloskion (Restio) tetraphyllum*) grows in the foreground.
PHOTOGRAPH SIMON GRIFFITHS

TOP RIGHT: Geale garden Tas. A touch of magic is added to any garden by a small reflective pool with adjacent rocks and water plants.
PHOTOGRAPH DIANA SNAPE

BOTTOM RIGHT: Guymer & Aitchison garden Vic. Designed by Douglas Blythe. This lake, with its water plants and low, boardwalk bridge, within weeks transformed this outer suburban garden with the birds it began to attract. The indigenous garden requires very little maintenance.
PHOTOGRAPH DIANA SNAPE

Wildlife

The control of nature is a phrase conceived in arrogance, born of the Neanderthal age of biology and philosophy when it was supposed that nature exists for the convenience of man.

Rachel Carson, *Silent Spring*, 1962

Australian gardens naturally provide habitat for Australian wildlife – or do they? Gardeners often comment on the birds that visit their garden. However, these frequently turn out to be the larger native species such as Noisy Miners, Wattlebirds, Singing or New Holland Honeyeaters, Pied Currawongs and Rainbow Lorikeets, or the unwanted intruders – Common Mynahs, Starlings, Blackbirds, House Sparrows and Turtle-doves. These hardy, often very territorial species are doing well in suburbia, but less common are small bush birds like wrens, robins, thornbills and finches with their excited calls and delightful activity.

And what about lizards, frogs, small ground mammals and all the fascinating insects and other creepy crawlies? There are always some tough ones like possums, or tiny souls who can live almost anywhere (in a crack in the wall or under a closely mown lawn), but what can we do for those native

animals in need of a more natural lifestyle? A patch of garden may seem insignificant in the wider wildlife picture but, if a few gardens in each street provided some wildlife habitat, then larger habitat areas such as bushland reserves and regional and national parks adjacent to suburbia, could be connected by backyards. Gardens can become links in the chain of wildlife corridors.

Responsible land managers consider the conservation and sustainable use of their land's resources – its soil, wildlife and vegetation – its biodiversity. Gardeners are looking after some of the most expensive land in the country, and their cumulative individual contributions are invaluable in maintaining this wonderful planet's life support system. When gardeners start looking out for wildlife they notice much more activity than ever before and derive enormous pleasure from what they learn and from the part they are playing in sustaining it.

General principles

The biggest problems for wildlife in suburban gardens are not caused by lack of knowledge about wildlife and its habitat requirements. Even a good general knowledge of wildlife and a willingness to consider its needs in a garden will be undermined by two wildlife-unfriendly traits of many people – impatience and an obsession with tidiness.

Impatience may show itself in the sudden removal of much of the garden's vegetation and other cover, that is, its wildlife shelter, feeding and breeding areas. Gardeners may dislike 'the mess' in the garden, or may have just moved in and want to make a mark quickly. However, when they suddenly convert a garden from an area with trees and shrubs, weeds

OPPOSITE: Densley garden Vic. The garden owner was excited to see this echidna (*Tachyglossus aculeatus*) in her garden rapidly heading for the shelter of a pink-flowering *Isopogon latifolius*, where it promply disappeared. PHOTOGRAPH CHERREE DENSLEY

and rubbish to what they believe will be a more wildlife-friendly garden, the transition period can be devastating, if not fatal, for the wildlife dependent on it. A garden may have been an important island of food or shelter in an otherwise inhospitable area. If this habitat is removed all at once, some animals will die during the removal process or while trying to escape. Others may get away but not return because they cannot find a safe route or because the new plantings take too long to mature and provide resources.

An obsession with tidiness can take the form of always picking up bark, twigs and leaves; constantly pruning, cutting and mowing; never leaving a pile of prunings to start breaking down and become warm and moist. Sometimes gardeners leave no corner or piece of habitat undisturbed ('no stone unturned') for any length of time so that no animal can feel safe enough to take up residence, or to forage or build a nest anywhere in the garden.

Here are three principles for establishing wildlife habitat in a garden. They are adapted from those identified by the Bradley sisters of Sydney in Joan Bradley's book, *Bush Regeneration*.

1 Work from areas of least important habitat to most important habitat.

2 Create minimal disturbance to habitat areas during your garden activities.

3 Don't overclear. Let the wildlife (and your time, physical fitness and ability to replace plants) dictate how fast you clear habitat.

To explain these principles more fully:

ABOVE: Snape garden Vic. Butterflies and other insects are attracted by tufted grasses such as poas and Kangaroo Grass (*Themeda triandra*), and also by daisies (brachyscomes and chrysocephalums). Here a tapestry of these replaces a grass 'nature strip' which usually does much less for 'nature'.

PHOTOGRAPH SIMON GRIFFITHS

1. From least to most

This principle means starting to clear the least important habitat for the animals you wish to retain in, or encourage to your garden. Ideally observe for at least a year to see how the wildlife's habits change with the seasons. Watch for birds, reptiles, mammals, frogs, invertebrates, and aquatic animals if you have water. Look for the areas of most activity for your most important wildlife. Remember that good habitat is not necessarily the most attractive or most desirable for you. To help you decide where to clear first, look at areas most used by unwanted wildlife such as introduced birds, overly territorial or predatory native birds, rats, cats, rabbits and foxes. Then establish habitat priorities:

- Least important – used by unwanted wildlife (work here first)
- Apparently unused
- Most important – used by desired wildlife (work here last)

2. Minimal disturbance

Tidying up – clearing, pruning, mowing, cleaning up, whipper-snippering, picking up leaves and bark, removing dead flower heads and plants – constantly affects wildlife using the garden. We dig up beetle larvae and skink eggs when we cultivate the soil. We expose nesting birds when we cut back dense shrubs during the breeding season. We carve up skinks and butterfly caterpillars during lawn-mowing. We remove Blue-tongued Lizard shelters when we finally take those old concrete blocks to the tip and we wrench Ring-tailed Possums out of their daytime shelters when we do big Lantana clean-ups.

ABOVE: Squirrel Glider on a banksia. The beautiful and rare Squirrel Glider (*Petaurus norfolcensis*) of eastern Australia feeds on insects (such as beetles and caterpillars), wattle gum, the sap of some eucalypts, nectar and pollen. If you are very lucky and your garden backs onto the appropriate coastal forest or woodland, you may receive night-time visits from this delightful small possum.

PHOTOGRAPH PAVEL GERMAN

People are usually aware that some wildlife is using their garden. However most seem to need reassurance that it is actual wildlife habitat and that they should not feel guilty about leaving 'the mess' and enjoying the wildlife.

3. Don't overclear

This principle is usually the hardest one to follow. It's about relinquishing total control of the garden and forming a partnership with nature. Just like any other relationship, it's not always in harmony but it is real and dynamic. All vegetation and wildlife communities are constantly changing and this principle allows gardeners time to take an interest in and feel good about these never-ending changes. By relinquishing apparent control you gain a true sense of control – but it's relaxed, flexible and enjoyable, not fraught with guilt or worry.

A cautious approach to wildlife habitat gardening, using these three principles, avoids disasters and allows time for reflection and possibly a change of direction.

Creating a habitat garden

A flexible garden design will provide resources for local wildlife together with a beautiful and functional yet not too obsessively neat garden. A plan for converting what you have to what you want should proceed in stages, while maintaining the habitat of existing wildlife. Allow time for this to work – possibly years rather than months! Your plan will need to be very flexible and take into account any changes in wildlife use.

The following strategies will assist in designing a wildlife habitat garden and implementing a work plan:

- Be fair – reconsider trying to attract wildlife to a garden where there are active pets or if neighbouring cats and dogs cannot be kept out.
- Limit clearing, heavy pruning and weed removal to no more than one-third of the total area at any one time. Try to do this work outside peak breeding times – especially spring.
- It is preferable to replace unnatural or unwanted habitat before you remove it. Use more natural and aesthetically pleasing habitat components such as rocks, logs, leaf litter and native plantings elsewhere.
- Plan to remove weeds in a mosaic pattern, leaving patches of undisturbed habitat adjacent to weeded areas to maintain shelter and food resources, and reduce predation and erosion. Waiting for new plantings to produce flowers and fruit will provide other shelter before removing further unwanted plants.
- Select plants that provide flowers, seed and fruit at different times of the year, especially during autumn and winter. Winter is a tough time for animals who don't 'shut up shop', as many reptiles do.
- Consider other aspects of habitat such as clean water that is safe to access, logs, rocks and leaf litter to provide shelter and foraging sites for lizards, frogs and invertebrates. Sanctuary areas that are never disturbed will provide important refuge and breeding sites.
- Before weeding, bagging, burning or otherwise altering recently undisturbed habitat (including weed piles), disturb by noise, agitate with sticks, or shake to give resident animals an opportunity to get away and find alternative homes. Preferably do this twenty-four hours (or at least some hours) beforehand.

Planting strategies

Local wildlife has evolved to live with plants indigenous to the area. Birds appreciate shrubs planted densely and in clumps of the same or similar species. The best shrubs for creating

OPPOSITE: An Eastern Spinebill (*Acanthorhynchus tenuirostris*) sips delicately from a grevillea flower. It is a delight to see this beautiful honeyeater visiting flowers in your garden and to hear its characteristic song. PHOTOGRAPH JOHN MOVERLEY (BIRDS AUSTRALIA LIBRARY)

habitat are dense and/or spikey and offer a range of resources such as seed, nectar, insects, nesting material and nest sites throughout the year. Around existing mature trees planting a dense, shrubby understorey or a group of the same or similar species of trees indigenous to the area will create a haven for wildlife. Small migratory birds such as Yellow-faced Honey-eaters and Silvereyes will head for groups of trees which provide rest sites, or from which they can locate safe feeding areas. Most mature trees (including weed trees such as Large-leaved Privet and Camphor Laurel) provide important food, shelter and nest sites for a wide range of native animals. Dead mature trees are particularly important and sought after.

Although fruit-bearing plants may provide food for small birds and other animals such as butterflies and flying-foxes, they may also attract many Pied Currawongs, which are a major predator of eggs, nestlings and occasionally adult birds. Where Noisy Miners and other large territorial honeyeaters are a problem, insect- rather than bird-pollinated plants, such as wattles, pea-plants and tea-trees, will increase shelter, nesting and foraging sites for small, insectivorous birds.

Planting around the base of large, outcropping boulders will improve shelter for lizards and other fauna. Take care to select plants appropriate to the levels of soil moisture. Weeding around the base may expose previously secure wildlife refuges leaving wildlife vulnerable to predation. Try to carry out the work over a number of weeks or, preferably, partially weed, revegetate and allow planting to mature and provide cover before repeating the process.

Plants stabilise the banks of waterways and provide corridors and habitat for aquatic life. Margins of drains and boggy areas can support Australian sedges, grasses, ferns and shrubs that can tolerate wet feet as well as occasionally drying out. You could create small, safe and clean wetland habitats where local birds, lizards, frogs and insects, such as dragon-flies, can drink, cool themselves, bathe or slough their skin. Take care to block possible sources of water pollution.

When you are removing branches from mature trees leave stumps, approximately thirty centimetres from the

ABOVE: A Jacky Lizard (*Amphibolurus muricatus*) reclines on a log on the ground, protected by its cryptic colouring. It is easy to miss seeing such a well-camouflaged animal.
PHOTOGRAPH TREVOR BLAKE

trunk. Hollows will form in these stumps and provide nest or shelter sites for fauna such as possums, parrots, owls or microbats. Artificial nest boxes for birds, possums and microbats can also be excellent homes but seek expert advice on construction, installation and monitoring.

Wildlife role

Most people are aware of plants providing food and shelter for wildlife but are often not aware that it is a mutually dependent relationship.

Groundcovers or lovely leaf litter harbour small creatures. Unmown lawn provides seed for finches and allows caterpillars to eat enough to turn into spirit-lifting butterflies. As well as providing food, flowers (including those in vegetable gardens) are pollinated by birds, small possums, flying-foxes and insects such as moths, beetles, flies, weevils, thrips, wasps, mosquitoes, sawflies and fungus gnats (all your favourites!). Seed and spore are distributed by birds, flying-foxes, ants and ground mammals such as bandicoots, native rats and potoroos.

Insect pests are eaten by birds, lizards, frogs and mammals such as gliders, microbats, bush rats, antechinus and bandicoots as well as by spiders, parasitic wasps and other invertebrates. Nutrients are recycled and soil improved by the activity of earthworms and other soil invertebrates and micro-organisms, by herbivorous insects and by lyrebirds, bandicoots and other diggers.

Native wildlife is an essential part of a balanced ecosystem and should be an inspiring and beautiful component of gardens as well as parks and urban bushland.

Animal needs

These are some very general habitat requirements for the various animal groups.

Birds need a diversity of habitat types such as forest with dense understorey, heathland, open grassy woodland with fallen timber, creeklines and open water with fringing vegetation. They require shelter and nesting sites such as tree hollows, floating vegetation, display sites and access to water. They need food such as seed, fruit and nectar, and a range of prey such as insects, reptiles, fish and small mammals.

Mammals need a diversity of habitats such as mature forest trees with hollows and connecting canopies (aerial pathways), dense, native understorey with deep leaf litter, open grassland and woodland, and rocky outcrops. Their food includes nectar, pollen, whole flowers, buds, seed, fruit, sap, stems and leaves of trees, shrubs and grasses, fungi, insects and other invertebrates such as earthworms, spiders and small mammals.

Reptiles need rocky outcrops, boulders, logs, leaf litter, sunny basking sites near dense vegetation, creeklines and swampy areas and termite mounds. Their food requirements range from insects and other invertebrates (for example snails and crayfish), to fruit, flowers, vegetation, fungi, frogs, lizards, snakes, mice, eels, fish and carrion.

Frogs need dense, moist vegetation with logs, rocks and bark, and access to clean water free of fish and other frogspawn-eaters. Some need sunny basking sites. Food includes insects and other invertebrates such as snails, worms and spiders, as well as small lizards and other frogs.

Insects and other invertebrates need minimal pesticide exposure and habitat such as vegetation, leaf litter, bark, rocks, logs, soil or water bodies to complete their life cycle. They need food such as plant material (nectar, leaves, roots, sap, wood, honeydew, leaf mould, moss, fungi and decaying vegetable matter). They also require prey including insects and other invertebrates such as slaters and spiders or animal material (feathers, blood, dung and carrion).

Freshwater and estuarine fish and other aquatic fauna need clean water. Objects in the water like rocks, logs and aquatic vegetation are a necessity. A range of water types is essential such as deep pools, riffles and backwaters. Bankside vegetation and stable banks provide shade, shelter, foraging and breeding sites. Intertidal areas such as mudflats are also sought after. Their food includes aquatic and terrestrial insects, crustaceans, molluscs, plankton, algae and other aquatic plants and fish.

Habitat plants

Most Australian plants provide valuable resources for wildlife. The best habitat plants provide some food, shelter and nest sites for a range of nectar-, fruit-, seed-, leaf-, insect- and prey-eating animals such as birds, mammals, lizards, frogs, insects and other invertebrates. The top habitat plant genera that provide many resources for a wide range of Australian animals are eucalyptus, corymbia, angophora, melaleuca, acacia, banksia, leptospermum and kunzea.

Shelter plants

Many species of acacia (wattles), leptospermum (tea-trees), melaleuca, kunzea, bursaria (for example *B. spinosa*, Sweet Bursaria), hakea, ceratopetalum (for example *C. gummiferum*, NSW Christmas Bush); vines – for example rubus (*R. parvifolius* is Native Raspberry), clematis – and any dense or spiky planting.

Insect-pollinated plants

Acacias, Australian peas (for example dillwynias, hardenbergias), leptospermums. Australian daisies (for example olearias) as well as hibbertias (Guinea Flowers), clematis, pomaderris.

Nectar plants

Banksias, grevilleas, hakeas, correas, lambertias (for example *L. formosa*, Mountain Devil), mistletoes, eucalyptus, corymbias, angophoras, melaleucas, callistemons, xanthorrhoeas (Grass Trees) and other plants with big, showy flower heads.

Seed plants

Eucalyptus, corymbias, angophoras, acacias, casuarinas and allocasuarinas (She-oaks), glochidions (for example *G. ferdinandi*, Cheese Tree), lomandras, Australian grasses (for example themeda, Wallaby Grasses) and sedges (for example, gahnia).

Fruit plants

Acmenas and syzygiums (Lilly Pillies), ficus (Figs), alphitonias, persoonias (Geebungs), dianellas (Flax Lilies), cissus (for example *C. antarctica*, Kangaroo Vine), breynias, saltbushes and many rainforest or wet forest species.

Native bee plants

Persoonias (Geebungs), Australian peas (for example hoveas, pultenaeas), Australian daisies (for example xerochrysum, rhodanthe), heath plants (for example epacris, leucopogons), tristaniopsis (for example *T. laurina*, Water Gum).

Native butterfly plants

Australian peas and daisies, Australian grasses (for example poas), sedges (for example carex), rushes (for example juncus), lomandras, dianellas, bursarias, macrozamias (for example *M. communis*, Burrawang), dodonaeas (Hop Bushes), zierias, cupaniopsis (Tuckeroos).

Nature needs time to show what's possible in a garden. Mowers, whipper-snippers, chainsaws, excessive clean-up days and overuse of chemicals will all overwhelm her. Patience and tolerance when making changes will ensure the consideration of wildlife and its habitat requirements.

OPPOSITE: Blake garden Vic. A lake in an outer suburban garden is the centre of a complete ecosystem, providing a small, floating island for ducks and attracting a great variety of birds and other animals. The creation of the lake changed the focus of this garden in a remarkable way. Landscaping the surrounding area required careful placing of trees with ample open space, to avoid crowding and to provide access and open vistas.
PHOTOGRAPH DIANA SNAPE

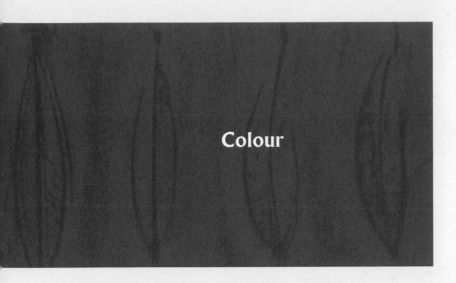

Colour

In the end, colour combinations come down to our personal preferences, which we must discover through observation and experiment.

Montagu Don, *The Sensuous Garden*, 1997

Clever use of colour is an integral part of garden design. This was well understood by Gertrude Jekyll, who had been trained as an artist. She brought her artistic experience to bear in planning her famous herbaceous borders that relied on a combination of perennial and annual plants for a great range of intermingling colours. The borders were planned to unfold in a gradual progression of blended tones as the viewer walked along.

Some of the French Impressionists were also gardeners, perhaps the most famous being Monet, and used colour in their gardens very skilfully. They generally planned their gardens to be viewed from particular spots, where they set up their easels. Their planting tended towards ribbons of colour, quite different from more formal styles that comprised blocks of solid colour in beds and parterres. Generally Australian gardens are closer to the Jekyll or Impressionist styles but differ in many ways, with the most available plants being perennial shrubs, though the range of annuals and biennials is widening. Understanding the properties of different colours and how to use them to maximum effect is very beneficial when designing a garden.

The colour wheel

Sunlight ('white light') contains all the colours of the spectrum, seen separated in a rainbow. A red flower reflects only red light to the viewer, absorbing all other colours. A white flower reflects all light falling on it while a black flower, for example *Kennedia nigricans* (Black Coral-pea), absorbs all and reflects none. Colour theory recognises three primary colours – red, yellow and blue. All other colours result from mixing these primaries. An easy way to visualize this is to use the Colour Wheel, with the three primaries equally spaced around it and the secondary colours (orange, green and purple) formed by mixing between each pair. The number of further mixed colours shown is a matter of choice and space; they vary with different proportions of each primary colour used.

Colour perception

Perception of colour is very subjective – blue/green foliage will appear blue when set against true greens, whereas against a blue wall it will seem green. If a colour is diluted progressively with white (tints) and also with black (shades) and these are arranged in rows of increasing dilutions, the original hue will look dark against the tints and light against the shades. So the colour we see is influenced by the setting in which we see it. In the bright, clear light of inland Australia and the tropics, pastels can seem washed out and insipid – strong hues are called for. In the soft light of a wet winter's day, whites, yellows and pastels will stand out.

Most animal groups have slightly different receptor pigments and therefore see a different range of colours. Over

OPPOSITE: Vivid orange and cerise flowers of *Chorizema cordatum* (Heart-leaved Flame-pea) – the shrub grows in sun or shade and will enliven a dull corner of any garden.
PHOTOGRAPH BRIAN SNAPE

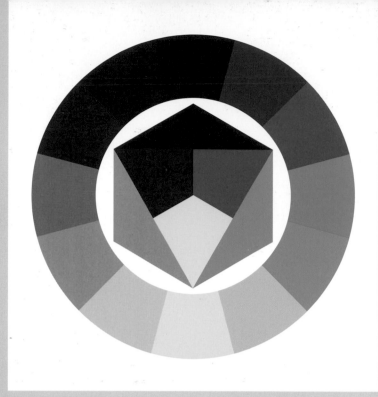

the millenia, plants have evolved pigments as well as scents and nectar in order to attract specific pollinators, so it is possible to predict the pollinator on which a plant relies by the colour of its flowers. Insects are sensitive to ultraviolet light (but not to red) and night-flying insects are drawn to pale flowers. Birds are more sensitive in the red area of the spectrum – a natural division of labour – and Australia is rich in honeyeaters and in red flowers. Honeyeaters are also able to find among the foliage greenish flowers that we hardly notice such as those of *Grevillea shiressii* and some forms of Common Correa (*C. reflexa*).

ABOVE LEFT: Colour wheel. The three primary colours, red, yellow and blue, are shown in the centre and then the secondary colours, orange, green and purple, made by mixing the primaries. Further mixing produces a spectrum of colours.

ABOVE RIGHT: Vivid new leaves of a syzygium species selected by Don Burke for his garden. PHOTOGRAPH LORNA ROSE

OPPOSITE: The lilac foliage of *Eucalyptus pluricaulis* is striking in combination with reddish stems and lemon buds and new leaves. PHOTOGRAPH BRIAN SNAPE

Colour personalities

People have their favourite colours but each colour has its own individuality and a situation in which it is just right. Characteristics are ascribed to groups of colours – blues are said to be restful and soothing, the cool colours; red has strength and warmth, yellow is vibrant and exciting. Cool colours tend to recede in the landscape and can make a small space look larger, especially if set off by touches of white. A silver-grey eucalypt placed against a dark background will give depth to a vista. There is no equivalent in exotic trees, although all floras have a variety of such shrubs. It is best to use these silver foliages selectively. The famous white garden at Sissinghurst in England, where flowers and foliage are all white, silver or grey, has dark-green yew hedges for contrast.

The warm colours, which tend to dominate and crowd small spaces by seeming closer to the viewer, can be softened with cream or tints. If they seem too bright and glary in a large garden, shades or dark colours will tone them down, as will plenty of green nearby. A Waratah in full flower can be a source of pride and joy yet can disrupt the proportions of the garden space unless carefully placed. Most Australian flowers are individually small and partly

surrounded by foliage that softens the effect of bright colours. Yellows, such as in hibbertias (Guinea Flowers), are invaluable for lighting up dark corners. On a larger scale, winter-flowering wattles can create a patch of sunlight on a dull winter's day.

True blue

Australia has some of the most beautiful pure blue flowers in the world. Although they are mainly small plants, you can use them in the front of garden beds to create a dazzling display and as ideal linking plants that will not clash with any other colour. Most well known is probably *Lechenaultia biloba* which has been cultivated for a long time. It can be difficult to maintain for more than a couple of years (unless given ideal conditions) but it strikes readily. Several colour forms have been selected, pale and deep blues and some with white flashes, so a mixed patch can be wonderful.

Halgania cyanea and *H. preissiana* are also lovely and easier to grow in the eastern states. They will sucker gently, flowering throughout the warmer weather. Some dampieras have equally true blues and are nearly as long-flowering.

Wahlenbergias can come and go. These are all low plants so for something taller members of the Iris family *Orthrosanthus multiflorus* (Morning Flag), *O. laxus* (Morning Iris) and *O. polystachya* and the climbers *Hardenbergia comptoniana* (Native Lilac) and *Billardiera variifolia* can give height. The many purple-blue flowers such as hoveas show up well in full light rather than shade, or with lemon or cream neighbours.

Colour harmonies

The most harmonious colour schemes are based on a pure hue with some of its tints and shades, or on a group of several adjacent colours on the wheel. Examples are red, orange and yellow, or blue, indigo and purple. You can make these more dramatic by introducing a complementary colour, one directly opposite on the colour wheel. Use such contrasts sparingly with only small amounts of the brighter colour. Red and green are a pair of complementary colours and red is very attractive on its own against green foliage. Other complementary colours, such as purple and yellow, are better together against green foliage than either colour is alone.

Red occurs frequently in Australian flowers. In the callistemons (bottlebrushes), with their dense floral display, the predominant colour, red, is striking against green foliage. *Hakea purpurea* with elegant flowers in brilliant red or purple-red also comes with an inbuilt contrast. Red is set off well by greyish foliage as in Granite Kunzea (*K. pulchella*). Possibly the best loved red/green combination is the common Kangaroo Paw *Anigozanthos manglesii*, with rich red stems and calyxes and bright-green floral tubes with a touch of gold in the anthers. The Red Kangaroo Paw *Anigozanthos rufus* is all red with stately flower stalks above dark-green leaves.

Because they share white in their composition, the tints (or pastels) all blend well together. With their light-reflecting capacity they suit situations of subdued light, though a bright colour is also a good feature in shade. You may choose to mix all hues in a garden but it is better not to, especially not with flowers that create a solid block of colour and obscure the leaves. Certain colours are diminished in proximity to each other and are best appreciated in different areas, separated by white, grey, or plenty of foliage. Tastes differ but yellows are generally preferred away from bright mauve pinks – this is easiest to achieve by growing them apart and not relying on flowering times to keep them isolated.

PREVIOUS PAGE: Kings Park Botanic Gardens WA. Strong hues show up well in bright sunlight. Mass plantings of red Kangaroo Paws and pink daisies are harmonious against a complementary background of many different shades of foliage green, creating a complex pattern of colours. Rounded, juvenile eucalypt leaves add silver-blue as an accent. PHOTOGRAPH DIANA SNAPE

TOP: Fringed Wattle (*Acacia fimbriata*) PHOTOGRAPH BRIAN SNAPE

MIDDLE: Common Dampiera (*Dampiera linearis*). Yellow and purple are complementary colours and look more effective together on a green background than either does alone. PHOTOGRAPH BRIAN SNAPE

BOTTOM: A coastal garden Vic. All gums flower, of course, but the Red-flowering Gum (*Corymbia ficifolia*) is brilliant and eye-catching in summer whether in red, pink, salmon or orange. Green foliage provides a complementary background to red flowers. PHOTOGRAPH BRIAN SNAPE

Using colour

No matter how carefully you plan a colour scheme, vagaries of the weather can upset flowering times and spoil a planned harmony or produce an unwanted clash, unless colour groups are planted in separate areas. This enables a succession of flowering times to carry through chosen colour schemes. Sometimes flower colour will differ from the expected due to soil type and some flowers can fade rapidly in strong light – *Callistemon* 'Injune' opens a very pretty pink but can rapidly become beige. Heat and sunlight appear to affect the rate of change. Other plants need lots of sun to flower prolifically.

Consider also the appearance of a plant throughout the year and site it accordingly. *Melaleuca fulgens* (Scarlet Honey-myrtle) has different forms with magnificent salmon or purple flowers but its somewhat stiff, twiggy shape cannot be completely cured by pruning. Like a rose, it is best placed between more leafy foreground and background plants.

You may seek peace and serenity in a garden but this need not be the whole story. The occasional colour clash or a bright section of 'fluorescent' colours can be very stimulating. Such outbursts usually only last a short time and serve to emphasise the overall effect of restfulness. Some of the small Western Australian kunzeas (*K. affinis, K. jucunda, K. preissiana*) are a shocking pink and reasonably long-lived, given good drainage. Bright pink forms of the Rice Flower *Pimelea ferruginea* are reliable and more readily available from nurseries. Climbing Flame-pea (*Chorizema diversifolium*) is a light climber with purple and orange flowers, vivid at close range, yet very beautiful. Other climbers, Red Billardiera (*B. erubescens*) and purple-flowered Native Sarsaparilla (*Hardenbergia violacea*), are spectacular entwined with both in bloom. All rules are made to be broken at times, so if you are ever dismayed that certain colours have not worked out as planned, look at their potential to be the shockers, the spot that wakes you up and emphasises the calm elsewhere. Pretend that you planned it all along, and do it again!

Adding sparkle

White is the big mixer and will freshen any other combination when used in restrained amounts. A solid patch of white in bright light can seem to punch a hole in the landscape and interfere with proportions and perspective, but small splashes of white add sparkle. The bracts of *Spyridium parvifolium* (Dusty Miller) glistening in the undergrowth of the mountain forest, or in your garden, are a shining example.

Iridescent or translucent petals also increase the shimmer, especially if planted to be seen with light filtering through. Examples are the waxy petals of some grevilleas, such as *G. tripartita, G. insignis* and *G.wilsonii* (Wilson's Grevillea) and Hakeas, such as *H. orthorrhyncha*, Bird Beak Hakea. 'Apple blossom' effects, pink buds opening to white flowers as in many leptospermums and philothecas, are especially pretty.

Ever-popular all-white gardens occur in nature too. In a good season, the mid-Tambo valley in Gippsland, Victoria, is like a bridal scene with Wax Flowers (philothecas), clematis, Burgan (*Kunzea ericoides*), olearias (Daisy Bush) and tea-trees (leptospermums) all contributing to the effect. Among low white plants are brachyscomes such as Basalt Daisy (*B. basaltica* var. *gracilis*); a little taller, Common Heath (*Epacris impressa*), *Woollsia pungens* or *Pseudanthus pimeleoides*; up to *Olearia passerinoides* (Slender Daisy-bush). White is very effective in toning down overbright colours and separating potential clashes. Like pale grey or silver, it is excellent in shade, especially against a dark-green backdrop.

Many gums have wonderful white trunks, memorable in inland scenes against sunset-coloured rock. *Eucalyptus scoparia* (Wallangarra White Gum) is magnificent against red scoria in the Hoffman Walk, near Melbourne. The striking use of *Corymbia* (*Eucalyptus*) *citriodora* (Lemon-scented Gum) to line the drive at Cruden Farm, Victoria, has often been celebrated. White trunks among a clump of mallees contribute interest and sparkle.

A galaxy of small flowers

The Australian flora is not rich in big, bold flowers – lovely hibiscus and *Rhododendron lochiae* with individual flowers; magnificent grevilleas (including many hybrids), Rock Orchid (*Thelychiton speciosus*) and Stream Lily (*Helmholtzia glaberrima*) are a few notable exceptions. Solid colours in the bush or garden are frequently due to masses of small flowers obscuring the leaves. Very often these flowers are multi-coloured like the chorizemas, where purple and orange form part of each flower. Seen from any but very close range the two shades meld, with the brighter predominating but softened. Such combinations offer the opportunity to juxtapose in nearby plants similar colours that might otherwise clash. More often the colours within each flower are harmonious, as in dainty *Hypocalymma angustifolium* (White Myrtle) and some of the exquisite verticordias (Feather Flowers). White or yellow adds a highlight and can make the flower more visible, for example *Grevillea georgeana* (reddish-pink flowers) and blue-rayed brachyscomes, each with yellow centres.

A similar blending of colours occurs in grasslands or daisy fields where the individual plants and their flowers are small but their numbers immense – a galaxy of small flowers. Again it is an overall impression that registers. The original cottage gardeners grew simple flowers higgledy-piggledy without any concern for colour clashes – they succeeded because there was plenty of green and only smallish areas of colour. While it is desirable to plant shrubs together for similar cultivation needs or foliage effects, which are relevant throughout the year, also choosing flower colours carefully will give you the greatest pleasure. Flowers from a harmonious range will enable each contribution to be appreciated, for example cream, lemon, gold, a touch of orange, ideally in drifts which mingle at their edges and with a few contrasting highlights of contrast (purple-blue). In suitable conditions you could try *Olearia teretifolia* (Cypress Daisy-bush), *Hibbertia cuneiformis* (Cut-leaf Guinea-flower), *Correa backhouseana*, *Callistemon pinifolius*, *Acacia drummondii* (Drummond's Wattle), with the smaller *Phebalium squamulosum* (Forest Phebalium) forms, *Hibbertia pedunculata* (Stalked Guinea-flower) and add life with the orange-red form of beautiful *Correa pulchella*.

The idea of planting in drifts originated with exotic herbaceous plants that are generally smaller than Australian shrubs, so it may not be easy to achieve in the space of a suburban garden. It looks natural to have no sharp boundaries between colours. The amount of accent colour need only be small and the brighter the colour, the less is needed. The effect is much reduced in a 50:50 balance.

Foliage – green and other colours

Green is undoubtedly the most important colour in the garden, a fact we tend to overlook because it is so ubiquitous and we 'see' only the flower colours. Not only are there many shades of green in leaves but buds, berries, fruit, twigs and trunks also contribute. Australian trees may not have the marvellous colours of many deciduous trees but the White Cedar (*Melia azedarach*) can clothe itself in gold and many other rainforest trees produce brilliant flushes of new growth in bronze, pink, red and even purple to mark seasonal changes, not just autumn.

Numerous banksias have soft bronze new growth – *B. baxteri* (Birds-nest Banksia) and *B. grandis* (Bull Banksia) from Western Australia and *B. robur* (Swamp Banksia) from the tropics are just a few. Many hakeas have their hour of glory – for example *H. pandanicarpa* subsp. *crassifolia* (Thick-leaved Hakea), *H. adnata* and *H. elliptica* (Oval-leaved Hakea), which can have superb bronze foliage for extended periods. During colder months the leaves of *Grevillea repens* (Creeping Grevillea) become a deep-plum colour while the new growth of *G. microstegia* is a beautiful bronze. A selected form of *Acacia baileyana* (Cootamundra Wattle) has smoky-purple new growth but, as noted earlier, excessive self-sowing in natural areas can be a problem. *Agonis* 'After Dark' has magnificent

ABOVE: A natural garden Vic. Wonderful foliage colours of Slaty She-oak
(*Allocasuarina muelleriana*).

PHOTOGRAPH DIANA SNAPE

dark-purple foliage. Such plants are just the tip of the potential for Australian flora, which have been selected and cultivated for only an extremely short time compared to exotic plants. Location, soil type, climate and exposure will all influence the degree of colour.

Awareness is growing of the potential of rainforest and rainforest verge plants, especially with their coloured growth flushes which occur throughout the year in response to water and nutrients. In frost-prone areas some rainforest plants may have to be restricted to pots. They seem to adapt readily to life in containers and are showing promise as indoor plants. Even in southern areas Lilly Pillies (acmenas) have long been recognised for their colourful berries, though both leaf and berry colour develop more dramatically in warmer regions.

There are also many reds in ordinary foliage and the pigments seem to lessen damage from frost and drought. It can be worth hunting through seedling trays of *Allocasuarina torulosa* (Rose She-oak) or *Leptospermum lanigerum* (Woolly Tea-tree) among others for the most coloured plants, or use *Leptospermum* 'Copper Glow' or 'Copper Sheen', selections already made by the nursery industry. A new series of colourful *Austromyrtus dulcis* (Midgen Berry) has recently been released. These new releases may appear in Garden Centres well before they become available at your favourite Australian plant nursery. There are wonderful pinks and reds in the new growth of callistemons, for example *C. salignus* (Willow Bottlebrush) and *C. citrinus* (Crimson Bottlebrush). To date many of these red-leaved plants belong to the Myrtaceae family but there are also candidates among the boronias. An outstanding example from the acacias is *A. glaucoptera* (Clay Wattle), especially if you can admire it with light behind its rich red tips.

The glaucous look of silvery-leaved eucalypts is due to waxy layers that reduce water loss or frost damage. Examples are *E. macrocarpa* (Mottlecah) from the dry areas and *E. pulverulenta* (Silver-leaved Mountain Gum) from the highlands. *Eucalyptus coccifera* (Tasmanian Snow Gum) is widely grown in England for its foliage, particularly the juvenile leaves which can be retained by annual coppicing. These and other beautiful silver-grey eucalypts are grown for the cut-flower market here and overseas.

Other desert, seaside or alpine plants protect themselves from desiccation with a heavy growth of leaf hairs that makes them appear silver-grey. The degree of silver can vary as rain and rapid growth produce a greener look that alters as summer proceeds. The Ray Flowers *Cyphanthera albicans* and *C. tasmanica* (two largish shrubs which benefit from tip pruning) also show this seasonal change. *Cyphanthera albicans*, in particular, displays a lovely fresh silver mound at the height of summer. While both flower profusely with creamy to white flowers, these are but a bonus after the beauty of the foliage. You can use low-growing silver-foliaged plants along a drive or pathway to make it more visible at night, for example Cushion Bush (*Leucophyta brownii*), forms of Common Everlasting (*Chrysocephalum apiculatum*), Lemon Beauty-heads (*Calocephalus citreus*) and Milky Beauty-heads (*C. lacteus*), both small, pretty groundcover plants with silver-grey foliage and lemon or cream globular flower heads.

TOP LEFT: *Acacia glaucoptera* (Clay Wattle) backlit.
PHOTOGRAPH DIANA SNAPE

TOP RIGHT: *Acacia glaucoptera* (Clay Wattle) frontlit.
PHOTOGRAPH DIANA SNAPE

BOTTOM LEFT: Anigozanthos 'Gold Cross' retains its vibrant colour from spring through summer.
PHOTOGRAPH BRIAN SNAPE

BOTTOM RIGHT: Cockburn garden NSW. Designed by Bruce Mackenzie. Light defines the contrasting foliage and form of *Banksia robur* (Swamp Banksia) and *Lomandra longifolia* (Spiny-headed Mat-rush). Both plants have bold leaves, the banksia's undulate, the lomandra's long and strappy.
PHOTOGRAPH DIANA SNAPE

The sensuous garden

The greatest gift of a garden is the restoration of the five senses.

Hanna Rion, *Let's Make a Flower Garden*, 1912

The enjoyment of sitting and walking in a garden is experienced not only through sight, but also through smell, hearing, touch and possibly taste. The sensuous appeal of a garden can be increased by choosing Australian plants that, when combined harmoniously, stimulate and engage the senses. Water, rocks, mulches and soil are visual features but titillate other senses too. The amount of light and warmth also contributes to the sensuous 'feel' of a garden. Appealing to instinctive human responses can help raise a garden to the sublime.

Gardens designed for people with deficient sight are very rewarding as other senses become more discerning. Whether in a hospital or at home, a sensuous garden is therapeutic for anyone who is ill, convalescing or not very mobile.

The sense of sight

A plant appeals to the sense of sight by its form and texture in addition to its colour. Forms vary enormously – forest giant to tiny lichen, tall or spreading, straight or gnarled, there is a vast array to choose from. The varying shapes of small shrubs and ground flora lend themselves to the unpretentious, cheerful effect of a sunlit wildflower, grassland or cottage garden. Soft, arching shapes of ferns and palms suggest the secret, shaded world of the rainforest gully.

We respond to the beauty of the smoothly moulded trunk and limbs of a Snow Gum (*Eucalyptus pauciflora*) and, at the other extreme, the delicate form of a Sundew (drosera), with its rosette of dainty, dew-dotted, hairy leaves and fragile stem of tiny, exquisite flowers. We enjoy the voluptuous movement in the wind of grasses or Grass Trees (xanthorrhoeas) as a wave of air passes through those finest of leaves. Movement always catches the eye – enchanting butterflies in erratic flight, darting skinks, and birds at home in the air, on land or water.

We react to many shapes in the garden with a feeling of satisfaction or pleasure. Some forms invite stroking – the rounded shape of small shrubs such as soft *Acacia cognata* 'Green Mist' and firmer dwarf *Babingtonia pluriflora*; and the neat doughnut shape of the Mat-rush *Lomandra confertifolia*. Other forms are intriguing – a mallee's rough lignotuber, shaped like a mushroom cap; the perky, upright foliage of prostrate Fern-leaf Banksia (*B. blechnifolia*); even the elegantly twisted stem of an old, woody climber. Pendent trees or shrubs have special visual appeal – for example, allocasuarinas, Weeping Myall (*Acacia pendula*), Willow Myrtle (*Agonis flexuosa*) and Weeping Pittosporum (*P. angustifolium*). Many shrubs have a fascinating pattern of trunk, branches and foliage, remarkably complex in form. Seen as a whole, foliage can have dense, overlapping structure, as in the dwarf syzygiums, with gradation in both size and colour of new foliage as a decorative bonus. The details of a plant's form give rise to its textures.

OPPOSITE: Red Mulga (*Acacia cyperophylla*) is a small tree with distinctive, intriguing Minni Ritchie bark. PHOTOGRAPH BRIAN SNAPE

Plants can be shaped to accentuate their sensuous qualities, to control the way a garden is viewed and therefore used, for example:

- a round shape on a corner tends to make one pause and look before proceeding;
- a branch trimmed to arch gracefully over a pathway has an enclosing and welcoming effect;
- a tree with its lower limbs removed gives a different message to one with its lower limbs intact – 'come and sit under me' rather than 'walk around me please, I'm sheltering something'.

The sense of smell

Smell is the most evocative of senses, capable of transporting us instantly into scenes from the past. Individual people differ in the perfumes they can detect and those they find most appealing. The plants described below are a small selection of those with flowers and leaves that will add that extra dimension of aroma. It is not difficult to create the 'smell of the bush' and no Australian garden is complete without it.

In *Old Days, Old Ways*, Dame Mary Gilmore wrote: 'At sea we smelt the rich scent of the country, different from anything we have ever known. We noticed the perfume long before we came to it. Those who had come home from Australia told us of it, and all who went to Australia looked for it.'

Fragrant plants are appreciated best when grown close to doors or windows, along paths, or in pots that you can move – not at the far end of the garden. Flower perfumes are

TOP: Belgamba Qld. The delicately fine foliage of Grass Trees such as *Xanthorrhoea latifolia* moves voluptuously in the wind, shimmering and dancing in the light.
PHOTOGRAPH DIANA SNAPE

BOTTOM: A natural garden Vic. The ornate, sculptural beauty of the unfolding fronds of Tree Ferns stirs memories of cool, shaded, rainforest gullies.
PHOTOGRAPH DIANA SNAPE

limited to seasons and flowers often release their fragrance at a particular time of day. For Native frangipani (*Hymenosporum flavum*) and Sweet Jasmine (*Jasminum suavissimum*) this occurs at dusk when their honey flow is strongest and their pollinators most active.

Leaves can be brushed against all year round – it is always tempting to crush a few leaves and test the scent. Fragrant oils produced in leaves reduce the water loss caused by strong sun and brisk air movement, so growing conditions can affect the quantity of perfume a plant produces. For example, the magnificent vanilla scent of *Acacia redolens* growing in sunny Western Australia may lose its richness if grown in a cool area of Victoria. Rain and strong sun cause plants to release aroma and the whole garden gradually develops a delicious but indefinable perfume throughout the day. Most fragrant is the scent when, after a dry spell, the first few drops of rain spatter onto the ground and the earth and its plants release their concentrated aromas into the atmosphere.

Fragrant families

Myrtaceae

The Myrtle Family – flowers and foliage – eucalypts, callistemons, melaleucas, leptospermums and many other popular genera belong to this aromatic family. One *Corymbia citriodora* (Lemon-scented Gum) and its fallen leaves can spread its delectable fragrance afar. Scent can repel insects and a form of *Leptospermum liversidgei* (Olive Tea-tree) has been marketed as 'Mossie Buster' – its aroma is one of a number that are lemon scented to some degree, including *Leptospermum petersonii* (Lemon-scented Tea-tree), *Darwinia citriodora* (Lemon-Scented Myrtle) and *Callistemon citrinus* (Crimson Bottlebrush), often not noticeably perfumed. Many small members of this family are highly aromatic, for example *Micromyrtus ciliata* (Fringed

Heath-myrtle), *Chamelaucium ciliatum* (Small Wax-plant) and *Hypocalymma robustum* (Swan River Myrtle).

Rutaceae

The Citrus Family – flowers and often foliage – boronias, philothecas, correas, leionemas, croweas and zierias. Boronias are possibly Australia's best known scented flowers, with a highly distinctive character. The Brown Boronia (*B. megastigma*) of Western Australia has been cultivated for many years for its fragrance and now has several appealing colour forms. It may be treated as an infill plant, as may Sydney's exquisite pink Native Rose (*B. serrulata*). Hardier boronias include Pinnate Boronia (*B. pinnata*) and Red Boronia (*B. heterophylla*).

Lamiaceae

The Mint and Sage Family – foliage – this family also includes lavender, rosemary, thyme and basil. Australian representatives are mentha, plectranthus, westringias and the wonderfully aromatic prostantheras, for example *P. ovalifolia*, *P. rotundifolia* (Round-leaf Mint-bush) and *P. incisa* (Cut-leaf Mint-bush). Prostantheras come in all shapes and sizes from many different habitats, arid to wet forest, so it is possible to find suitable species for any garden. Once established some prostantheras and boronias with strong-smelling leaves are immune to rabbit attack.

Mimosaceae

The Wattle Family – flowers – for many Australians the sight and smell of wattle blossom is the herald of spring. Acacias have many different perfumes though some are odourless. *A. farnesiana*, the Mimosa of the French Riviera, smells of violets; *A. nervosa* (Rib Wattle) and *A. redolens* of vanilla; *A. leprosa* is Cinnamon Wattle; *A. suaveolens* (Sweet Wattle) is not the only one described as sweet.

Proteaceae

The Protea Family – flowers – banksias, grevilleas, hakeas, dryandras and lambertias have a variety of honey scents to attract their range of pollinators.

Rainforest species

Many of the larger species can be successfully grown in pots for quite a few years.

Scented flowers: Leatherwood (*Eucryphia lucida*); Narrow-leaved Gardenia (*Randia chartacea*); Smooth Clerodendrum (*C. floribundum*); Native Frangipani (*Hymenosporum flavum*).

Scented foliage: Aniseed Tree (*Anetholea anisata*); Lemon Ironwood (*Backhousia citriodora*); Blue Lilly-pilly (*Syzygium oleosum*) – lemon; Blueberry Ash (*Elaeocarpus reticulatus*) – licorice; Oliver's Sassafras (*Cinnamomum oliveri*) – camphor-scented; Southern Sassafras (*Atherosperma moschatum*).

There are many other fragrant plants. The creeper Sweet Jasmine (*Jasminum suavissimum*) does well in cold areas despite its northern origin and flowers for months on end, given good conditions, a little water and an occasional 'haircut'. Its delightful perfume is more noticeable in warmer weather. Individual flowers of the Chocolate and Vanilla Lilies (arthropodiums) have to be held close for their scent but, if grown in a drift, the whole atmosphere will be permeated with it. An outstanding plant of the coastal heaths is Wedding Bush (*Ricinocarpos pinifolius*) with massed display of perfumed white flowers set against dark-green foliage.

A spectacular plant appreciated more overseas than here is *Calomeria amaranthoides* (Incense Plant), a member of the Daisy family in disguise that comes from the moister gullies of the east coast. This biennial plant has very large leaves and produces a dramatic plume of small flowers in reds, pinks and tans, with an all-pervading, heady perfume. In Victorian times pots of the Incense Plant were placed in ballrooms for its supposedly aphrodisiac powers. Some beautiful shrubs are better planted away from the house. Two layered plants with musky smelling flowers are the graceful Slender Myoporum (*M. floribundum*) and the sculptural *Homoranthus papillatus*, called Mouse and Honey Plant. The flowers of lovely White-plumed Grevillea (*G. leucopteris*) have a spicy aroma during the day but a less pleasant smell at night, when they attract night-flying insects for pollination.

The sense of touch

Texture is both a visual and tactile dimension – how often do we look and appreciate but not actually touch? Texture is provided by every part of a plant – bark or smooth trunk, foliage, buds, flowers and fruits – and we can enjoy the experience of touching. Natural, decorative and practical features like rocks, water, walls, fences, paving, pebbles, mulch and soil all contribute to the textural content of a garden. The materials of vertical and horizontal surfaces provide a textural background or stage against which plants are seen and we can mentally 'feel' contrasts.

Trunks and bark provide the most obvious contribution to the textures of a garden. Allocasuarinas, banksias (especially *B. serrata*) and xanthorrhoeas all have interesting corky hides. Some melaleucas and callistemons have beautiful flaky trunks like layered filo pastry. Tree Ferns and also *Allocasuarina inophloia* have matted, hairy trunks, of great interest in a small garden. Some acacias, for example *A. cyperophylla* (Red Mulga) from inland areas, have fascinating curly 'Minni Ritchie' bark. Some persoonia trunks are coloured a beautiful coppery red under a dark, flaky exterior.

OPPOSITE: Ford garden, Fülling, Vic. Designed by Gorden Ford. The winding path with its graceful and aromatic eucalypts seems entirely natural but each tree has been carefully sited. The thick understory planting along the edges reflects the influence of Edna Walling.
PHOTOGRAPH TRISHA DIXON

ABOVE: Joyce garden Vic. Designed by Paul Thompson. The effects of light can introduce a sensuous quality to a garden. Here it casts softs shadows, colours wattle blossom and allocasuarina foliage, and highlights pale eucalypt trunks. The corners of hard surfaces can be rounded for a softer effect.

PHOTOGRAPH PAUL THOMPSON

Eucalypts recommended for their bark or trunk textures

Non-shedding, rough-barked: angophoras, for example *A. floribunda* (Rough-barked Apple); corymbias, for example *C. eximia* (Yellow Bloodwood), eucalyptus, for example *E. microcorys* (Tallowwood), *E. paniculata* (Grey Ironbark), *E. sideroxylon* (Mugga).

Partial shedders: *Eucalyptus haemastoma* and *E. sclerophylla* (Scribbly Gums); *Corymbia maculata* (Spotted Gum), *E. pilularis* (NSW Blackbutt), *E. punctata* (Grey Gum), *E. pauciflora* (Snow Gum), *E. camaldulensis* (River Red Gum), *E. caesia*.

Complete shedders: *Angophora costata* (Smooth-barked Apple), *Eucalyptus deanei* (Round-leaved Gum), *Corymbia citriodora* (Lemon-scented Gum).

There are hundreds of others.

Foliage

Foliage varies enormously and ranges from the large and dramatic leaves of banksias, waratahs and rainforest plants to the tiny, fine and delicate leaves of heathland and grassland plants. Rainforest plants can provide a garden with textures other than the soft, smooth glossiness usually associated with them. The rough leaves of the Sandpaper Fig (*Ficus coronata*) were used by Aborigines to sharpen their tools. Red Jacket (*Alectryon tomentosus*) has tough, hairy leaflets and capsules with red-coated seeds each resembling a bird's eye (its other common name). Oliver's Sassafras (*Cinnamomum oliveri*) has outstanding crinkly-edged, pink, new growth.

Ferns also are wonderful textural plants, as shown by a variety of common names – Maidenhair, Birds-nest, Gristle, Rough, Soft, Scaly and Tender Ferns. Clubmosses, small plants which resemble tiny forests, live happily with ferns in damp conditions and can add yet another textural dimension to a garden. Mosses and lichens decorate surfaces with fine and intricate textures. Prickly or spiky plants suggest that you stop and admire them from a respectful distance, though you can touch warily to help identification. In contrast, softly drooping foliage like that of *Acacia cognata* (Bower Wattle) is calming and beckoning. Some plants encourage touching or stroking – many banksias have new growth that looks and feels like rufous velvet. *Adenanthos sericea* (Woollybush) is also true to its appearance with fine, soft foliage reminiscent of silk. *Persoonia pinifolia* (Pine-leaved Geebung) is another. However *Scleranthus biflorus* (Knawel) looks like a soft, low, mossy cushion but feels almost prickly.

The sense of hearing

Sound can be created both naturally and artificially in a sensuous garden. Introducing a waterfall or fountain, windchimes or music, is one way. Planting trees and shrubs, which by their form and texture create windsong, is another. Allocasuarina groves sigh and whisper as winds disturb their foliage – a soothing and stimulating sound. Eucalypts and conifers tinkle, growl or whistle, palms and hanging bark rustle. A flowering eucalypt or leptospermum invites the whir and hum of insects and the songs of birds attracted by food, either in the flowers or on the wing. The evocative calls of magpies, willie wagtails and other birds create a distinctly Australian soundscape. By providing habitat and food sources for native birds, frogs, reptiles and insects you create the most joyous sound of all – nature in harmony.

The sense of taste

Australian plants have been providing people with a wide variety of edible fruits, nuts, shoots and tubers for thousands of years. Rainforests produce a large amount of this food and their bush tucker plants can be included in a garden for taste in addition to other senses. An edible landscape can be laid out following permaculture principles. Plants that are highly ornamental as well as valuable in a serious bush food collection include:

- Brush Cherry (*Syzygium australe*), Riberry (*S. luehmannii*) and Blue Lilly-pilly (*S. oleosum*).
- Davidson's Plum (*Davidsonia pruriens*) – the purple plums can be made into jam.
- Finger Lime (*Citrus australasica*) – tangy lemon fruit for jam or drinks.
- Small-leafed Tamarind (*Diploglottis campbellii*) – excellent for shade; reputedly the best eating tamarind.
- Walking Stick Palm (*Linospadix monostachya*) – an attractive small palm with edible red fruit.
- Peanut Tree (*Sterculia quadrifida*) – peanut flavoured seeds eaten directly from leathery pods.
- *Backhousia citriodora* and *Anetholea anisata* – chew, brew or tear the leaves for flavouring teas or salad dressings.
- Bush Nut (macadamia): Rough-shelled (*M. tetraphylla*) and Smooth-shelled (*M. integrifolia*) both grown commercially.
  Among smaller plants:
- Mountain Pepper (*Tasmannia lanceolata*) – all parts have a hot flavour, concentrated in the dried fruits.
- Midgen Berry (*Austromyrtus dulcis*) – tasty small fruits that make a good jam.

All parts of a plant contribute to the sensuous appeal that is an intrinsic part of a garden's design – the fragility of a flower, the ripe solidity of a fruit, the smoothness of a tree trunk. An Australian garden relies heavily on evergreen foliage as its most constant and significant sensuous component. Foliage is particularly important in linking a garden into a visually cohesive whole whilst capturing windsong and providing intriguing textures and delightful scent. As a heightened awareness frees the imagination, gratifying all our senses will become an innate part of the Australian garden.

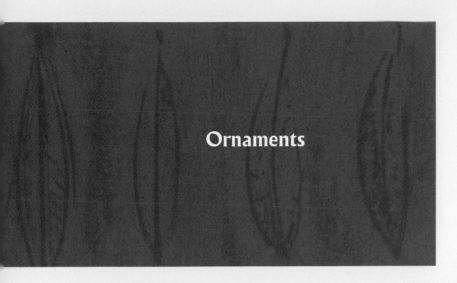

Ornaments

Garden sculpture should mirror its environs. There is nothing wrong with pink flamingos or plaster gnomes, providing the garden is located in flamingo or gnome country.

Roger B. Swain, 'Christmas Goose', *Horticulture*, December 1985

Furniture, sculptures, containers or lighting enhance a garden and give it a dimension beyond just plants. This aspect of garden design is very personal and you may choose to wait until the garden is mature, or something inspires you.

Designer and author Russell Page says:

'Analyse the underlying structure and rhythm of the scene. Is a feature where it is because it is necessary and useful, underlining a compelling rhythm, form, shape, pattern of texture? Or is it a decorative whimsy copied from elsewhere with no real relevance? Stick closely to the material in use on the site and when designing details keep it simple.'

Most ornamental pieces have an association with garden styles of the past. Italian and French gardens have left a legacy of classically inspired statues, fountains and sundials; the English cottage garden the birdbaths, seats, arches and wells; the Japanese garden the calming simplicity of raked pebbles, placed rocks and the famous red bridge. Paving, tiles, archways and water features in strict geometric pattern come from ancient Islamic gardens. You can incorporate versions of these elements successfully into a garden of Australian plants, providing they harmonize with their environment. Garden art, decorative or functional, can be made of local material or a quite different material that complements the surroundings. Its size, shape, colour and texture should relate to the overall picture. Ornamentation is limited only by the width of your imagination and the depth of your pocket.

Garden furniture

Garden seats are usually among the most important, early additions – it is a shame not to be able to sit and relax while enjoying your garden. Garden furniture can be decorative as well as functional. A seat can be as natural as a log, a rock or a sawn-off tree stump, though these may not remain comfortable for very long. Timber seats in many styles are widely popular, some carved out of a single trunk or woven from flexible branches. A simple bench made from railway sleepers is easy to construct (though heavy to move) and blends in a natural garden. Timber seats can have a natural finish or introduce a strong colour. Old seats painted bright purple-blue or deep red can look striking, a splash of colour like the flowers of an eremophila or the flash of a Crimson Rosella. Fine, light steel or wrought-iron seats can almost disappear against fine foliage. Furniture can be beautiful – the luxury in both comfort and appearance of Margot Knox's mosaic sofa in Melbourne is memorable. Nearby plant forms and foliage need strength to match the solidity of substantial seats like this sofa.

Seats can entice the gardener or visitor – in a quiet, sheltered position, perhaps shaded by a tree; beside a pond, where birds will come; with a garden vista to enjoy, or a view over the countryside. Ideally the seat will be somewhat screened from weather and the outside world but it will need

OPPOSITE: Don & Marea Burke's garden NSW. Stylish lily pads add elegance to this area of an indigenous garden. PHOTOGRAPH LORNA ROSE

sufficient open space for you to admire your garden handiwork. Tables are less important but may also be useful and will complement seating.

Sculpture

In the past natural structures such as rocks and logs have provided the main ornamental decoration in gardens of Australian plants. A few, very large granite boulders could create a place for meditation, reflection and contemplation. An expert with a chain-saw can carve a bold design in timber. Garden designers tend to restrict the use of more formal ornaments to formal gardens. In contrast to furniture, sculpture has no obvious function in a natural garden but is further evidence of human intervention.

It is exciting when any sculpture, realistic or abstract, has its own intrinsic value through the skill and artistry of its creator. Simplicity of line and form, as in truly classical styles, is always effective. If architectural plant forms don't exist, a sculpture can be a striking focal point. It can close a vista or be a point of diversion and interest. You can beautify a quiet corner with a sculpture, or tuck it away in an inconspicuous spot to be dis-

covered with surprise and delight. Its material – stone, wood, metal, glass or concrete – can contrast with and complement foliage textures and the vitality of living plants. Its shape can reflect, relate to, or deliberately differ from, nearby shapes in the garden. It can emphasise height, weight, intricacy or space. Achieving such effects may be intuitive at first and develop further over time.

A unique piece of sculpture may be expensive but, alternatively, a friend or family member could create it quite cheaply. Something mass-produced can also have great appeal if it looks 'just right'. A sculpture needs to be well sited for best effect so consider its position carefully, especially if it is heavy.

ABOVE: Margot Knox's garden Vic. A fabulous mosaic sofa, luxurious and comfortable, invites relaxation in a blended garden featuring plants with large leaves and strong forms, including dianellas (Flax Lilies). PHOTOGRAPH DIANA SNAPE

OPPOSITE: Royal Botanic Garden, Cranbourne Vic. A number of these unique, highly decorative sculptures by David Wong were first displayed in the International Flower and Garden Show standing in a formal pool, which related visually to a large lake beyond. The sculptures explore the textures of dried plant materials – stems, foliage, fruits and nuts layered in intricate arrangements in large wire cages. PHOTOGRAPH DIANA SNAPE

A sculpture can epitomise some aspect of the garden or its locality, for example in a coastal garden a metal cormorant with its wings outstretched to dry, atop a pole. Sculpture colour can be neutral or strong, such as bright red to complement the garden's green. In or beside water, it will emphasise the beauty of water with its reflection. It might enhance the garden throughout the year or just disguise an occasional bald patch, or even add a touch of humour. Modern sculpture is as varied as modern art. There are many intriguing artworks (or 'junk sculpture') made from pieces of wrought iron and old machinery parts. If creatively made and in the right setting, these can introduce an element of Australian quirkiness or flair.

Ornaments

Fountains are sculptures linked to water and their variety is great, with simple or ornate designs, geometric, abstract, or based on organic shapes. They introduce the sound and light play of moving water and can provide an attractive focal point, especially in a tiny townhouse garden. Windchimes in gardens are small sculptures that embellish the sound of the wind. Their size, appearance and tones differ greatly – some need more wind to activate them and are less intrusive than others that respond to the slightest air movement. Wall plaques, mosaic work and mirrors can enhance vertical surfaces – the interface between house and garden – and mosaic work can also decorate paving, birdbaths and even artificial rocks. A mirror reflecting part of the garden can appear to double its apparent space.

Stone, cement and metal animal sculptures are numerous, and it can be fun to hunt for one that takes your fancy at weekend markets or nurseries. They can be romantic, kitsch or quite idiosyncratic – sheep, kangaroos, lizards, frogs or birds.

Our flora is unique yet exotic plants (even ivy!) still feature in garden hardware and in decorations on pots. For a distinctively Australiana look, garden beds could be created in unique boomerang shapes. Another quintessentially Australian symbol – a large, constructed 'termite mound' – could feature in a small urban garden alongside a brightly painted house. A garden and its ornamentation may be quite idiosyncratic – garden design can be fun!

Practical ornaments

Sundials and floral clocks express fascination with time, the fourth dimension of gardens. A sundial is more than a decoration; if it is properly built and sited, you may leave your watch inside. A terracotta sundial in an inland garden, on top of a black tree stump, matches the red dirt and provides a wonderful contrast near grey and silver foliage. Weather vanes are also practical as well as decorative.

A birdbath is an integral part of an Australian garden. It may be as simple as a discarded shallow pan, a pottery bowl set in the top of a terracotta pipe, or a designed birdbath, such as a slightly curved dish placed on top of a wrought-iron stem, or a ceramic creation. If there are cats in the neighbourhood, a tall stem (a metre or more) is essential. Siting is important, with provision for clear flight paths, a branch for birds to observe from and shelter to retreat to. Silky Hakea (*H. sericea*), or Bushy Needlewood (*H. decurrens*) and *Grevillea rosmarinifolia* are good 'pricklies' that birds appreciate and cats do not.

Found objects (which once were useful) can give pleasure too. Disused farm machinery, an old farm cart or hand-plough can give a country garden local 'feel'. However, if larger objects do not fit the 'sense of place', the effect may be kitsch. If you have less space, you could create an interesting corner with a harrow among groundcover plants, for example scaevolas. In a coastal garden, discarded tackle from fishing boats, old lobster pots or net floats look 'at home'. Many collected articles such

OPPOSITE: Sculpture Garden, National Gallery ACT. Designed by Harry Howard. In one area of the Sculpture Garden, strong and elegant sculptures by Robert Klippel stand in shallow water against a splendid backdrop of handsome River Oaks (*Casuarina cunninghamiana*). These superb gardens were designed on a grand scale and with visionary foresight in 1982.
PHOTOGRAPH DIANA SNAPE

ABOVE: Box Hill Community Centre Vic. A whimsical fence carved by members of the local community.

PHOTOGRAPH DIANA SNAPE

as terracotta jars, old chimney-pots, bottles on a table or pieces of tile, make intriguing pictures within a garden. They are evocative reminders of past adventures and good times and also provide a cosy home for reptiles and insects.

Containers

Plants in containers add ornamentation to any garden, rather like pictures in a house, and may be moved to try different conditions. In a very small garden they give scope for wonderful design. You can bring a plant in bloom out to a conspicuous position. Plants that die in containers are easily replaced and a container plant can temporarily fill an unexpected 'hole' in the garden. A pot may be used to grow a single plant, highlighting its attractive form and foliage. A large, low pot or half-barrel can grow two or three plants together to create a miniature garden. In either case, design aspects such as choosing the proportions and degree of symmetry or asymmetry are important. Containers should complement the plants in both size and colour. You can prune a single plant to a spherical or other defined shape, allow it to run riot, or somewhere in between. Choosing the plants to combine in a miniature garden is a delight, similar to designing a much larger one but more focused.

Most containers are small, formal structures that provide a link between the house and garden. In any large garden centre the choice of shapes, sizes and materials is immense; some potteries sell 'seconds'. Pots may come in a natural material such as terracotta, ranging from low bowls to tall pipes; or be highly glazed in white, black or bright colours. Barrels are large and solid and suit more substantial plants. The insides of old coppers are almost as ample and the outsides more colourful. Hollow logs or old tree stumps seem part of the garden. You can place a pot into the hollow or plant directly into it.

Pot plants need far more regular watering than those growing in the ground. Containers need to be placed where they are easy to water and can enjoy the required shade or

ABOVE: Tootell garden Vic. A metal cormorant dries its wings in a coastal garden, its colour matching that of leptospermum foliage and toning with grevillea flowers. It does not object to being rusty.

PHOTOGRAPH DIANA SNAPE

sunlight. Pots make attractive barriers and you can use them as traffic controllers. Among smaller or more delicate plants the bulk and/or height of a container will tend to be a focal point.

If you introduce a number of containers and plants into a garden, design is necessary. A scattering of pots without any planning is unattractive. An example of extremely formal design is an evenly spaced row of similar pots with similar plants (nowadays often dwarf Lilly Pillies) lining a front path. A matched pair might appeal, on either side of a door or seat, or at symmetrical focal points. In a less formal arrangement, with variations possible in sizes of both pots and plants, either an even or odd number of pots can look good. A grouping could range from low pots in the front to taller ones at the back; or be a cluster of pots of similar sizes with one very large or tall one; a group of pots here and a couple over there; and so on. The scope for design is tremendous. In a focal area, you could group plants in pots with logs, stumps and terracotta birdbaths, or a small water feature.

Imaginative displays can reflect the special nature of Australian plants, for instance simple iron stands and terracotta pots beautifully display Bird's-nest Ferns. The ferns can sit at any height in rows or in a pattern. The result emphasises the unique character of these ferns, their large, simple leaves spreading umbrella fashion as if suspended in space. It mimics the growth of these ferns high in forest trees but enables much better viewing, and you can control their conditions. The range of outstanding Australian plants for pots is huge, with unique appearance, long life and minimal maintenance needs. Desirable but fussy plants can be tended easily in a container. Even large trees such as some conifers and rainforest trees will adapt well to life in a large pot.

Many small, decorative Australian plants are very well suited to growing in a hanging basket or window box – a few examples include *Scaevola aemula* (Fan Flower), *Dampiera diversifolia*, *Hibbertia dentata* (Trailing Guinea-flower) and *Brachyscome angustifolia* (Stiff Daisy).

Lighting

Lighting can embellish a garden at night and also increase safety and security. However one disadvantage of lighting is its disrupting effect on night-flying insects and possibly micro-bats and owls, so avoid using lights unnecessarily. Lights that are activated by movement are useful and economical. Areas far away from house electricity can now have lights powered by solar energy. Lamps can suit the part of the garden you wish to show – carriage lights beside the drive, round lights for softer plant shapes in the garden. Low down-lighting or side-lighting using soft yellow lights, well spaced, may be best for paths and particularly steps. Avoid glare by hiding or screening the light source, for example behind foliage or in a corner of a low wall.

Lighting the foreground and midground of a garden scene creates a superb picture with a three-dimensional effect of plants in the landscape. A ground-level spotlight shining upwards works magic on a handsome eucalyptus trunk and branches in the background. Evenly lit areas should balance well with smaller darker areas to produce a subtle and intriguing effect, as shadows contribute interest and a better perception of depth.

Accent or feature lighting shows up beautifully the forms and textures of a variety of shrubs and trees. You can backlight the fronds of a tree-fern using a low light concealed behind its trunk, or uplight the corky trunk of *Allocasuarina torulosa* (Rose She-oak), the felty underleaves of *Banksia marginata* (Silver Banksia), or a coppiced *Eucalyptus polybractea* (Blue Mallee). Accent lighting will display a special sculpture or water feature and fascinating effects can be obtained by designing with light from fibre-optic light sources and mist.

Ornamental structures

A range of ornamental structures including arches, pergolas and gazebos can be built as part of the initial hard landscaping or as additions. In traditional cottage gardens, arches over the entrance were usually wooden lattice work. Nowadays they are available as coated metal arches which, until covered with plants, can look rather raw. Many Australian climbing plants will grow over an arch very quickly but, the faster they grow, the more pruning they may require to keep them trim. *Clematis aristata* (Austral Clematis) and *Pandorea pandorana* (Wonga Vine) both have glossy leaves and creamy white flowers, *P.* 'Golden Showers' slightly smaller orange-gold flowers; vigorous *P. jasminoides* (Bower Vine) larger pink; *Kennedia coccinea* (Coral Vine) showy orange and pink flowers.

A pergola can be attached to the side of a house, or be free-standing, or provide a covered walk leading to another 'room' in the garden. Traditionally an arbour, it is usually flat-topped with trellis supporting climbing plants similar to those recommended for covering an arch. Construction may be rustic, using unshaped tree branches of tea-tree (lepto-spermums) or Raspberry Jam wood (*Acacia acuminata* ssp. *acuminata*); or more formal, using treated timber. In summer a pergola can also support shade-cloth over a hot patio, sheltering delicate plants or a seat. Shade sails are a popular, modern alternative with an Australian feel.

A gazebo is a more substantial roofed structure, quite separate from the house and suitable for a spacious garden. It usually includes seats for admiring a view and, in an exposed garden, provides shelter.

Ornaments in gardens range from the practical and useful to the purely whimsical and decorative. Your choice of ornament is a personal thing – follow your heart as well as your head. Ornaments will gradually become an integral part of the garden, an object you love adding beauty to a place you love.

OPPOSITE: 'Offshore' Vic. Designed by Jane Burke. In this coastal garden, a craypot's rounded form mimics that of a Cushion Bush (*Leucophyta brownii*) or a White Correa (*C. alba*), with Knobby Club-rush (*Ficinia nodosa*) and Coast Spear-grass (*Austrostipa stipoides*) as contrasting linear forms. The ornament quietly introduces a human note into the garden.
PHOTOGRAPH SIMON GRIFFITHS

Learning along the way

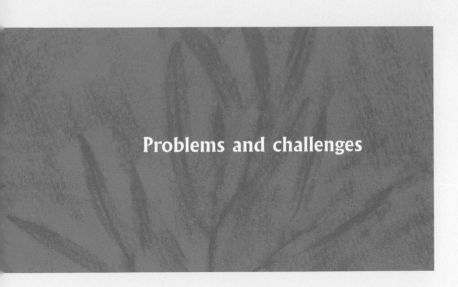

Problems and challenges

Unlike people, gardens never strive for perpetual youth –
they want to look old from the day they were born.
Their greatest glory comes with maturity.

Thomas D. Church, *Gardens are for People*, 1955

Whatever size your garden, problems may arise to challenge you. The more extreme the environment the greater will be the limitations. However the fewer the choices, the more effective the resulting design may be.

While accepting your garden's limits and exploiting its strengths, you may still need to find planting solutions to specific problems. Some commonly experienced difficulties are discussed below. In looking for solutions you will need to be mindful of the size of plant that you want and how it fits into the overall design. The more remote and extreme the environment, the more helpful will be advice from keen Australian plant gardeners living in your district. A publication likely to be of great value in identifying plants suitable for a range of specific conditions is *Grow What Where* by the Australian Plant Study Group. This information is also available on CD Rom.

From sunshine to shade

As a garden matures and ages, the growth of trees will result in more shade. Sun-loving plants like grevilleas will start to look unhealthy and, at some stage, need to be removed and replaced by shade-tolerant plants. Because of thirsty tree roots a shady garden area will more typically be dry. Examples in nature of shady dry areas are dry sclerophyll forests, while shady moist areas exist in some rainforests and mountain or coastal gullies.

Decide whether your garden has dry or moist shade, and select the most appropriate plants. Refer to those listed on page 217. In shady, moist gardens, rainforest trees will grow well under established trees as a middlestorey for they rarely achieve their full height out of their normal environment.

Dry sites in a mild climate

Plenty of dry sites exist in gardens in areas of Australia that receive reasonable rainfall. Plants suggested for a dry, sunny site are listed on page 217. Steep embankments can prove difficult and so too can gardens with many large, established trees. The challenge is increased if these factors are combined. Terracing across a steep slope will help retard water run-off, or you can partially bury large rocks to provide water storage and a cool root run for nearby plants. You can also use such rocks to help create a sloping creek bed and maybe even waterfalls.

One way of trapping water is to dig trenches behind planting sites and fill them with hidden stone or mulch. Water then travels quickly below surface level to where it can be stored away from the drying elements of sun and wind, and

PREVIOUS PAGE: A natural forest garden NSW. Dramatically textured Burrawangs (*Macrozamia communis*), tolerant of shade, form an impressive understorey beneath magnificent Spotted Gums (*Corymbia maculata*). An individual macrozamia is an excellent feature plant for a garden and massed as here they are stunning. PHOTOGRAPH DIANA SNAPE

OPPOSITE: Aitken garden NSW. A steep, shady and moist slope has been stabilised by the introduction of many rocks to form a creek bed to channel water run-off and prevent erosion. Planting of a selection of ferns and flowering Rock Orchid (*Thelychiton speciosus*) has created a beautiful and natural effect. PHOTOGRAPH DIANA SNAPE

used by plants through upward capillary action. Another successful method is to bury large, plastic drink bottles quite close to the plant. With nail holes punched in the bottoms and screw tops firmly on, water will be released slowly. This also encourages roots to reach down, away from the dry surface. You can fill the bottles in stress times and totally hide them with mulch.

To nurture plants through their first critical year of life, choose a favourable time of year for planting. After the first seasonal rains when there is moisture in the soil is ideal; soak pots in water before planting and water in well. Planting in autumn gives a plant six to nine months to establish before it meets the stress periods of summer. In cold climates, spring is favoured for planting. You can closely monitor water needs for a while after planting. If necessary a soil-wetting agent can help attract water molecules to soil particles. Mulch is also invaluable (see following chapter).

Planting under established Australian trees

Except in a wet rainforest environment, planting under large trees can be a problem because the soil will be dry. There are two reasons for this. First, rain collected on the canopy is lost through wind and sun evaporation. Only persistent rains over long periods enable a reasonable amount of water to reach the ground. Secondly, mature trees use a large quantity of water from the surrounding area for their survival. If you have a number of large trees then shade may further limit the range of suitable plants. Enjoying and appreciating a tree garden with some grasses in the understorey may be a simple and appealing solution. Another possibility for a small area is an irrigation system to be used only sparingly.

Plants for dry shaded and dry sunny situations are listed below.

Windy sites

Windbreaks cannot always eliminate the problems of windy sites and regular exposure to strong winds presents a challenge for the gardener. However, frequent strong winds are likely to produce plants that are stronger and more compact in their growth habit than plants growing in protected situations. To maximise the chances of a plant surviving long enough to establish a strong root system, choose plants that are compact rather than leggy. Look for strong growth at the base, multiple branching just above the soil level, or evidence of new growth near the base. Plants will grow stronger without the support of stakes. If stakes are unavoidable, use three with a tie around all, leaving the plant free to move within this triangle until its roots have strengthened. If a plant is leggy, or grows too quickly, prune it to allow root development to keep pace with growth above ground. Placing plants near rocks may provide them with physical protection and a means of anchoring their roots. Wind is a greater drying element than sun and mulch or groundcover plants will conserve a substantial quantity of moisture.

Microclimates

Different microclimates within the garden can provide areas of shelter for plants that are sensitive to wind, frost or excessive sun. To some extent wind and temperature can be controlled by structures, partially buried rocks and protective planting. Solid walls facing north provide reflected and stored heat that varies with the change in angle and temperature of the sun. Trees shade areas from heat and light but also create partial rain shadows. Certain plants can be used as indicators, surviving but not thriving in conditions that may harm other plants, for example prostantheras (Mint Bushes) quickly indicate a need for water.

OPPOSITE: Larkin garden Vic. Designed by Roger Stone. Orange-flowering *Grevillea tenuiloba* cascades over large rocks which help retain a steep slope. The small mat plant, Stalked Guinea-flower (*Hibbertia pedunculata*), benefits from the cool root run provided.
PHOTOGRAPH DIANA SNAPE

RIGHT: Guymer and Aitchison garden Vic. Designed by Douglas Blythe. Groundcovers and tufted plants follow the contours of the slope and stabilise it. Small grassland plants make use of shelter – shade and moisture – offered by rocks.
PHOTOGRAPH DIANA SNAPE

Plants for difficult sites

The following three lists provide a few examples of plants with different characteristics and qualities for use in design in a range of climatic conditions and problem sites. Exhaustive lists would be impossible as geological, geographic and climatic differences are too great over the whole of Australia.

1. Dry and Shaded

Groundcovers: various correas, hardenbergias, kennedias, Common Emu-bush (*Eremophila glabra*), Woolly Grevillea (*G. lanigera*), Rough Halgania (*H. cyanea*), Velvet-bush (*Lasiopetalum floribundum*), *Einadia nutans*

Shrubs: various acacias, correas, phebaliums, philothecas, thomasias and westringeas, also Silver Banksia (*B. marginata*), Coast Banksia (*B. integrifolia*) and Hairpin Banksia (*B. spinulosa*), *Senna artemisioides*, also try *Babingtonia densifolia* and *B. pluriflora*, boronias such as Forest Boronia (*B. muelleri*), Tall Boronia (*B. molloyae*), Fraser's Boronia (*B. fraseri*) and *B. denticulata*, NSW Christmas Bush (*Cera-topetalum gummiferum*), Austral Indigo (*Indigofera australis*)

Accent plants: many grasses, Spreading Flax-lily (*Dianella revoluta*), Paroo Lily (*D. caerulea*), Spiny-headed Mat-rush (*Lomandra longifolia*) and Wattle Mat-rush (*L. filiformis*)

2. Dry and Sunny

Groundcovers: as in (1) except the lasiopetalum; in addition Rough Guinea-flower (*Hibbertia aspera*), Creeping Myoporum (*M. parvifolium*), Mat Bush-pea (*Pultenaea pedunculata*) and prostrate forms of the following acacias, Flinders Range Wattle (*A. iteaphylla*), Sticky Wattle (*A. howittii*), Ovens Wattle (*A. pravissima*)

Shrubs: as in (1) except thomasias; in addition various acacias, for example Gold Dust Wattle (*A. acinacea*) and *A. aspera*, Saw or Old Man Banksia (*B. serrata*), Hop Bushes (dodonaeas), for example *D. sinuolata* (syn. *D. adenophra*) and *D. viscosa* ssp. *cuneata*, Silky Hakea (*H. sericea*) or Bushy Needlewood (*H. decurrens*).

Accent plants: as in (1)

3. Moist and Shaded

Groundcovers: Hop Goodenia (*G. ovata*) and Swamp Goodenia (*G. humilis*), Climbing Guinea-flower (*Hibbertia scandens*), Swamp Mazus (*M. pumilio*), Matted Pratia (*Lobelia pedunculata*), violas

Shrubs: Cinnamon Wattle (*Acacia leprosa*) and Bower Wattle (*A. cognata*), *Astartea fascicularis*, Wiry Baurea (*B. rubioides*) and Grampians Bauera (*B. sessiliflora*), Fern-leaf Baeckea (*Babingtonia crenulata*), Swamp Banksia (*B. robur*) and Hairpin Banksia (*B. spinulosa*), various callistemons, hibiscus and leptospermums, Yellow Hakea (*H. nodosa*), Royal Grevillea (*G. victoriae*), melaleucas, for example Showy Honey-myrtle (*Melaleuca nesophila*), Scented Paperbark (*M. squarrosa*), Thyme Honey-myrtle (*M. thymifolia*) and *M. violacea*

Accent plants: Morning Flag (*Orthrosanthus multiflorus*) and Morning Iris (*O. laxus*), Slender Palm-lily (*Cordyline stricta*), Black Bristle-rush (*Chorizandra enodis*), Purple Flags (*Patersonia occidentalis*) and Grass Flags (libertias).

PREVIOUS PAGE: A natural woodland garden. A bushfire can bring rejuvenation and a spectacular display of a pioneer infill plant. *Calomeria amaranthoides* or Incense Plant, can help restore morale. This is a member of the Daisy family from the moister gullies of the east coast.
PHOTOGRAPH DIANA SNAPE

OPPOSITE: Larkin garden Vic. Designed by Roger Stone. Massed plantings of Marsh Banksia (*B. paludosa*) (foreground) and groundcover plants such as *Grevillea* 'Poorinda Royal Mantle' and *Lasiopetalum micranthum* will cover large areas of embankments to dramatic effect. Organic mulch covering bare soil is supplemented as it gradually breaks down.
PHOTOGRAPH CHRIS LARKIN

ABOVE: Joyce garden Vic. Designed by Paul Thompson. Dry, shady areas under established trees can be a problem in a garden for later planting. Here the borders to a driveway lined with acacias and eucalypts have been left with few understorey plants for a pleasant, relaxed look. Otherwise a number of tolerant understorey plants may be chosen from those listed.
PHOTOGRAPH DIANA SNAPE

Managing your garden

The secret of landscapes isn't creation ...
It's maintenance.

Michael Dolan, 'Public Works', *Garden Design*, July/August 1992

Once your garden is established, its continuing management involves maintenance, renewal and redesign. Garden maintenance includes somewhat mundane activities such as weeding, mulching, grass cutting, raking gravel paths, sweeping hard surfaces and controlling pests. These activities need to be carried out fairly regularly to keep the garden pleasing so you can fully enjoy the design.

Redesigning a garden suggests major changes – removal of a tree or lawn, reshaping a garden bed, establishing a new path or pond. On the other hand, renewal of a garden involves more minor changes such as the ongoing work of pruning, removing plants and planting new ones. It includes being ruthless with unhealthy plants or those that 'don't work' with their neighbours. It is impossible to predict precisely how most plants will grow, nor their health in the short or long term. Factors such as soil and climate variations (on the macro and micro level), normal ageing, disease and death of plants, weed and pest invasion, even falling leaves and broken branches, contribute quite naturally to effect

change. Both redesign and renewal are part of the process of ongoing design that is at the heart of good gardening. 'A garden designed to present a certain appearance and to remain this way is doomed to failure', said designer John Stoward. This is why gardening is so attractive – it is a creative past-time that can fully engage mind, body and soul.

Plant knowledge and vision

Continuing to learn about plants, particularly local ones, will help you successfully manage your garden into the future. There is often room to experiment and take risks in trying out less well-known plants – isn't this part of the fun? However, a healthy, vigorous garden cannot be based on risky plants. They are infills, not framework plants.

Professional help may be valuable but you will want to acquire your own skills and knowledge to develop a sensitivity for using plants effectively in your garden. Achieving a beautiful garden is a process, a journey without a destination but with many points of beauty along the way. This is true largely because the plants, so central to successfully realising any garden design, will continue on their unstoppable life cycles of growth, expansion and death.

As there are relatively few Australian plant gardens it is not always easy to see the growth habits of plants that will work for you. Visiting nurseries and Open Gardens, using the local library and buying Australian plant books are ways to learn but you may still feel that you don't really have a clear visual picture of what the plants will look like. Becoming a member of a local branch of the Australian Plant Society (or

OPPOSITE: Jacobs garden Vic. A well-managed garden including a wonderful variety and combination of form, texture and colour. Pruning is carried out where required. In the foreground on the right is a fine-leafed form of *Lomandra longifolia* (Spiny-headed Mat-rush) and, nearer the house, *Eucalyptus leucoxylon* (Yellow Gum) has been coppiced.
PHOTOGRAPH IAN LITTLER

Society for Growing Australian Plants) can provide opportunities to visit gardens and discuss particular plants in detail.

You can also learn about designing with plants by observing how they relate to each other and the environment in their natural settings. One of the great rewards from Australian plant gardening is an increased ability to appreciate the natural beauty of our land.

Learning the names of plants is a challenge but the rewards are many and the task will become much easier over time. A major benefit of knowing botanical names is that to distinguish the plant you need to pay attention to its specific characteristics – its foliage, floral display and growth habit. Such knowledge then better equips you to make informed decisions about how to use the plant in the design of your garden.

Learning about plants is only part of the story. Being able to use plants effectively in garden design is the real challenge. Many factors should be borne in mind when choosing plants for specific spots. In a well-managed garden the physical

work follows on from research, contemplation, thinking and decision-making as a means of realising your vision.

Organic mulches

Mulching is one of the secrets in successfully maintaining a garden, particularly a large one. The structure of both sandy and clay soils will benefit from the addition and working in of organic mulch for different (almost opposite) reasons. In a freely draining sandy soil mulch will help retain moisture and provide nutrients; in a clay soil it will improve structure and drainage.

In open areas and garden beds, organic mulches on the surface have definite advantages and a key one is the suppression of weeds. Mulches supply nutrients on decomposition and create a more favourable environment for beneficial soil organisms such as worms and fungi. They help retain moisture in the soil that would otherwise be lost through evaporation from wind and sun. However you will eventually need to re-mulch parts of the garden because this

natural material breaks down sooner or later in time depending on the type of mulch, the microclimate and the activity of animals such as the common blackbird or, if you are lucky, bandicoots or lyrebirds. Organic mulch absorbs water and to some extent hinders the penetration of rain into the soil. In the driest mulched sections mulch should be scraped back to allow good rains to soak in. After seasonal rains the mulch can be spread again. If you are on tank water and have an excess in winter, watering dry sections during rainy periods will help water penetrate below the surface level of the soil. Groundcover plants can effectively replace the need for mulch, especially if they have good dense foliage.

Organic mulches can have disadvantages. Fine materials, such as sawdust, can matt and prevent water penetration. Light rains may do no more than wet the surface of the mulch while underneath a dry crust forms. This is a problem on garden beds but on paths or small openings in the garden it becomes a virtue, as water is shed onto plants around the edge. Sawdust can be used on beds if soil-wetting agents and

nitrogenous fertiliser are added. This enables soil micro-flora to break down the wood fibres eventually enriching and improving the soil underneath. Sawdust is also guaranteed free of weed seeds. Other organic mulches may limit self-seeding of all plants (not just the unwanted weeds) but introduce weed seeds. Such mulches are not suitable for frost-prone garden beds (again this does not matter on paths or open spaces) – it seems a completely flat surface attracts less frost.

Eucalypts provide (free of charge) attractive and appropriate leaf, twig and bark litter, to mulch and integrate garden beds or open space. You can either rake them for a tidy surface or leave them where they fall to weather over time. Although not characteristic of all natural areas of Australia, eucalypt mulch can be attractive when it complements the garden style. Organic mulches such as pinebark look less formal than hard surfaces and weather fittingly. Optimum thickness of the layer of mulch varies depending on the local conditions and the type of material – 100mm is probably too thick except for very coarse materials; for finer materials, a maximum of 50mm is preferable. In any area, you can apply organic mulches when needed and rake them back when not. They should be kept away from plant stems to reduce risk of collar rot.

OPPOSITE LEFT: Armstrong garden Vic. A small to medium tree of an appropriate size for a suburban garden, *Eucalyptus polybractea* (Blue Mallee) in this garden is coppiced every fifth year to enhance its mallee form.
PHOTOGRAPH DIANA SNAPE

OPPOSITE RIGHT: Cleaver garden Vic. The lower branches of a group of *Leptospermum laevigatum* (Coast Tea-tree) have been removed to give the effect of small trees. Light – an important element in design – shines through their fine trunks.
PHOTOGRAPH DIANA SNAPE

ABOVE: Pruning in front of a barber's house NSW.
PHOTOGRAPH JO HAMBRETT

Pests

Pests in a garden of Australian plants are rarely a concern. Birds keep most problems under control as part of the natural ecosystem. The butterflies we enjoy were once caterpillars and few of these or other insects do enough damage to require intervention and treatment. Occasional real problems, such as slugs and snails damaging young plants, may require control.

Pruning

Pruning is necessary to maintain the health and shape of many plants. It contributes to regular maintenance and is often vital in garden renewal. As plants perform according to their specific microclimate, it is often difficult to choose the right plant for each spot, though greater knowledge does lead to greater success. The first experience of pruning for many gardeners is when they are forced to cut plants back, because groundcovers are spilling out on to walkways or larger plants are restricting a pathway. When foliage is weighed down by rain you will see whether you have pruned these plants sufficiently.

If you are pruning from necessity, carefully observe what happens to the plants in about six to twelve months. Most plants will respond with new healthy growth. Gardeners are sometimes far too anxious about when and how to prune. Books are available on the subject and you can gain confidence by cutting back plants to bring neatness and order to the garden. As you learn from experience you can apply the technique of pruning more generally as a way of managing and enhancing the beauty of individual plants and the garden as a whole.

Australian plants have evolved over time and have adapted to being pruned by fire, frost, wind and the appetites of Australian marsupials. Plants are frequently fast growing and will need to be kept in check to stop them quickly becoming 'leggy' and unsightly. Judicious pruning can modify a plant's growth habit and regular tip pruning from an early age will produce a tidier, healthier, more bushy specimen. Untidy plants may blend into the landscape of the bush but they rarely look appropriate in the artificial situation of a garden. Pruning will increase the number of flowers on a plant and sometimes even the frequency of flowering. For example, deadheading spent callistemon flowers may cause plants to flower in autumn as well as spring. However some gardeners like the unpruned, natural, open look of callistemons, with the distinctive seed capsules but fewer flowers.

In the extreme situation of having to either remove a plant or prune it savagely, it is worth trying the latter (almost to ground level and into hard wood) to give the plant a last chance. Some Australian plants will not tolerate this harsh treatment but others respond amazingly well – *Babingtonia pluriflora* (Tall Baeckea), *Leptospermum petersonii* (Lemon-scented Tea-tree) and *Melaleuca lateritia* (Robin Red-breast Bush) are a few examples.

Pruning should be used to give definition to the many individual plants that make up a garden. While it is sometimes attractive to have plants intermingle, many do better with their own space so that their unique structure and individual beauty can be well appreciated.

Turning shrubs into small trees

Beautiful and even elegant results can be achieved by removing the lower branches of suitable shrubs so that they resemble a tree. The interesting lines and textures of the exposed trunk(s) will be emphasised. Shrubs such as *Melaleuca lateritia* (Robin Red-breast Bush), *M. incana* (Grey Honey-myrtle) and *Banksia spinulosa* var. *cunninghamii* (Hairpin Banksia) can be pruned to trunks with mop tops like miniature trees. (*B. spinulosa* var. *collina* has a lignotuber and shoots will continue to grow from this.) You can prune larger shrubs, such as *Callistemon rugulosus*

(*C. macropunctatus*) (Scarlet Bottlebrush), *Leptospermum petersonii* (Lemon-scented Tea-tree), *Melaleuca nesophila* (Showy Honey-myrtle) and *Babingtonia pluriflora* (Tall Baeckea), to trunks with a canopy of foliage above head height. This will allow large shrubs to be espaliered along walls or trellises or to fit into narrow garden beds with smaller plants growing at their base. You can shape large shrubs as shade trees, to provide a canopy of foliage along a path or to frame a vista.

Coppicing

Coppicing or cutting a tree to encourage numerous slender trunks to regenerate from the root-stock may be used to good effect in garden design. For instance, you can coppice a single tree or a group of trees to produce the effect of a small forest in a very limited space. All mallees do this naturally to some extent but coppicing can enhance the effect. Cutting back to near ground level can also control a tree that is growing too tall and instead produce a beautiful small tree with a number of slim trunks – *Eucalyptus leucoxylon* (Yellow Gum) and *E. macrandra* (Long-flowered Marlock) are excellent candidates. Not all trees will respond well to this treatment but it is worth a try if you have a small garden, or if you are thinking of removing a tree but would be happy with a smaller version.

Leaning shrubs and trees

A leaning shrub is always susceptible to damage from a combination of water and wind – if the weight of wet foliage causes it to lean further, pruning the low side can help restore a more upright position. Unusual or idiosyncratic shapes such as a leaning trunk or twisted branches can either be made less conspicuous or highlighted as a design feature by pruning.

Hedging and topiary

Hedging and topiary are cases where pruning is essential and ongoing from the time the plant is quite young. Suitable Australian species are listed in the section 'Formal gardens'.

Success in managing a garden depends on ever increasing knowledge and sensitivity or 'eye'. As you gain these you will continue learning to design your garden with its strong sense of place, its own Australian style and its own unique sense of harmony and beauty.

ABOVE: Floyd garden Vic. Plant knowledge and vision helped in the creation of a 'Stairway to the Stars', which is still being extended. Pruned plants include (in the front) newly planted *Westringia fruticosa* (Coast Rosemary), *Homoranthus papillatus*, *Acacia subulata*, *Calytrix tetragona* and *Ochrosperma lineare*.
PHOTOGRAPH DIANA SNAPE

APPENDIX

UK NURSERIES STOCKING AUSTRALIAN AND NEW ZEALAND SHRUBS AND TREES

Abbotsbury Sub-Tropical Gardens
Abbotsbury
Nr. Weymouth
Dorset DT3 4LA
Phone/Fax: +44 (0)1305 871344
e-mail: gardens@abbotsbury.co.uk

County Park Nursery
Essex Gardens
Hornchurch
Essex RM11 3BU
Phone: +44 (0)1708 445205

Garden Cottage Nursery
Tournaig
Poolewe
Achnasheen
Highland
Scotland IV22 2LH
Phone/Fax: +44 (0)1445 781777
e-mail: sales @gcnursery.co.uk
www.gcnursery.co.uk

The Iris Garden
47 Station Road
Barnet
Hertfordshire EN51PR
Phone/Fax: 020 8441 1300
e-mail: theirisgarden@aol.com
www.theirisgarden.co.uk

The Old Walled Garden
Oxonhoath
Hadlow
Kent TN11 9ss
Tel: +44 (0)1732 810012
Fax: +44 (0)1732 810856
e-mail: amyrtle@aol.com

Pantiles Garden Centre
Almners Road
Lyne
Chertsey
Surrey KT16 0BJ
Phone: +44 (0)1932 872195
Fax: +44 (0)1932 874030
e-mail: pantiles@telinco.co.uk
www.pantiles-nurseries.co.uk

Plantbase
Lamberhurst Vineyard
Lamberhurst Down
Lamberhurst
Kent TN3 8ER
Phone/Fax: +44 (0)1892 891453
e-mail: graham@plantbase.freeserve.co.uk

Stenbury Nursery
Smarts Cross
Southford
Nr. Whitwell
Isle of Wight PO38 2AG
Phone 07909 525343
e-mail:
stenburynursery@netscapeonline.co.uk

Trevena Cross Nurseries
Breage
Helston
Cornwall TR13 9PS
Phone: +44 (0)1736 763880
Fax: +44 (0)1736 762828
e-mail: sales@trevenacross.co.uk
www.trevenacross.co.uk

Other Plant Finding Sources

Europe

PPP Index (of nurseries throughout Europe and the plants they stock) is available on CD-Rom. There are six language versions on one disc: English, German, French, Spanish, Italian and Dutch. The 4th edition published in 2001 listed 100,000 plants available from 2,000 suppliers.
PPP Index is available in the UK from:
Plant Press Ltd
10 Market Street
Lewes
East Sussex BN7 2NB
Phone: +44 (0)1273 476151
Fax: +44 (0)1273 480132
e-mail: john@plantpress.com
www.plantpress.com
or in Germany from:
Verlag Eugen Ulmer
Wollgrasweg 41
D-70599
Stuttgart
Tel: 0711 4507 0
Fax: 0711 4507 120
e-mail: info@ulmer.de
www.ulmer.de

The RHS Plant Finder, compiled by The Royal Horticultural Society and published by Dorling Kindersley Ltd., is available in book form or on CD-Rom. The 16th edition, published in 2002, lists over 70,000 plants from the catalogues of over 800 nurseries in the UK, many of which operate mail order service to the Continent. The book and CD-Rom are available from Plant Press Ltd., as above.
Plant Finder is also available on line:
www.rhs.org.uk/rhsplantfinder

Netherlands

Plantenvinder voor de lage landen is
available from:
Uitgeverij Terra
Postbus 1080
7230 AB Warnsveld
Netherlands
Tel: 0575 581 310
Fax: 0575 525 242
e-mail: terra@terraboek.nl
www. terraboek.nl

North America

The Pacific Northwest Plant Locator,
compiled by Hill and Narizny, lists
nurseries in Oregon, Washington, Idaho
and Canada.

Available from:
Black-Eyed Susans Press
PMB 227
6327-C SW Capitol Highway
Portland
OR 97239-1937
USA
e-mail: susans@blackeyedsusanspress.com
www.blackeyedsusanspress.com

PlantFinder, a monthly magazine produced
for the wholesale nursery and landscape
industry, gives listings of plants in the
southern United States
Available from:
Betrock Information Systems Inc.
7770 Davie Road Extension
Hollywood
FL 33024–2516
USA
Tel: 1 800 627 3819
Fax: 1 954 981 2823
e-mail: betrock@betrock.com
www.hortworld.com

The Plant & Supply Locator, a monthly
magazine produced for the wholesale
nursery and landscape industry, gives
current listings of plants in the south
eastern United States.
Available from:
Hutchinson Publishing Corp.
102 East Lee Road
Taylors
SC 29687
Tel: 1 864 292 9490
Fax:1 800 611 4588
e-mail: info@plantlocator.com
www.plantlocator.com

The Canadian Nursery Landscape
Association provides an online finder
service:
e-mail:cnla@canadanursery.com
www.canadanursery.com

New Zealand

Gaddum's Plant Finder, 30,000 plants from
200 nurseries are given in the 2000 edn.
Later editions are produced when there is
sufficient demand.
Available from:
New Zealand Plant Finder
PO Box 2237
Gisborne
New Zealand
Tel: 646 863 1594
Fax: 646 862 3111
e-mail: info@plantfinder.co.nz
www.infogarden.co.nz

Australia

The secretaries of the various regional
organisations listed on page 227 can
supply more detailed information on
Australian plants.

Bibliography

Garden design

Those marked with an asterisk * have no Australian content but are included for their exposition of universal principles and their power of inspiration.

Bailey, Ralph & Lake, Julie 2001, *Gardening with Australian Rainforest Plants,* Bloomings Books, Hawthorn

*Brookes, John 1991, *Your Garden Design Book,* Lothian, Melbourne

*Brown, Jane 1985, *Gardens of a Golden Afternoon,* Penguin, Harmondsworth

*Church, Thomas 1955, *Gardens are for People,* Reinhold, New York

*Colvin, Brenda 1970, *Land and Landscape,* Murray, London

*Crowe, Sylvia 1994, *Garden Design,* Garden Art Press, Suffolk

Dixon, Trisha & Churchill, Jennie 1998, *The Vision of Edna Walling,* Bloomings Books, Hawthorn

*Druse, Ken 1989, *The Natural Garden,* Crown, New York

Elliot, W. Rodger 1984, *Pruning, A Practical Guide,* Lothian, Melbourne

Elliot, W. Rodger 1992, *Coastal Gardening in Australia,* Lothian, Melbourne

Elliot, W. Rodger 1990, *Gardening with Australian Plants,* Lothian, Melbourne

*Eliovson, Sima 1991, *The Gardens of Roberto Burle Marx,* H. N. Abrams/Saga Press, New York

*Fell, Derek 1994, *The Impressionist Garden,* Angus & Robertson, Pymble

Ford, Gordon 1999, *The Natural Australian Garden,* Bloomings Books, Hawthorn

Garnett, T.R. 2001, *From the Country,* Bloomings Books, Hawthorn

Hunt, John 1986, *Creating an Australian Garden,* Kangaroo Press, Kenthurst

*Jellicoe, G. & S. 1987, *The Landscape of Man,* Thames & Hudson, London

Latreille, Anne 1990, *The Natural Garden: Ellis Stones, His Life and Work,* Viking O'Neil, Ringwood

Maloney, B. & Walker, J. 1966, *Designing Australian Bush Gardens,* Horwitz, Sydney

Molyneux, Bill & Macdonald, Ross 1983, *Native Gardens: How to Create an Australian Landscape,* Nelson, Melbourne

Oldham, John & Ray 1980, *Gardens in Time,* Lansdowne Press, Sydney

*Page, Russell 1962, *The Education of a Gardener,* Collins, London

Pfeiffer, Andrew 1985, *Australian Garden Design: In Search of an Australian Style,* Macmillan, Melbourne

Pizzey, Graham 1988, *A Garden of Birds: Australian Birds in Australian Gardens,* Viking O'Neil, Ringwood

*Pollan, Michael 1991, *Second Nature,* Atlantic Monthly Press, New York

*Price, Suzanne 1986, *The Urban Woodland,* Lothian, Melbourne

Snape, Diana 1992, *Australian Native Gardens: Putting Visions Into Practice,* Lothian, Melbourne

*Stevens, David 1994, *The Outdoor Room,* Hodder & Stoughton, Sydney

Stones, Ellis 1971, *Australian Garden Design,* Macmillan, Melbourne

Stowar, John 1992, *In Sunshine and Shade,* Kangaroo Press, Kenthurst

Thompson, Paul 1991, *Water in your garden,* Lothian, Melbourne

Thompson, Paul 2002, *Australian Planting Design,* Lothian, Melbourne

Urquhart, Paul 1999, *The New Native Garden: Designing with Australian Plants,* Lansdowne, The Rocks

Walling, Edna 1943, *Gardens in Australia* (Facsimile Edition, 1999), Bloomings Books, Hawthorn

Walling, Edna, ed. Margaret Barrett 1980, *The Edna Walling Book of Garden Design,* Ann O'Donovan, Melbourne

Watts, P. 1982, *The Gardens of Edna Walling,* National Trust, Victoria

Wilson, Glen 1975, *Landscaping with Australian Plants,* Nelson, Melbourne

Environmental concerns

Flannery, Tim 1994, *The Future Eaters: An Ecological History of the Australian Lands and People,* Reed, Chatswood

Landy, John 1985, *Close to Nature: A Naturalist's Diary of a Year in the Bush,* Curry O'Neil, South Yarra

Rolls, Eric 1981, *A Million Wild Acres,* Nelson, Melbourne

Seddon, George 1972, *Sense of Place,* University of Western Australia Press

White, Mary E. 1997, *Listen ... Our Land is Crying Australia's Environment: Problems & Solutions,* Kangaroo Press, Kenthurst

Australian plants and their cultivation

The pre-eminent reference is *The Encyclopaedia of Australian Plants* 1980 by R. Elliot and D. Jones, Lothian, Melbourne, of which 7 volumes to the end of Po are available to date. Many municipal libraries carry it – all should.

Australian Daisy Study Group 1987, *Australian Daisies for Gardens and Floral Art,* Lothian, Lothian

Australian Plant Society, ed. W. H. Payne 1960, *Australian Plants* – 21 volumes to date – the Australian Plant Society, SGAP, NSW

Australian Plant Study Group 1980, *Grow What Where*; 1982, *Grow What Wet*; 1987, *Grow What Small Plant*, Nelson, Melbourne

Corrick, Margaret & Fuhrer, Bruce 1996, *Wildflowers of Southern Western Australia,* Five Mile Press, Noble Park

Corrick, Margaret & Fuhrer, Bruce 2000, *Wildflowers of Victoria*, Bloomings Books, Hawthorn

Cunningham, G.M., Mulham, W.E., Milthorpe, P.L. & Leigh, J.H. 1981, *Plants of Western New South Wales,* NSW Government Printing Office

Elliot, Gwen 1979, *Australian Plants for Small Gardens and Containers,* Hyland House, Melbourne

Elliot, G. & R., Kuranga Nursery 1996, *The Kuranga Handbook of Australian Plants,* Lothian, Melbourne

Fairley, Alan & Moore, Philip 1989, *Native Plants of the Sydney District,* Kangaroo Press & SGAP, NSW

Greig, Denise 1996, *Flowering Natives for Home Gardens,* Harper Collins / Angus & Robertson, Pymble

Handreck, Kevin 1983, *Gardening Down Under,* CSIRO Publishing, Collingwood

Jones, D. & Gray, B. 1977, *Australian Climbing Plants,* Reed, Sydney

Jones, D. & Clemensha, S. 1980, *Australian Ferns and Fern Allies,* Reed, Sydney

Jones, David 1984, *Palms in Australia,* New Holland, Sydney

Jones, David 1986, *Ornamental Rainforest Plants in Australia,* Reed, Sydney

Launceston Field Naturalistics Club 1981, *A Guide to Flowers and Plants of Tasmania,* Reed, Sydney

Mansfield, Darren 1992, *Australian Rainforest Plants for your Garden,* Simon & Schuster, East Roseville

Nicholson, H. & N. vols 1 – 5, 1985 – 2000, *Australian Rainforest Plants,* Terrania Rainforest Publishing, The Channon, NSW

Olde, P. & Marriott, N. 1994, *The Grevillea Book*, 3 vols, Kangaroo Press, Kenthurst

Romanowski, Nick 1992, *Water and Wetland Plants for Southern Australia,* Lothian, Melbourne

SGAP Maroondah Inc. 1991, *Flora of Melbourne,* SGAP Maroondah Inc.

Wrigley, J. & Fagg, M. 1979 and later eds, *Australian Native Plants,* Collins, Sydney

Wrigley, J. & Fagg, M. 1989, *Banksias, Waratahs, Grevilleas and all other Australian Proteaceae,* Collins, Sydney

Wrigley, J. & Fagg, M. 1993, *Bottlebrushes, Paperbarks and Tea-trees,* Angus and Robertson, Pymble

Further Information

The secretaries of the following regional organisations can supply more detailed information on Australian plants.

Australian Native Plant Society
Canberra Region Inc.
PO Box 217, Civic Square, ACT 2608
www.anbg.gov.au/sgap/

Australian Plant Society
New South Wales
PO Box 744, Blacktown, NSW 2148
www.austplants-nsw.org.au

Society for Growing Australian Plants
Queensland Region Inc.
PO Box 586, Fortitude Valley, Qld 4006
www.sgapqld.org.au

Australian Plant Society
South Australia Region Inc.
PO Box 304, Unley, SA 5061
www.iweb.net.au/~aps

Australian Plant Society
Tasmania Inc.
PO Box 75, Exeter, Tasmania 7275
www.trump.net.au~/joroco/sgaptas - index.htm

Australian Plant Society
Victoria Inc.
PO Box 357, Hawthorn, Vic 3122
www.vicnet.net.au/~sgapvic/

Wildflower Society of Western Australia Inc.
PO Box 64, Nedlands, WA 6909
www.ozemail.com.au/~wildflowers/

The Australian Society for Growing Australian Plants national web site:
farrer.csu.edu.au/ASGAP/

Australian Plants, quarterly online magazine:
farrer.csu.edu.au/ASGAP/apoline.html

Index

Note: Page numbers in bold indicate photograph